MÉXICO

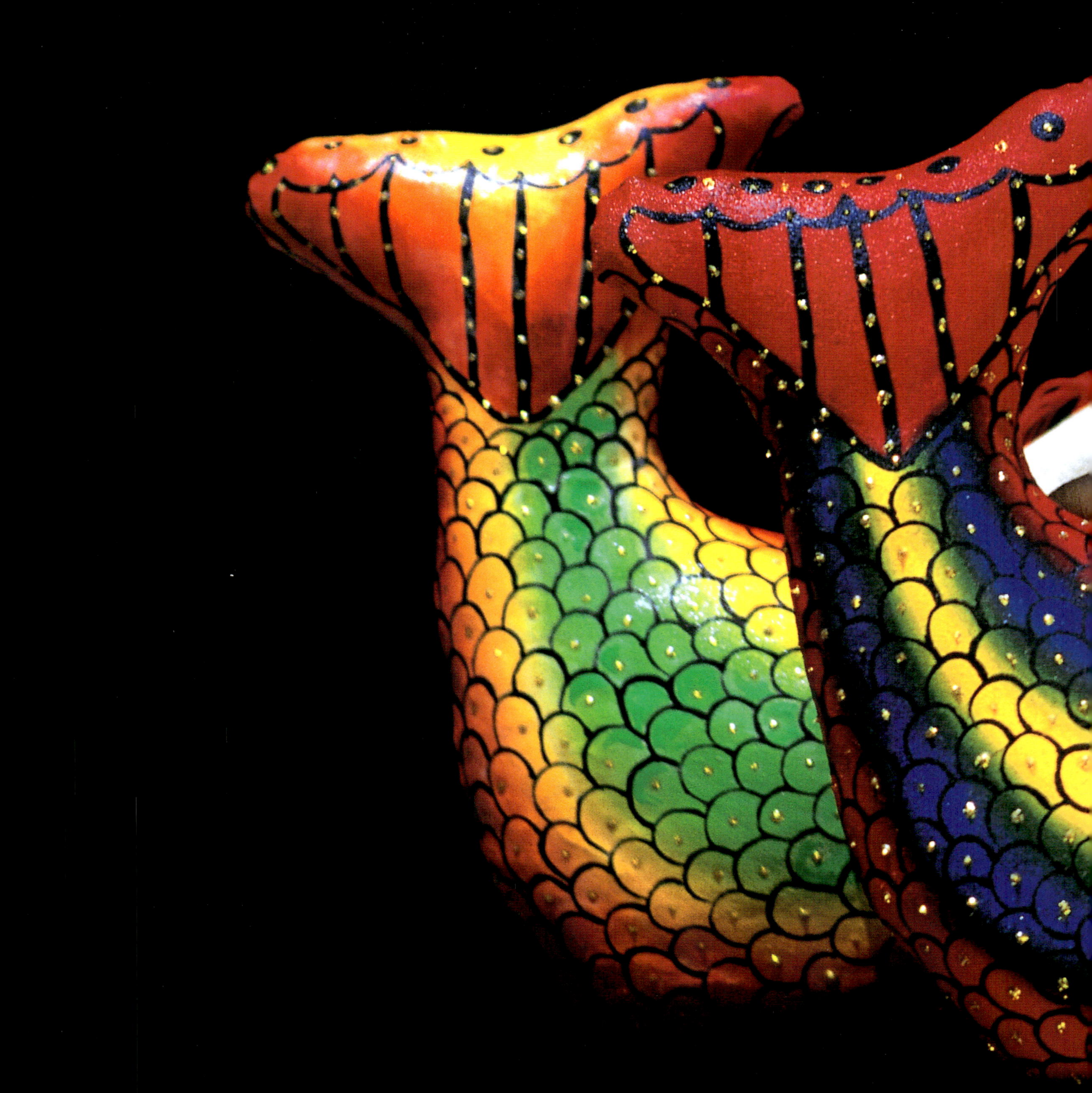

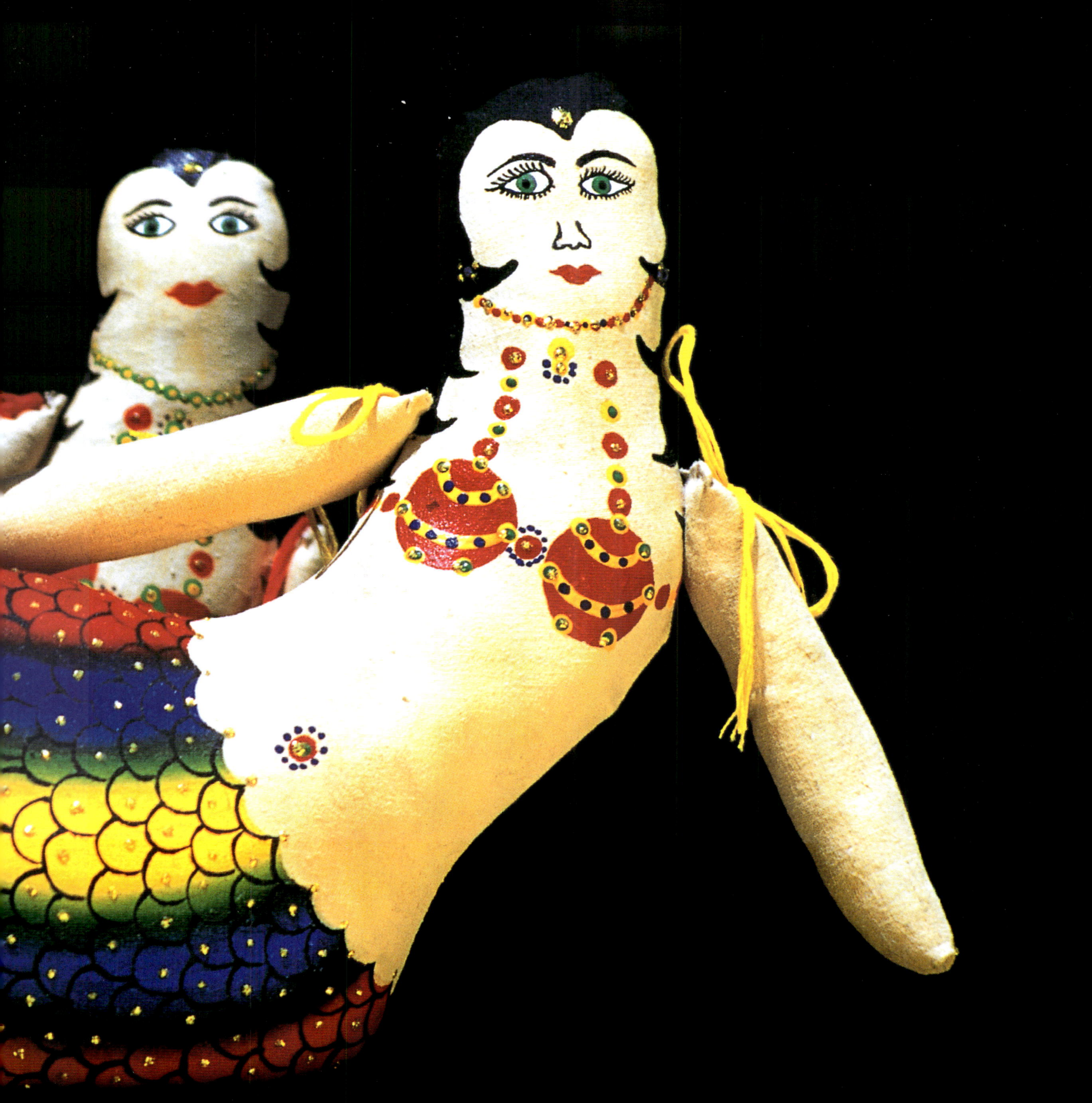

ABRACADABRA
mexican toys

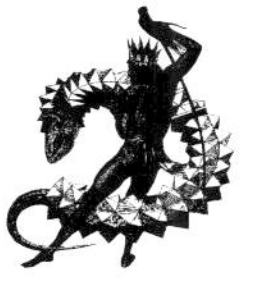

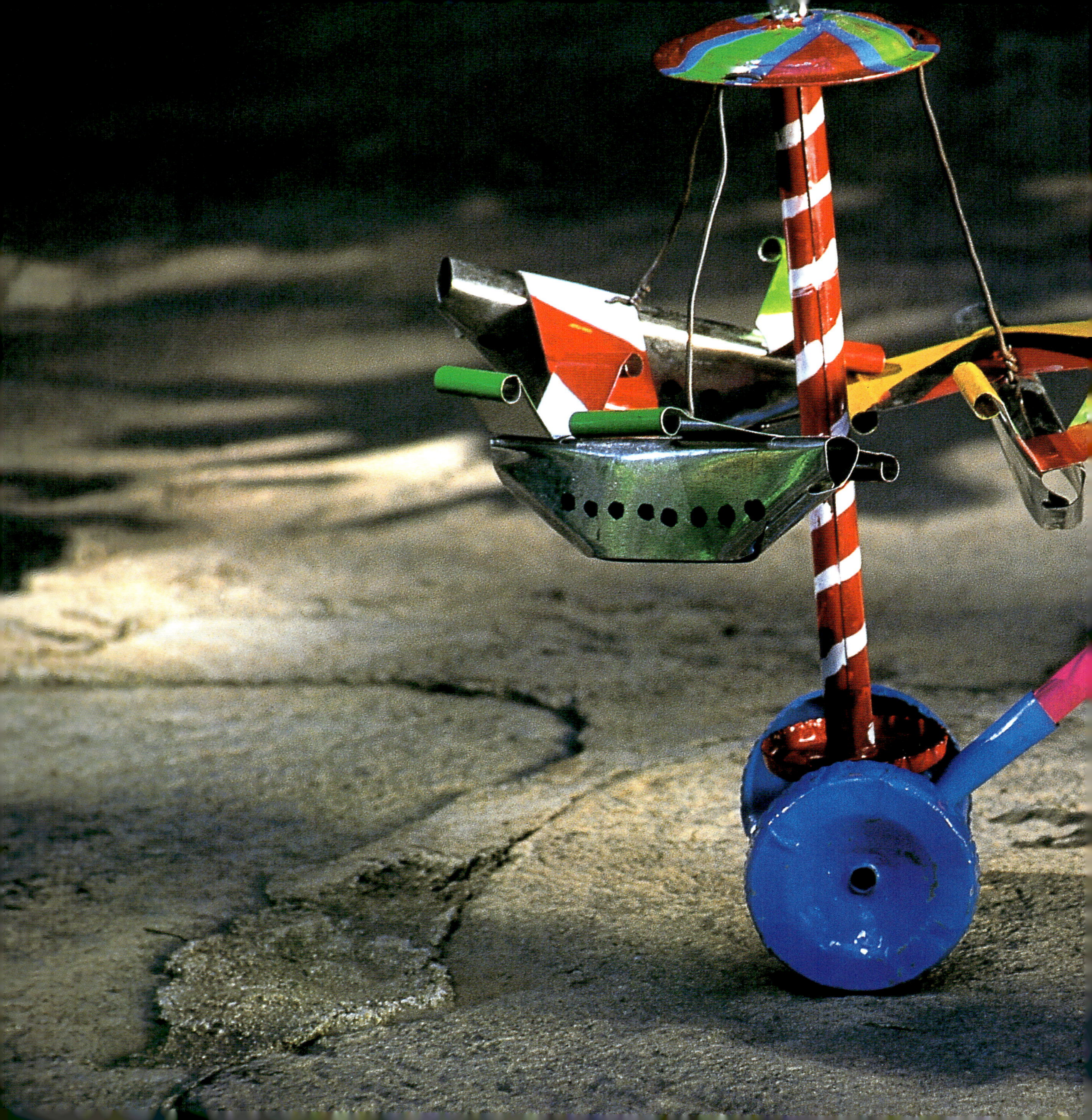

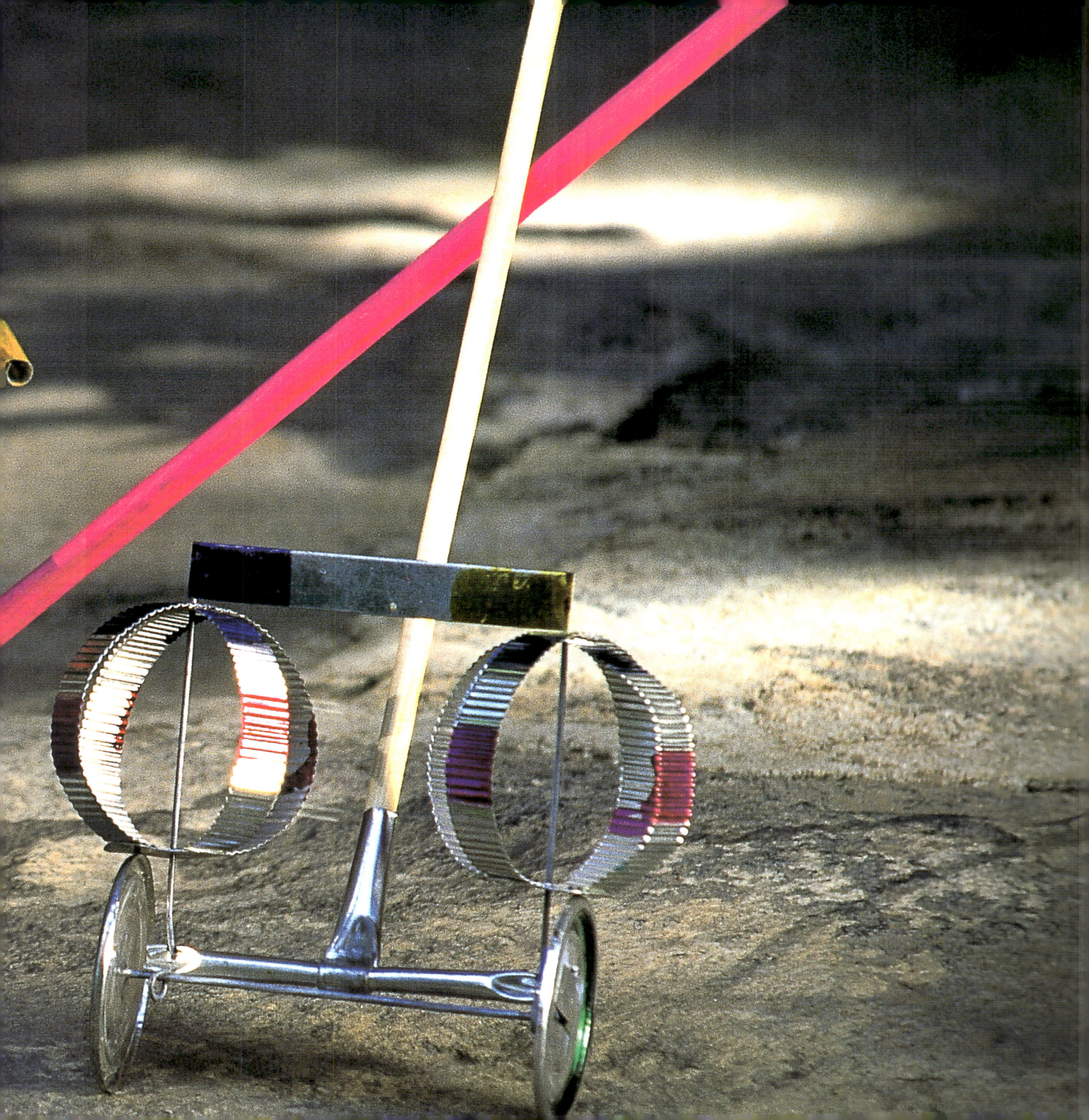

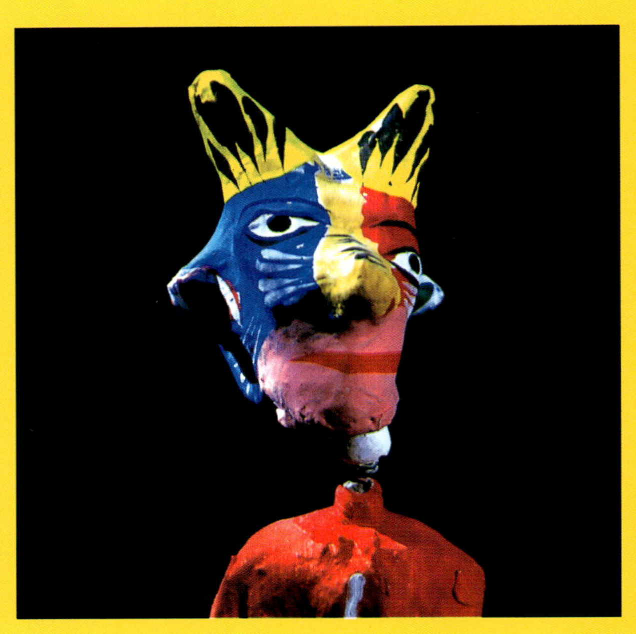

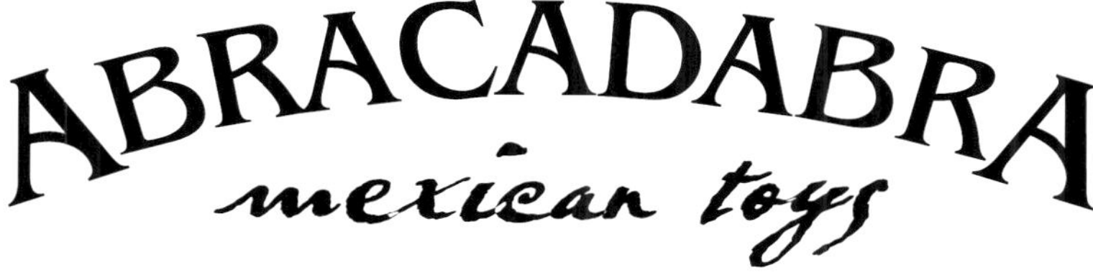

ABRACADABRA
mexican toys

Project Development and Direction
Mauricio Martínez

Photography
Rigoberto Moreno
José Martínez Verea
Carlos Díaz Corona

Texts
Gutierre Aceves
Raúl Aceves
Rubén Páez

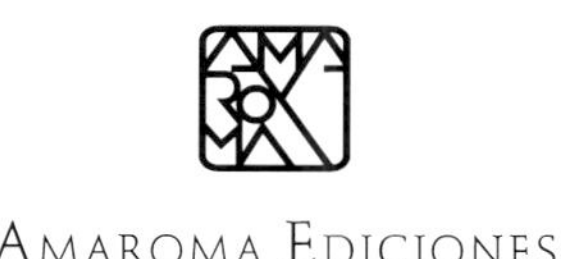

Amaroma Ediciones

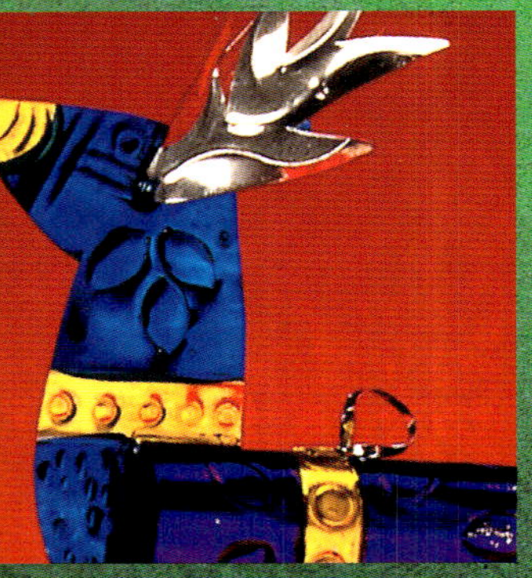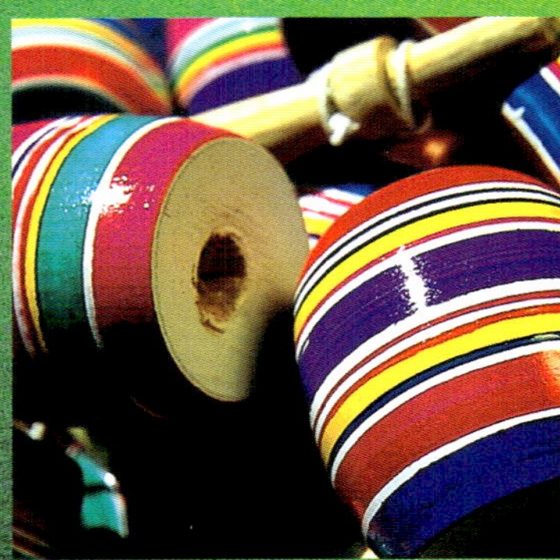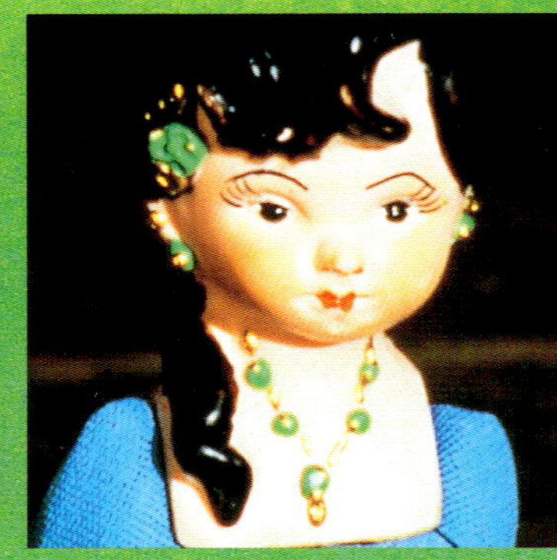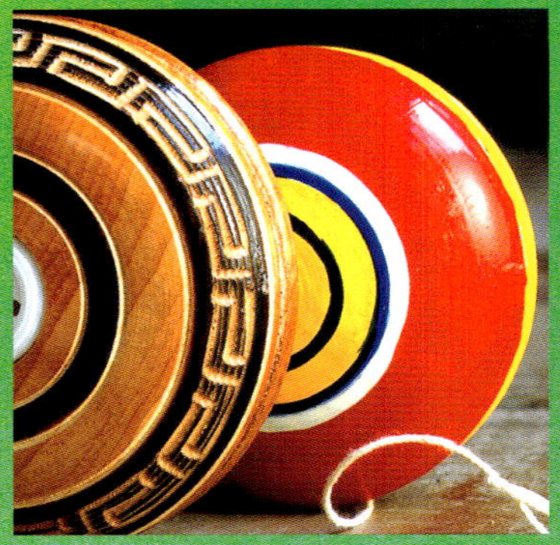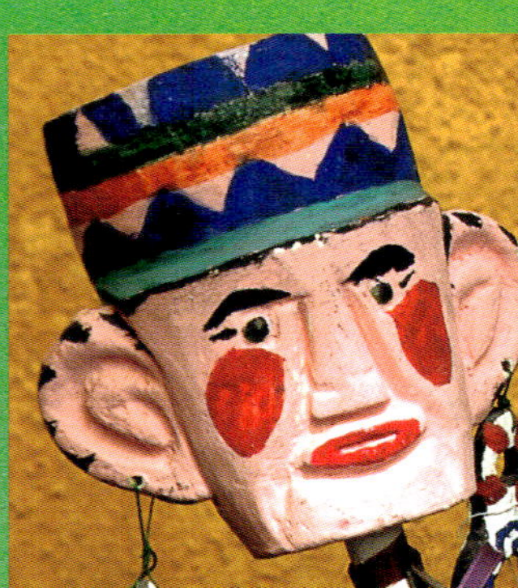

Design
Mauricio Martínez Rosas
Rocío Guillén

Executive Production
Amaroma Ediciones

Editing
Adriana Díaz Romo
Augusta Cobar
Rocío Guillén

Translation
Lucinda Mayo

Pre-press
Groppe

Published by: *Amaroma Ediciones*
Av. Vallarta 1835-2, Col. Americana
44140 Guadalajara, Jalisco, Mexico.
Tel. 36 16 53 43 Fax 36 16 53 46
E-MAIL: amaroma@vinet.com.mx
            amaroma@prodigy.net.mx

Spanish edition, Hardcover: ISBN 970-92410-4-4
English edition, Hardcover: ISBN 970-92410-5-2
English edition, Paperback: ISBN 0-89013-423-5
Printed in Hong Kong by *Global Interprint, Inc.*
Distributed in the U.S. by *Museum of New Mexico Press*

ABRACADABRA
mexican toys

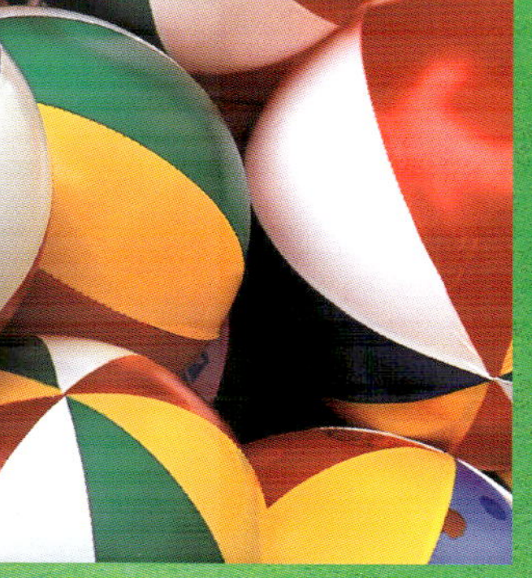 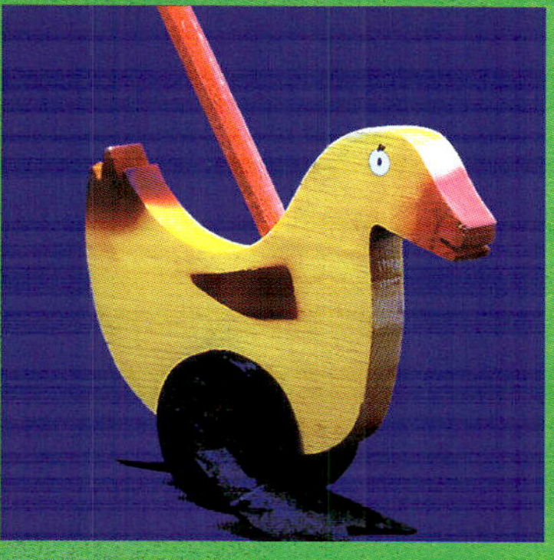 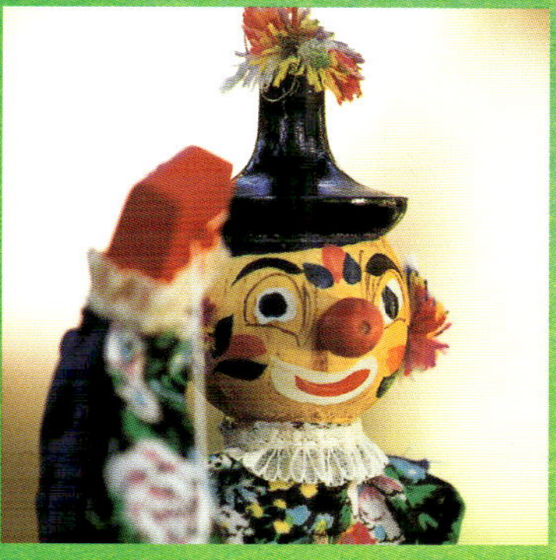

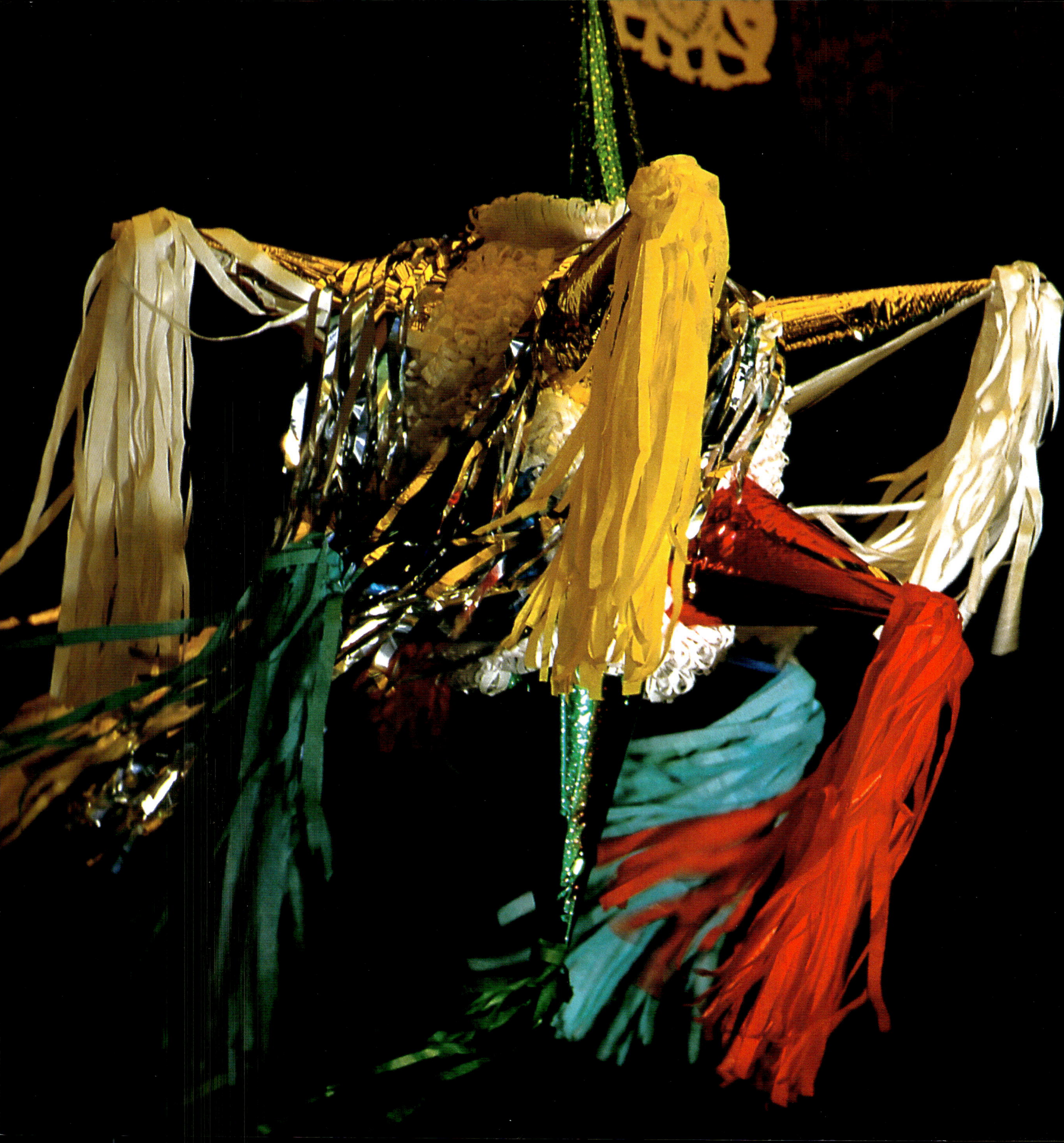

All life begins with one game, and ends with another. Human existence describes an arc between the two extremes. In this life which we know as precarious, which is lent to us for an always too-brief lapse of time, child's play is a defense par excellence. A disinterested defense, it has no business beyond the pure celebration of this wondrous instant. But the small universe of play is also the image and likeness of the great game that the gods, those immortal children, started to play on a day before memory began, and which they continue playing so that the cosmos won't stop in its tracks. Battles, cycles of creation and destruction, regimented presence or haphazard improvisation, mock-flight, disguises, coming to know the world, rhythms and chants, dialogue with the invisible... Playing with dolls has something to do with fertility rites; the child who sends a kite into the air, takes a symbolic soul-voyage that frees the body and yet keeps it attached by a thin string; the airplane that is drawn with chalk in the patio, or the street, provides a tour of the initiate's labyrinth...

It is not impossible to see the ancient origin of games and toys on a scale of magical dimensions, profoundly mysterious. Mircea Eliade would tell us that all play is essentially linked with the world's sacred aspect as is, at heart, every human activity, down to the most profane, and the most spontaneous. Children play. There is not one of them who doesn't put all their being into play, their souls and voices into their toys. Perhaps, if we watch children attentively, it is possible for us to recover that first sense of order we believed we had lost, but which inhabits children and is recreated in them, in incomparable ways.

Jorge Esquinca

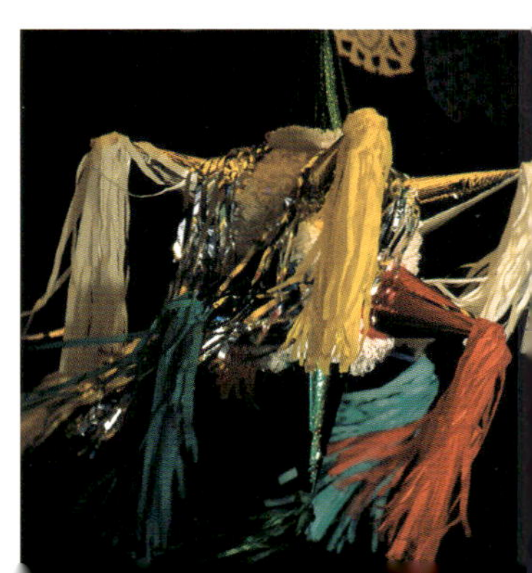

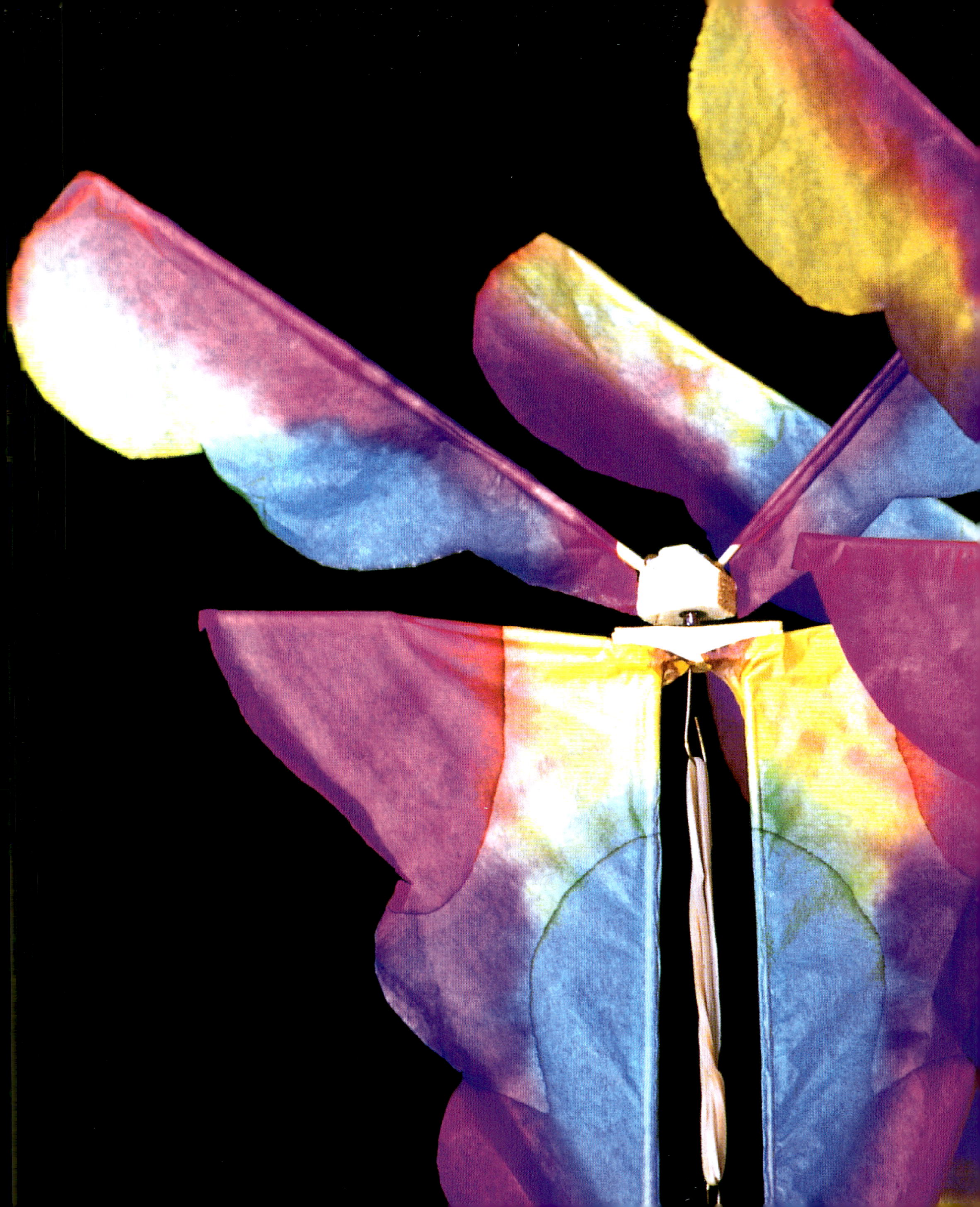

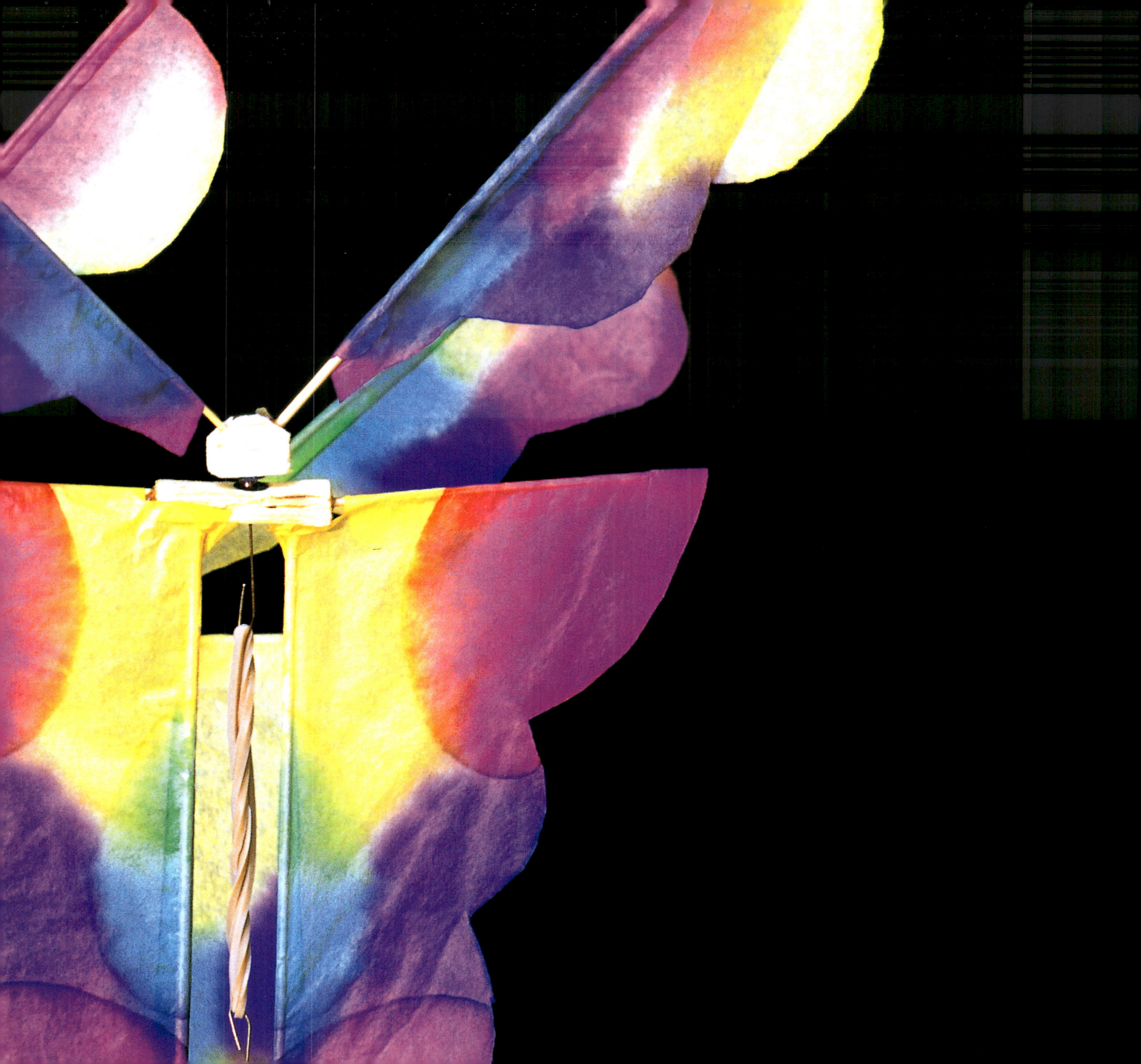

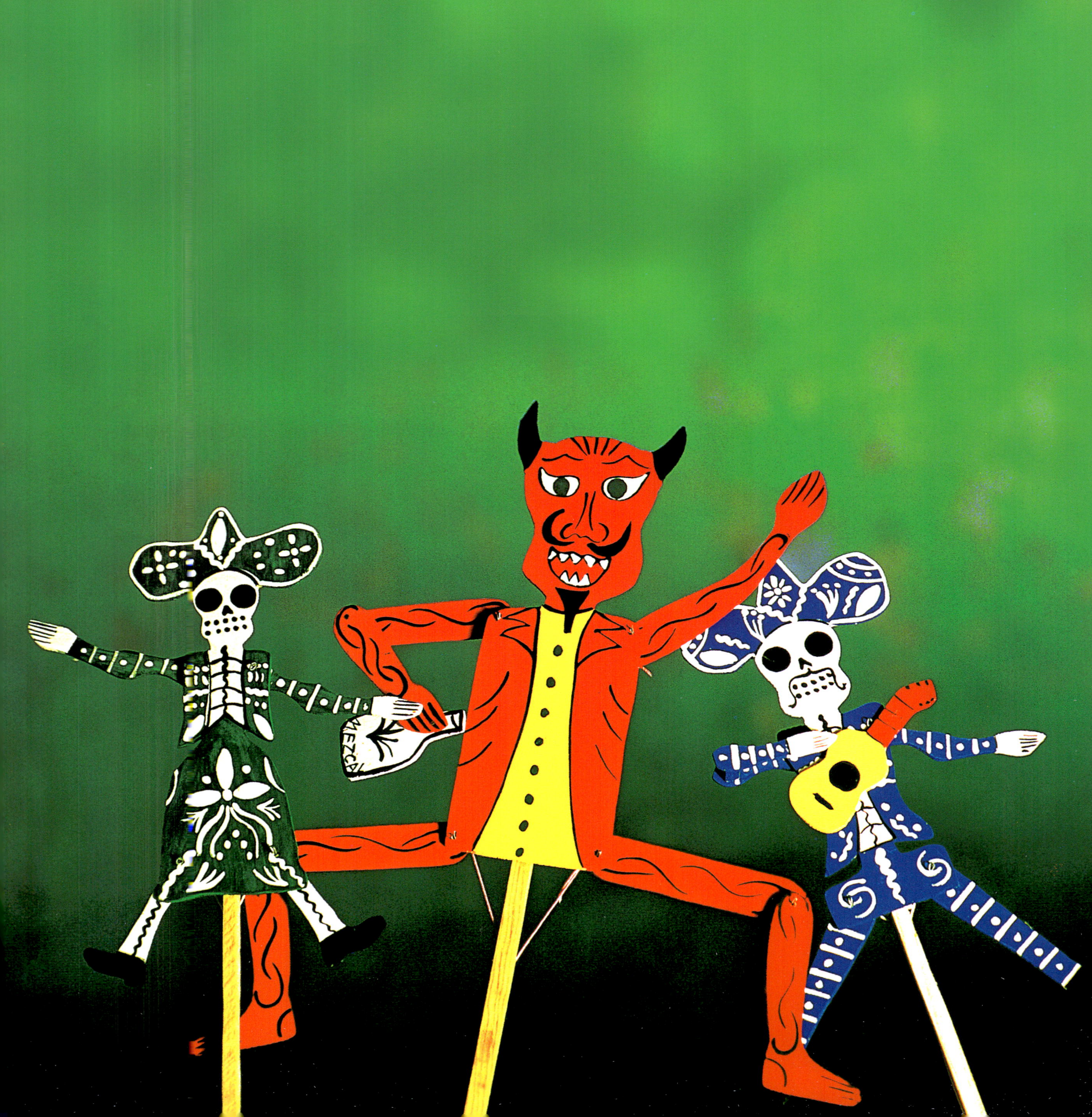

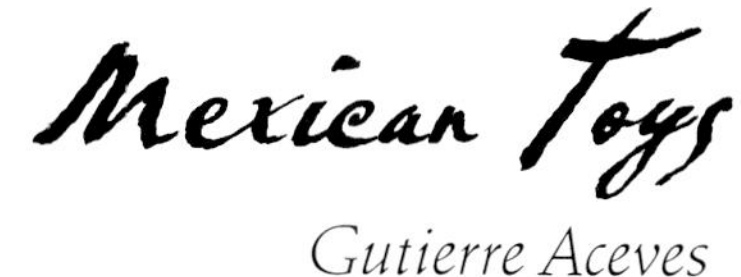

Mexican Toys

Gutierre Aceves

In Mexico, toymaking continues to be among the most fascinating of the traditional arts. Still, it is difficult to set boundaries: how to hazard a definition that takes in the whole variety of so-called popular toys? How to know the moment at which the rattle stops chasing away the bad spirits bent on marauding, and devotes itself to the sheer cajolery of a child's ears? How do we classify those toys which we call popular, "of the people", and which were actually, as Walter Benjamin has said, "the cultural belongings of the dominant class, which have been shipwrecked and reborn upon being picked up by the most numerous social group."

Given the anonymity of popular arts, locating the actual models among the adopted styles is part of a history that is yet to be written: the history of the toy in Mexico, abounding with highly diverse influences from outside Mexico as well.

It is possible, though, to specify the characteristics which traditional toys share. Qualities which stand out are the simplicity of their manufacture, the ability of the artisan to balance refined techniques with unrefined materials, and the toymaker's capacity to adapt foreign models to native resources. Traditional toys are also distinguished by the harmony of their strong colors, and the variety of their forms.

Low selling prices and the time the artisan takes to make traditional toys are creating an unfortunate tendency for this kind of production to die out.

Beyond entertainment and recreation, play and playthings permit us to have fun: to follow another track, we might say. Removing ourselves, departing from what is considered pressing and necessary, we can favor activities which are pleasurable in themselves, and free of specific purposes.

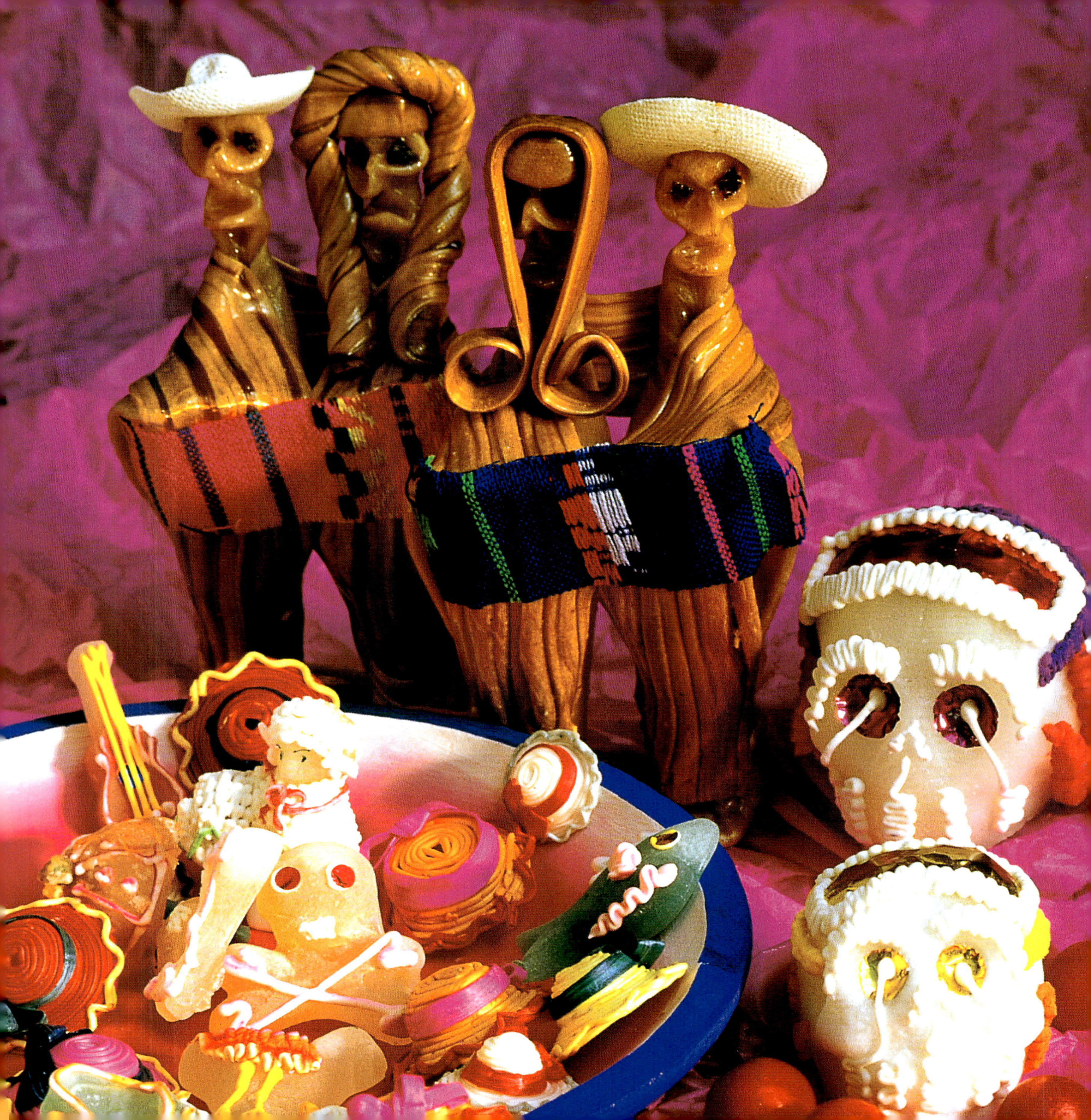

The pedagogical intentions imposed upon toys are no obstacle to their capacity for seducing the imagination and yielding themselves to the contours of play. That territory of agreeableness, that aimless land where useful ends are inconsequential and free time is exalted, enriches the creation of other worlds.

All of us have played, and succumbed to the suggestive power of toys. None of us is a stranger to the joy of exercising our gift for playfulness, and each of us can talk about games and toys based on our own experience.

Still, something so habitual and so much a part of everyday life passes unperceived by countless adults: once we outgrow childhood, play is associated with idleness and given a limited place in our lives. Play is thought to be something far from the real priorities of existence: it is conceived as something more akin to therapy, a pause in the aridity of routine, an uneasy truce between responsibility and the search for well-being. We forget the intense enjoyment of play.

We might go to the extreme of understanding play as a necessary evil, as fleeing life's seriousness. The impulse to play, considered childhood's bailiwick, loses it importance the nearer we get to "maturity": that unequivocal signpost of having reached the moment for replacing the happiness of play with the "happiness" of work.

"Why don't we let play," asks Eugene Fink, "become an 'oasis' of happiness which appears in the desert of our struggle for happiness?"

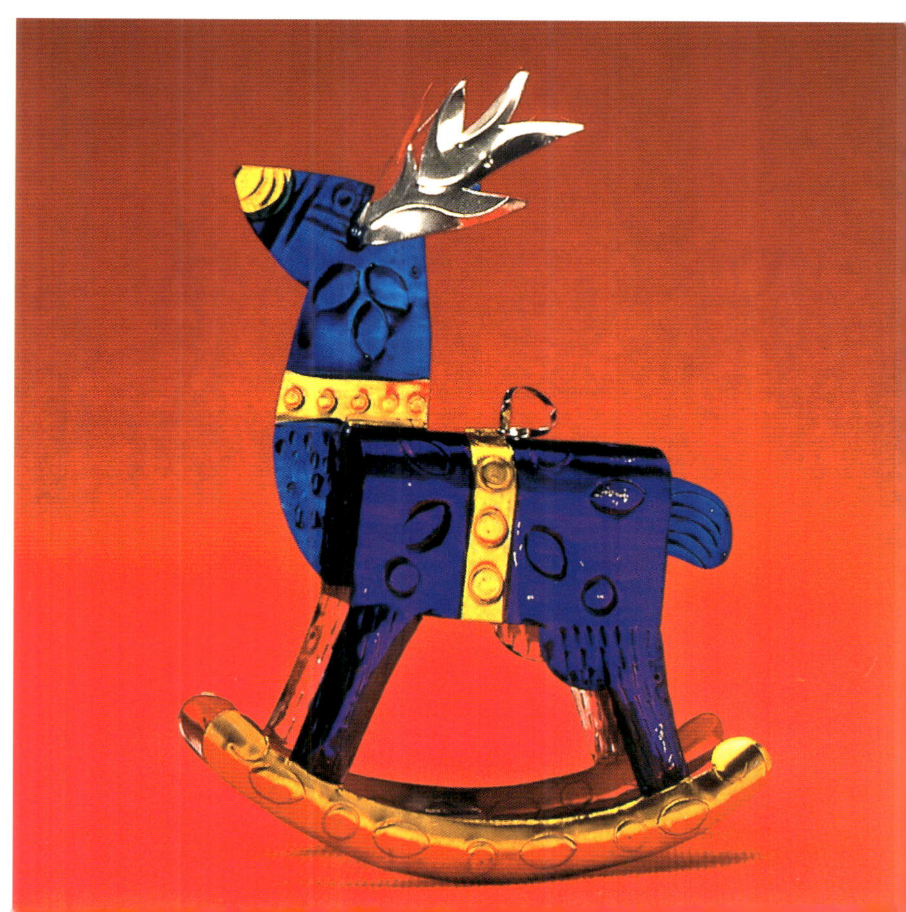

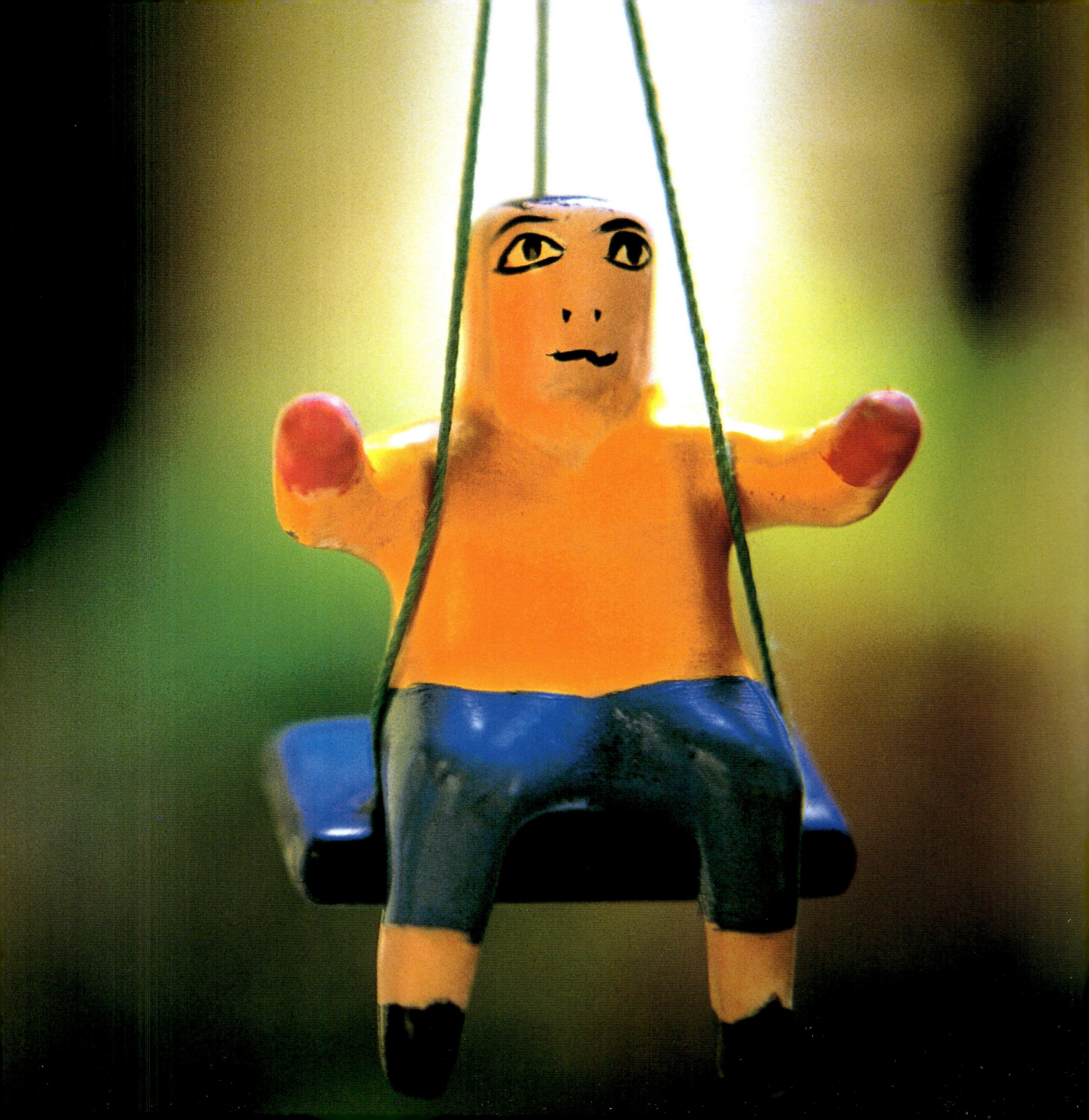

Maybe we don't allow ourselves to play because we consider it as dealing with "toys", and these are abandoned in childhood. Toys are the instrument of play, the incarnation of fantasy, the tangible manifestation of man's power for amusement.

Toys and Ritual

Although we lack the archaeological or documentary information sufficient for reflecting completely upon toys and games in the prehispanic world, we can be certain that some of today's toys have their origin in the past before Cortes' arrival, and we have still more proof that certain indigenous techniques and materials have prevailed since the days of the viceroys in Mexico.

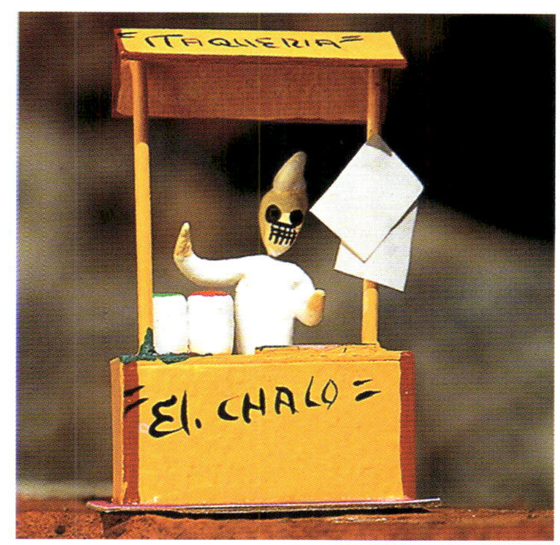

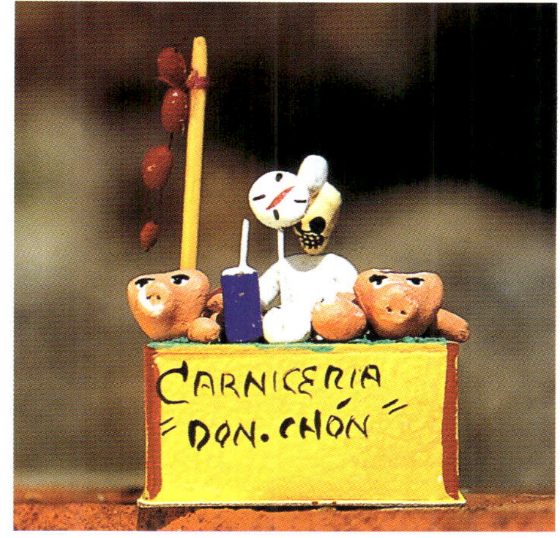

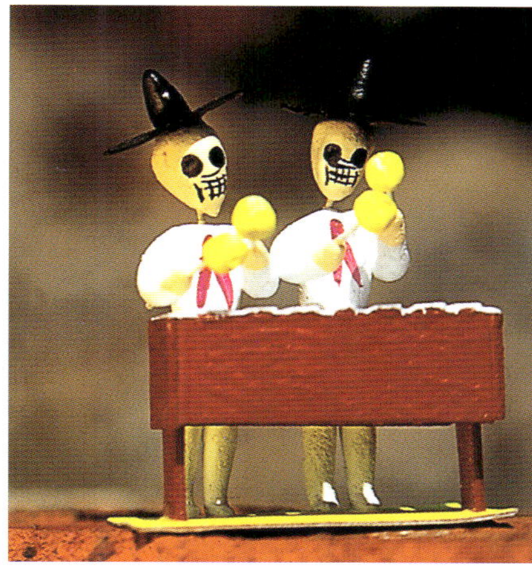

From the Colonial period on, toys and liturgy have gone together; entertainment and newborn faith implicitly joined in toys. The origin of the festival cycle relating to Jesus' birth provides a good example of this. When Friar Diego de Soria, prior of the San Augustine monastery in Acolman, asked Pope Sextus V to authorize special year-end masses, the tradition of posadas was born. Posadas take place during the nine days before Christmas. Once the traditional "pilgrims to Bethlehem" have their petitions answered by other celebrants, play itself takes center stage: with confetti, whistles, paper streamers, and above all piñatas, dressed up in brilliant tissue paper and pregnant with surprises and treats.

In Tlaquepaque, Jalisco, figures are created in clay to commemorate the redemptive promise of the Christ Child's birth. By the middle of each November these nativity

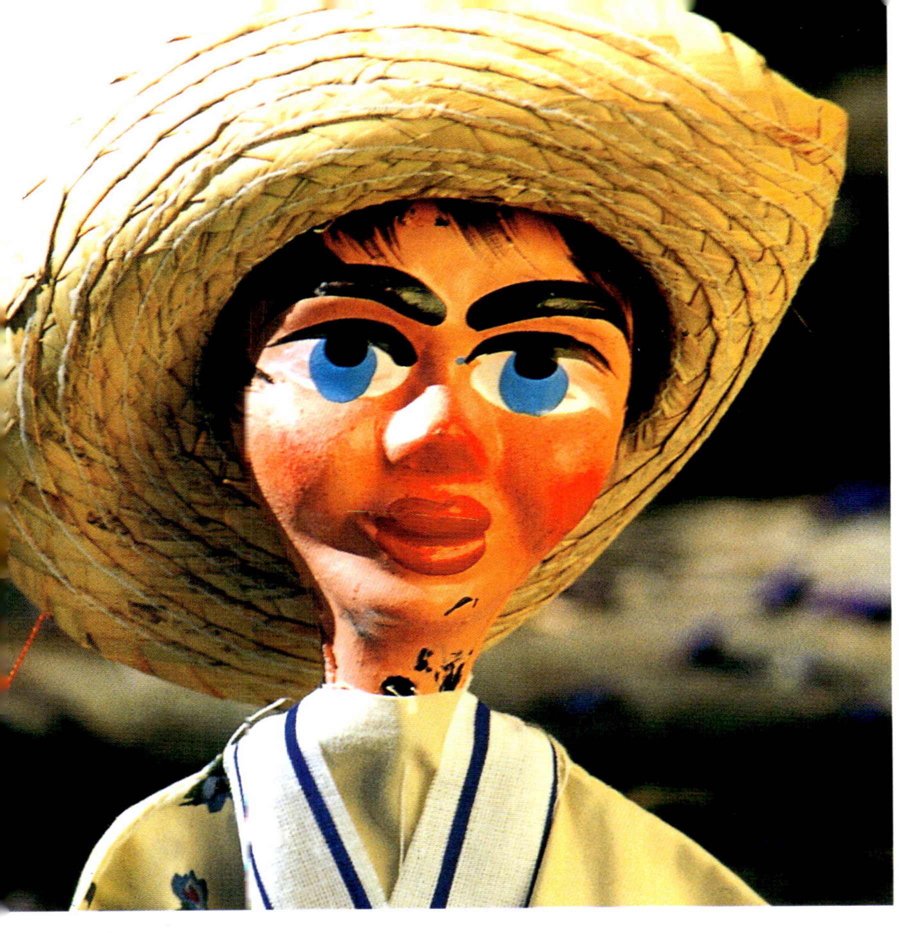

figures begin to populate markets throughout the country.

Along with small sculptures that recall the life of Jesus, there are figures representing popular characters or evoking customary scenes. All are brought together in the *nacimientos* that each family sets up for display according to its own tradition, and this activity is always one in which the children take part.

Tiny deserts and mountains, lakes, houses and animals are arranged as the setting for a cast of traditional characters, including representatives of the most varied endeavors: vendors of flowers, fruits, firewood, crockery, cardboard, tortilla makers and chocolate grinders, *charros* or rodeo riders, muledrivers, harness makers, ice sellers, and so on.

Captivating the hearts of children and adults, these groups of figures on the one hand present edifying religious themes: on the other hand, the naturalism of the little sculptures and their minute depiction of reality make them eye-catching in themselves.

After Christmas, on January 6th, the commemoration of the Wise Men's visit to the newborn is the day on which children receive toys. Returning from their star-guided trip to pay tribute to the Child of God, Melchior, Gaspar and Balthazar visit little ones to reward their good behavior during the year with gifts.

The enjoyment begins with preparations for the holiday. Children repay the Holy Kings by leaving fodder and water for their mounts, and then set out shoes to hold their presents: wooden swords, small carts, balls, helmets, and always-delightful rag or

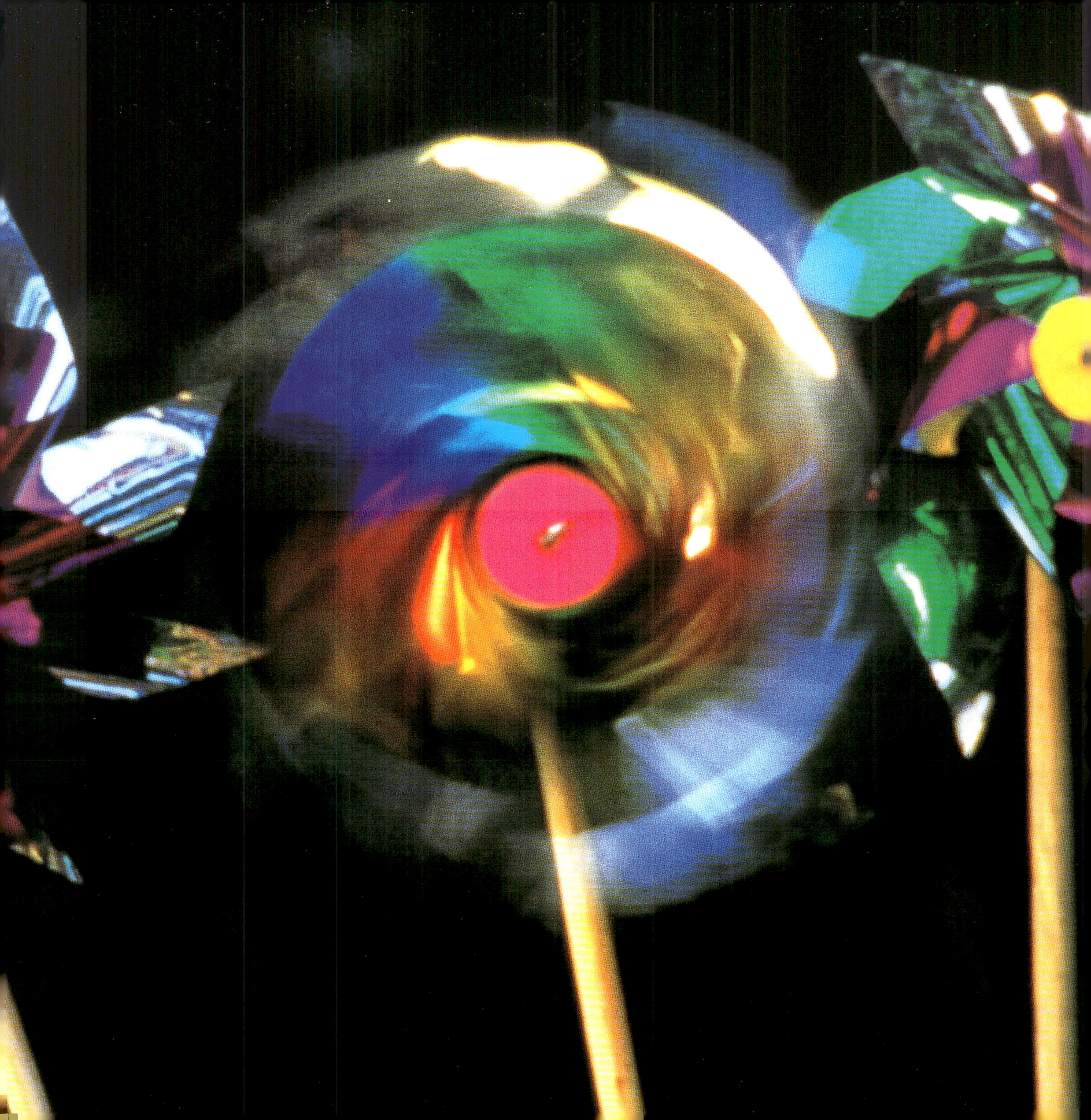

cardboard dolls, such as those which are molded and painted with tempera in Celaya, Guanajuato.

After the reflective period of Lent, with its austerity and abstinence from pleasures, Holy Saturday arrives with wooden noisemakers and tin rattles, as well as cardboard and papier-maché Judas-figures – which explode to drive away the anxious monotony of the earlier season and herald the joy of Resurrection.

From Santa Ana Acatlán, Jalisco, come aniline-tinted cornhusk dolls and little mules, which become part of Holy Thursday's celebration of Christ's presence in the Eucharist.

Most astonishing to foreigners' eyes are the traditional toys that are produced for All Saints' and All Souls' Days. Viewed from a cultural distance, it may seem startling that a father would give his child a sugar skull with his offspring's name written on its forehead.

During the same season, craftsmen create many little skeleton figures, of diverse and humble materials, to depict the activities of the living. Eating skull-shaped breads and candies banishes the grim side of death. Much-loved by Mexicans are toy coffins, each with its own skeleton which suddenly comes to life when activated by a simple mechanism – not to frighten, but to provoke surprise and smiles.

Playing and Learning

We cannot confine traditional toys only to the area of entertainment. In addition to creating them for this basic function, and to serve religion, toymakers have also traditionally built bridges between children and education.

What greater civics lesson is there than the one expressed by "September's toys"? Every year during the Independence Day celebrations there are red, green and white balls with the national emblem, miniature flags, pinwheels that dizzily blend the patriotic

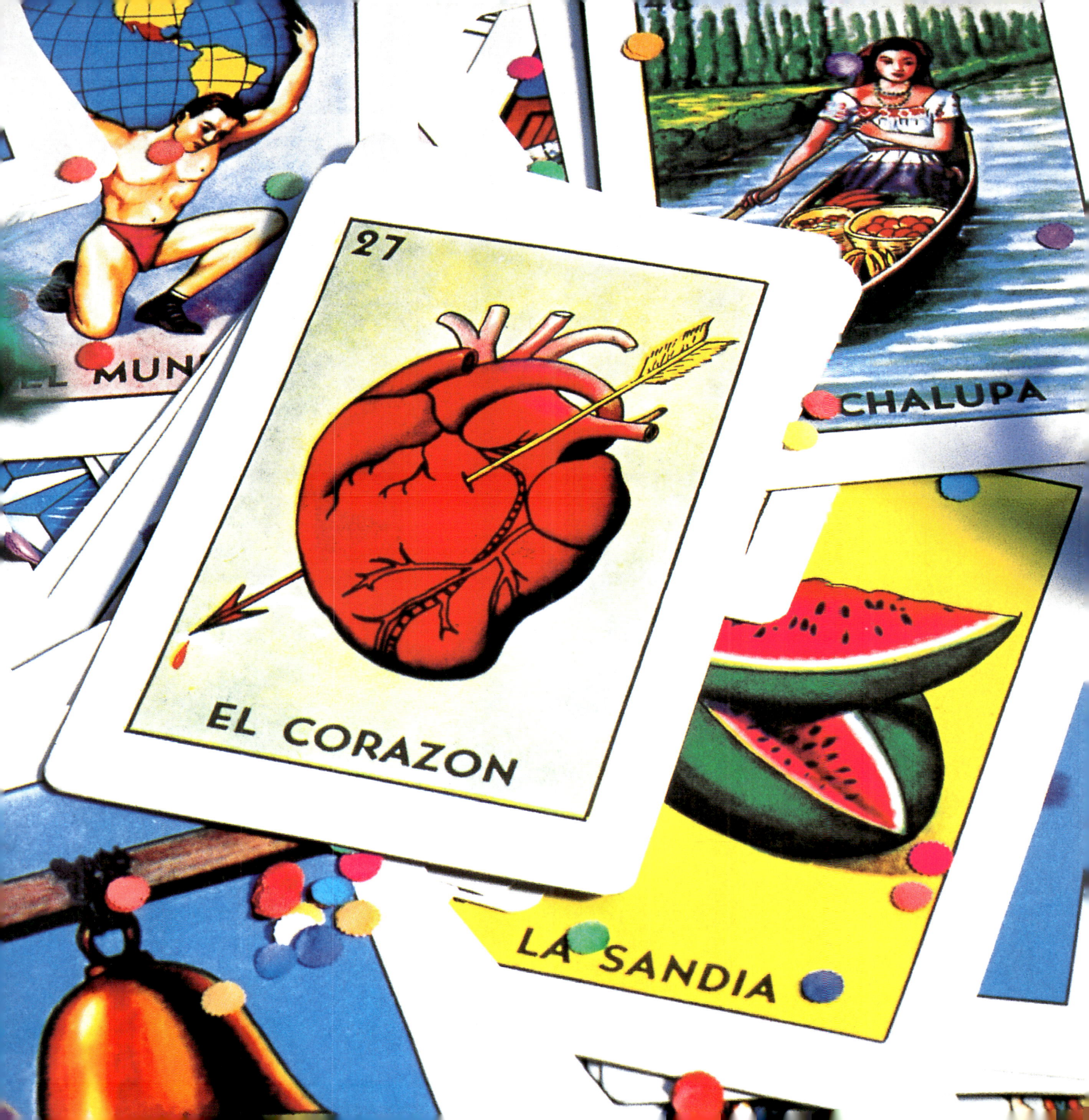
EL MUN
27
EL CORAZON
CHALUPA
LA SANDIA

colors, and interlacing tin hoops which respond to our finger-impulses, creating a moving sphere that ascends a wire-spiral.

What to say of the learning that takes place when children use toys to imagine their future roles as grownups? Dolls and kitchen utensils may wake a girl to her future life as mother and housewife, and for modeling the character and aspirations of men there is an array of work tools, armies of lead soldiers, and ingenious wooden pistols and rifles which "fire" by means of rubberbands.

Passion for progress, faith in science, our certainty that technology will make us better, these also begin with toys. Modern images proliferate in boats, trains, automobiles and airplanes, all conceived in materials dictated by tradition: wood, clay and tin. The airplanes made in the state of Veracruz, of woven and aniline-dyed palm, are light as air and will always evoke flight.

Besides being interrelated with ritual and education, the popular toy has links to secular celebrations. We find toys that reproduce fiestas, popular diversions and spectacles exclusive to adults or those in which children participate: fairs, circuses and puppet shows. In the state of Guanajuato, especially in Silao and Celaya, aniline-painted *copalillo* wood continues to be carved into comical "action figures": fighting roosters, boxers and bullfighters come to life at the touch of a button. *Maromero* tumbling figures have a special charm as they execute the most dangerous feats when varying degrees of hand-pressure are exerted on the thin wooden

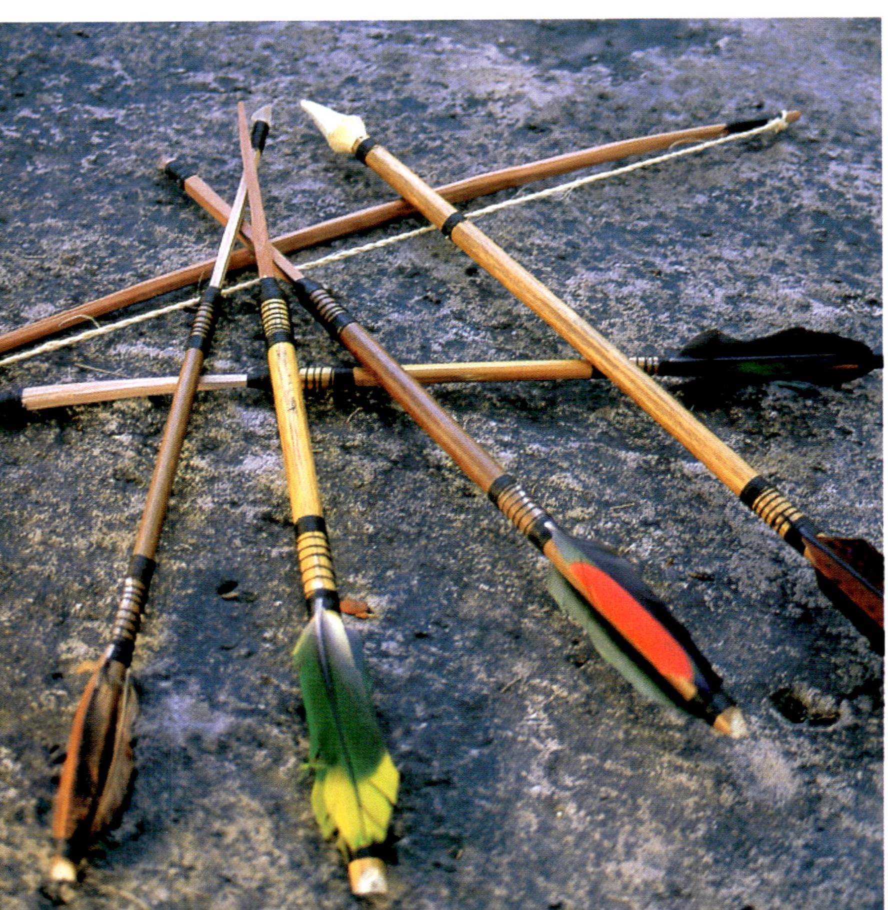

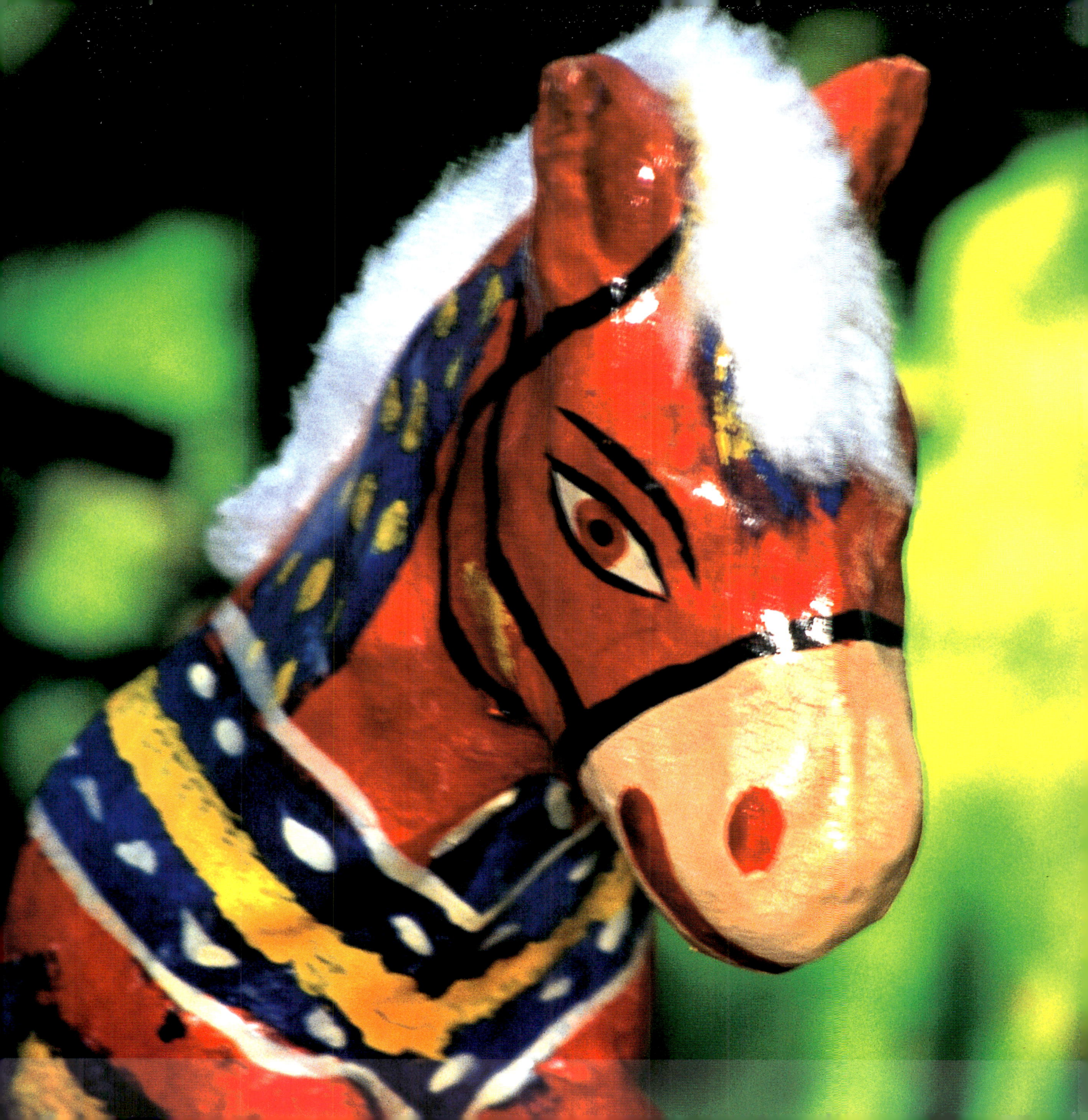

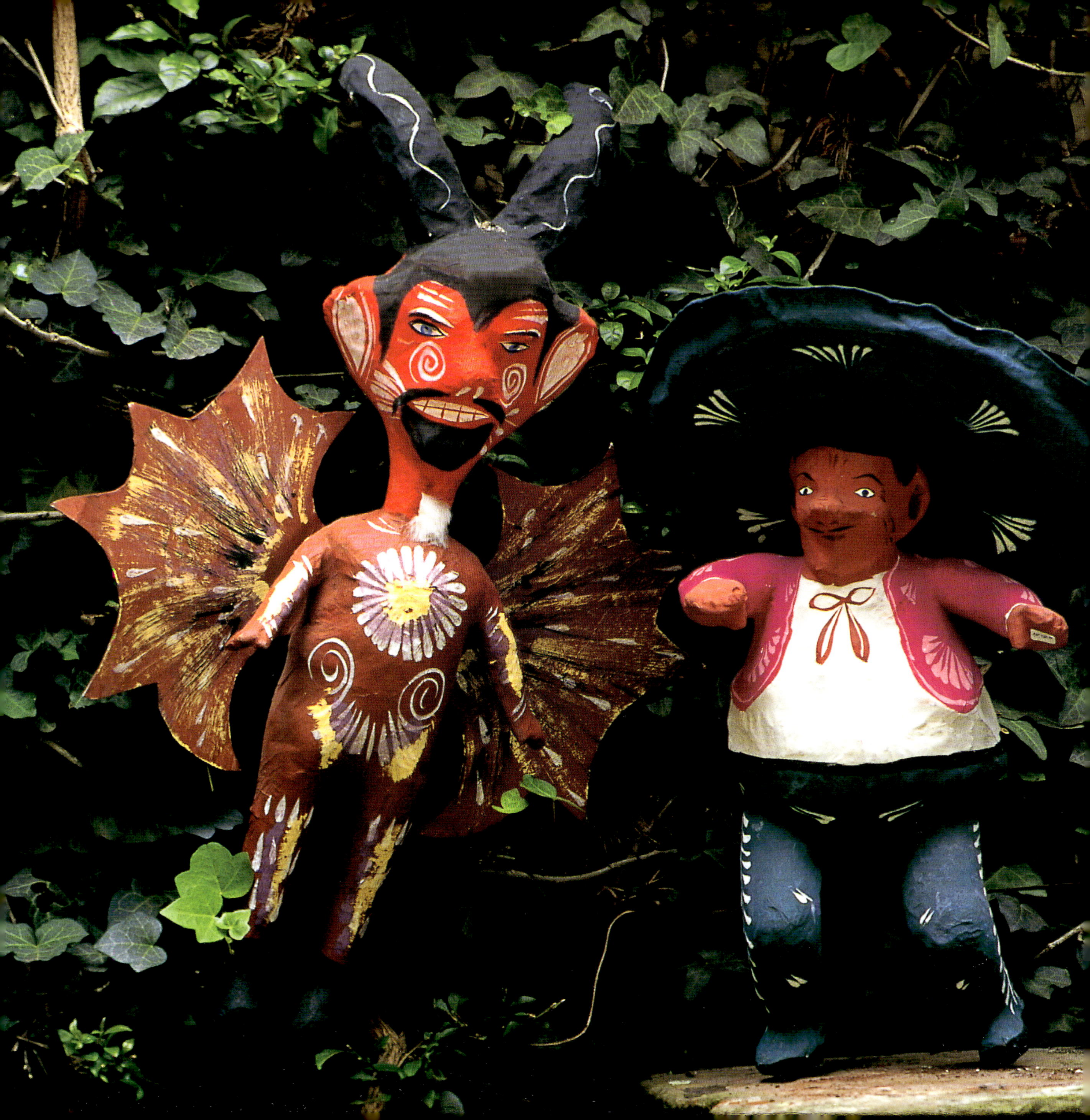

bars from which they are suspended. From town fairs come toy imitations of carousels, ferris wheels and roundabouts, such as those in lacquer-work from the state of Guerrero.

From copper, chicle, lead, wood, glass and clay a miniature universe is made in the image and likeness of the model it reflects. In their tiny verisimilitude, these small objects attract the vision and touch of the child as well as the adult. Soon they become valued collectors items, full of the possibility of creating a world to scale, where the child rules. We treat them with the same affection with which we use the diminutive forms of words.

With the utmost care we handle wardrobes, tables, chairs, sets of dishes, and all the other furnishings that make up a dollhouse. The same care is taken with the small tools and metal animals that the boy carries around as if they were amulets.

Toys that are dear to our hearts

Other toys, of larger dimensions, are made child-sized by the special character the child confers upon them. Clay "piggybanks", whether in the form of a piglet or a piece of fruit, allow a child to save coins that will inspire yet another fantasy.

Also beloved are rocking-horses whose tireless equilibrium takes children on tours of the imagination. Humble hobby-horses, their heads smelling peculiarly of cardboard and glue, are content with their wooden stick or cane bodies, upon which children "ride horseback".

What greater joy than to fly a kite, to feel the wind in your hand, to hear the air buzz with its lighthearted leaps? What an incomparable sound a tin drum makes! What excitement in catching a girl's finger with the tricky little woven-palm tube called a *pescanovia,* or "girlfriend-catcher".

With bodies of the most varied materials, puppets – those which fit the hand like a glove as well as those which require invisible strings – provoke special feelings in children

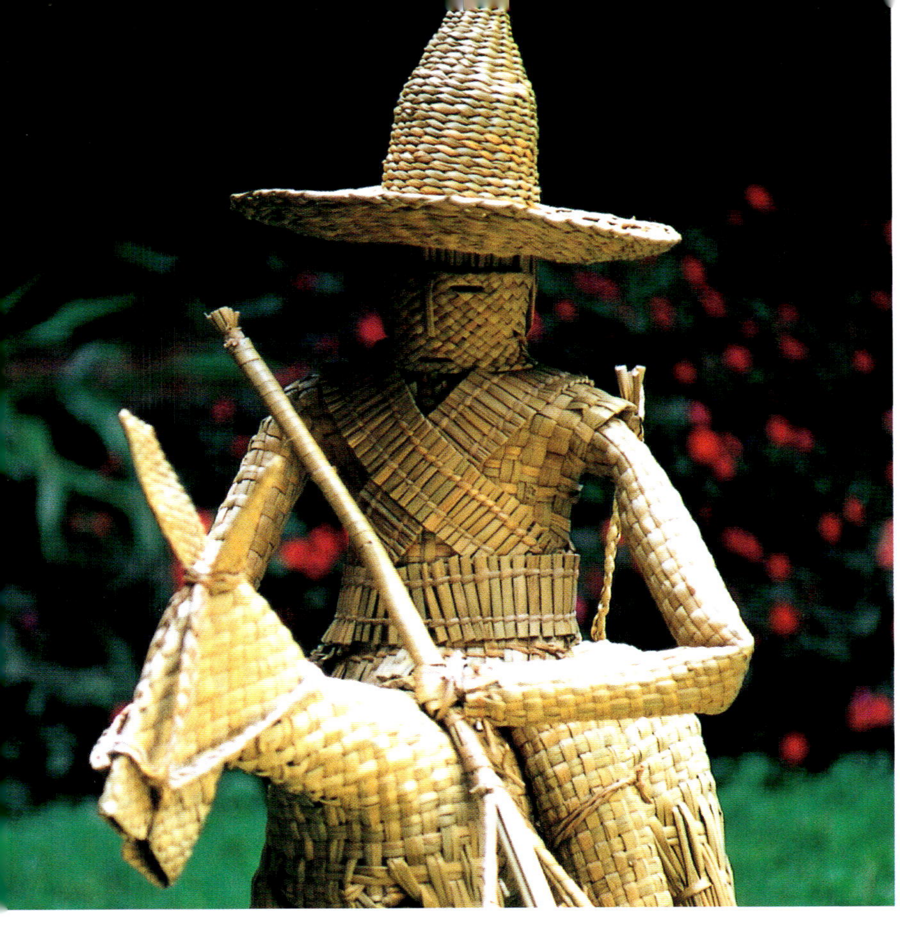

and adults. The worlds of the puppeteer are perennially remembered by all who contemplate them. The puppet-shows of Rosete Arandas are proverbial, even among those who never had the chance to see his animated operas and recreations of Mexican history. They endure in the collective memory.

Fragrant cardboard masks are applied over faces to play at being someone else – or perhaps, more accurately, to allow the true face of the child to emerge. Wolf, rabbit, skull, clown or monkey, all are other facets of the word "I".

Walter Benjamin considers that the soul of play is in repetition. Nothing makes a child happier than "once again", "over and over". "The dark eagerness of reiteration in play is no less powerful, nor less astute, than is the sexual impulse in love."

Toys like the yo-yo, the *balero* (game of skill played with a cup attached by string to a stick) or marbles, all carry the implication that they will be played with again. Feeling the dizziness of a spinning top in the palm of the hand is an emotion to be enjoyed more than once. So it is with victory over a rival playmate: managing to remove an adversary's "sleeping" top from the ring with an accurate blow is a experience that wants to be endorsed through repetition. The same thing happens when we find the lucky balance in a top that hums when we pull its cord.

In Michoacán, such *pirinolas*, as well as other tops and turned-wood *baleros*, are famous for their lively colors. These toys, along with marbles, re-appear periodically in today's children's games, for they still preserve the rhythm of an ancient calendar – though one

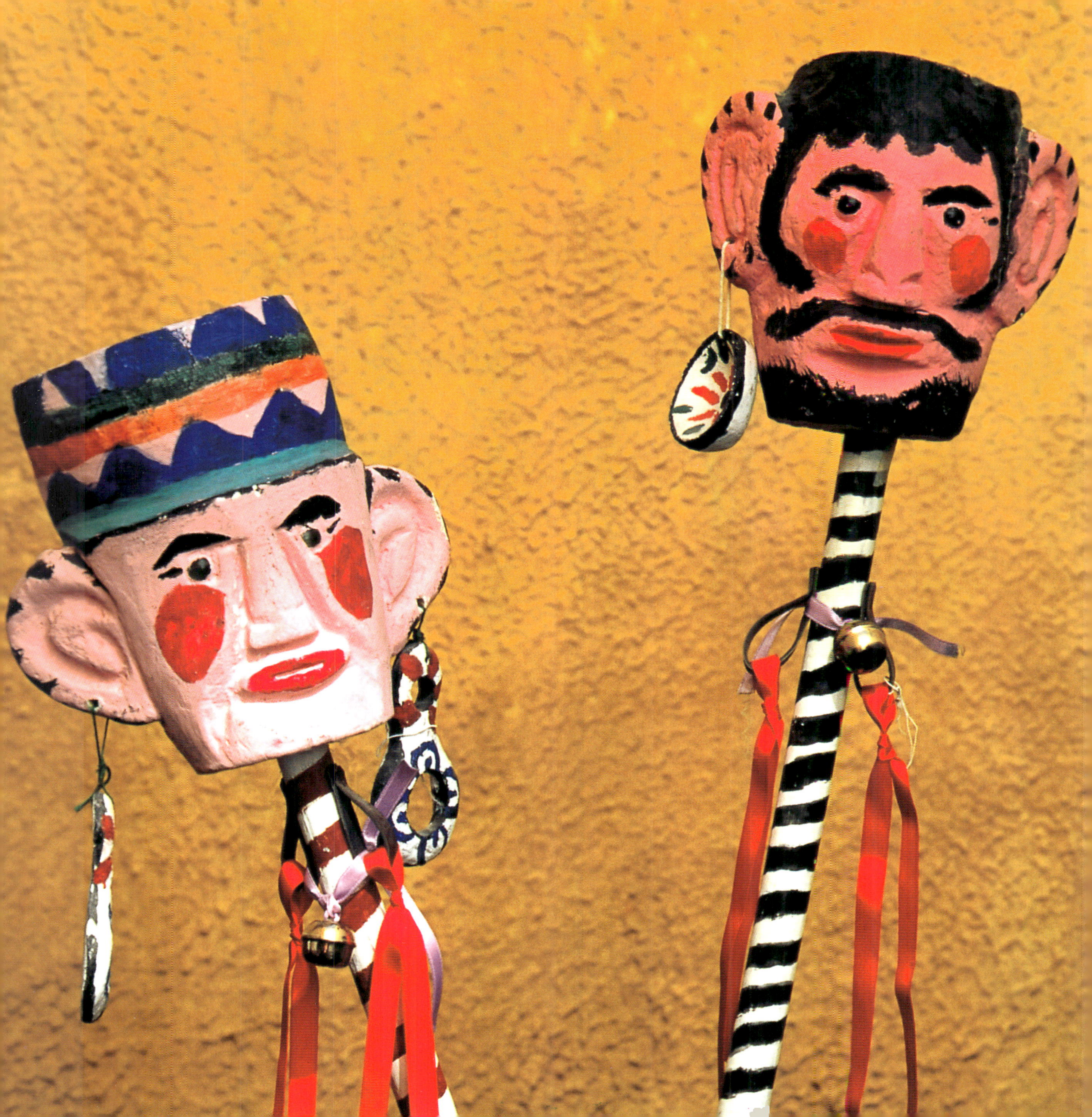

whose original meaning has been lost. Despite that, these games continue to add a playful character to the seasons of the year.

Toys and Memory

Incessant renovations and breathless updates are not made to the traditional toy, because it possesses the soul of permanence. It encompasses childhood memories handed down from one generation to another, and is thus both a symbol of identity and a vehicle that preserves tradition.

Given its durability, we can entrust our affection to a handmade toy. There is no doubt that when we as children were especially fond of a certain marble or *balero,* that toy permitted us to acquire special skills.

The industrial toy, on the contrary, is subject to fashion, to constant change. It is based on other premises: usefulness, sameness in its manufacture and above all, newness. Its role is to disappear, to be replaced by a "better" toy, as rapidly as possible.

In the traditional toy, collective persistence is interwoven and "tainted" with everyday concerns: manufactured toys are antiseptic, striving for the uniformity imposed on them by marketing edicts. Still, all toys are individualized when we infuse them with an emotional charge or strong symbolism. Once rescued from forgetfulness, a small train or a set of jacks which has been saved jealously over the years will by its mere presence revive the past, or recreate our passage through childhood.

By tradition, the handmade toy lives in Mexico's markets, its regional festivals and *tianguis* – neighborhood streets given over to selling and socializing. The customary jurisdiction of the industrialized toy is the huge warehouse store, and we hear about it on television, or in mass-market magazines.

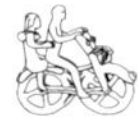

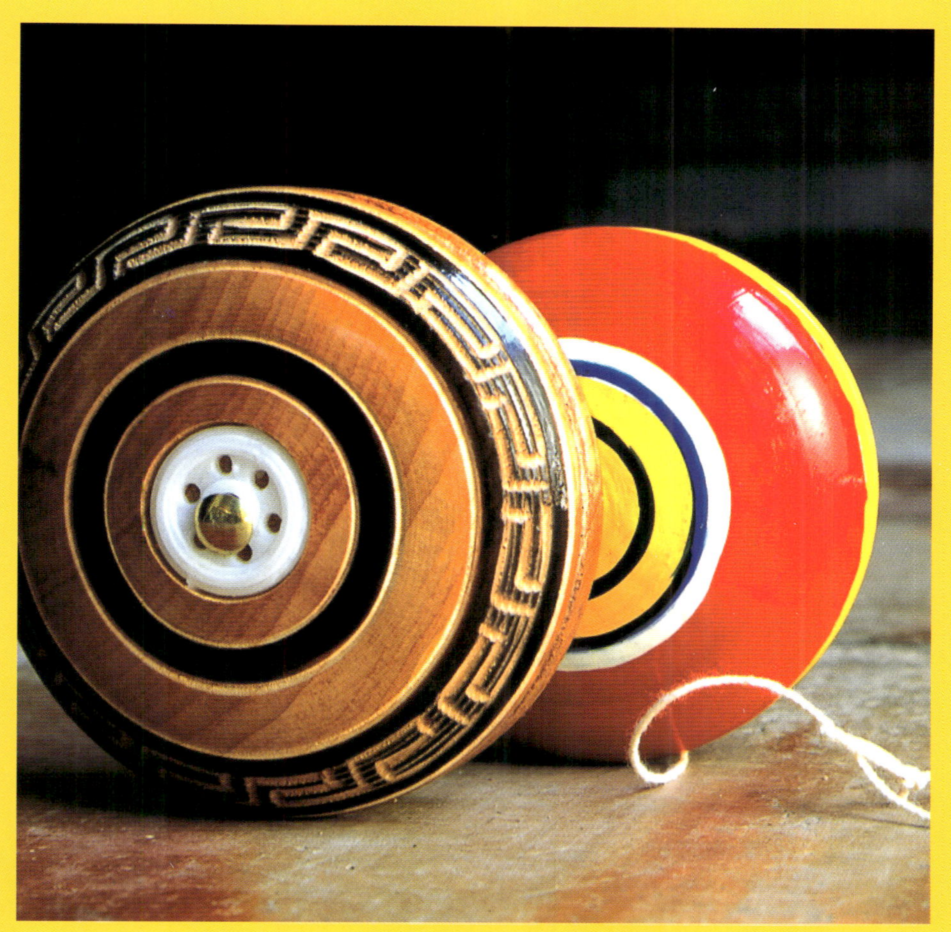

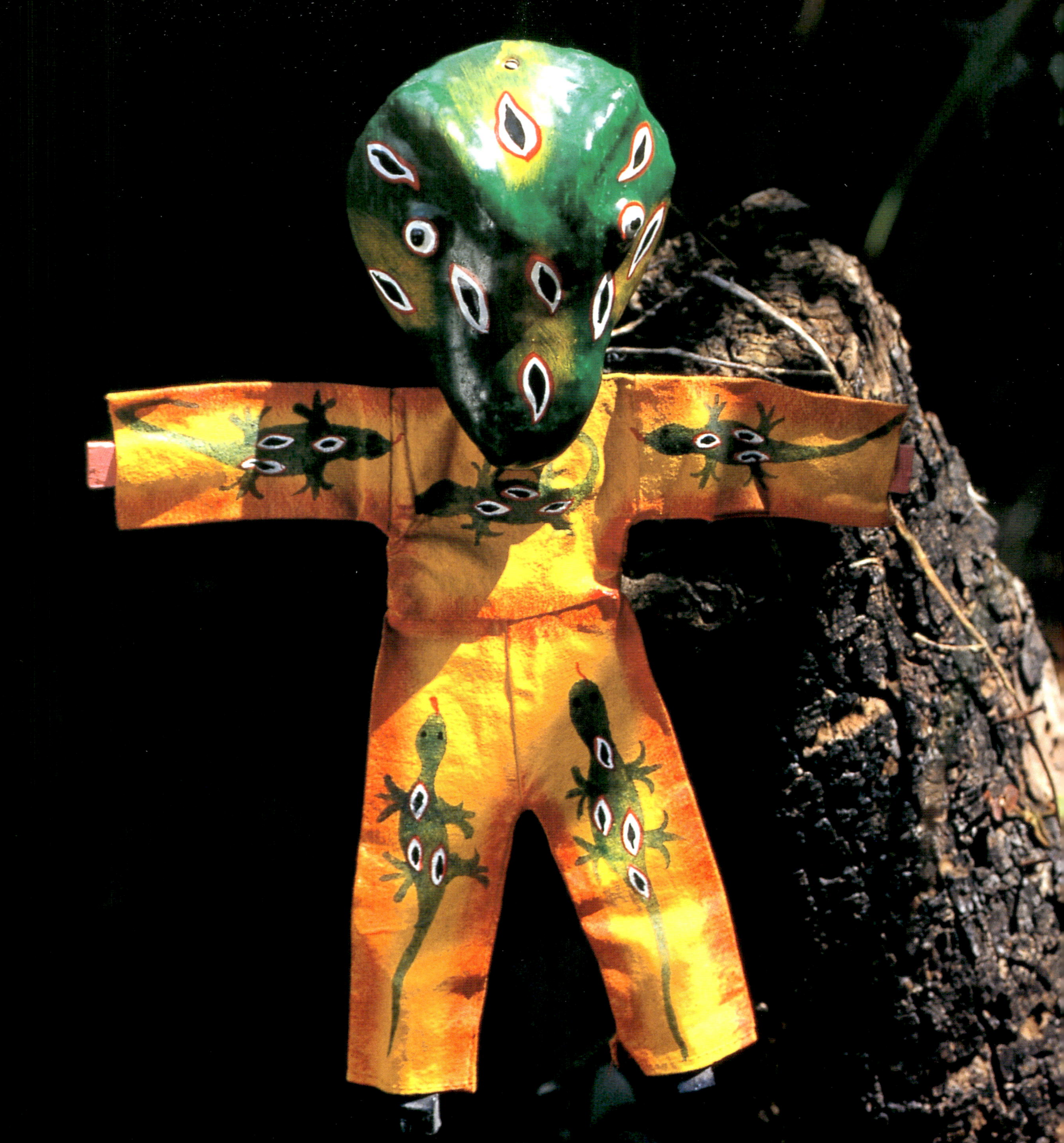

For those artisans who still dedicate themselves to the creation of traditional toys, work and play comprise a single process. In the toys they produce, we see the fantasy, wit and imagination of men who play while they work. It is not so strange, then, that these artisans have decided to give substance to figures with deep popular roots, to dreams, myths and chimeras which come alive in toys that are appreciated as much for their craftsmanship as for the memories they evoke.

It is well known that the effects of illusion never completely end when the game does, for at that moment these objects become fetishes to conserve the splendor of the living moment. Surely this is why many travellers are seduced by traditional toys, and smitten with fantastic forms. Away from the time and place of the game – or, once the trip is over– these toys become decorative objects charged with preserving memories of each place visited.

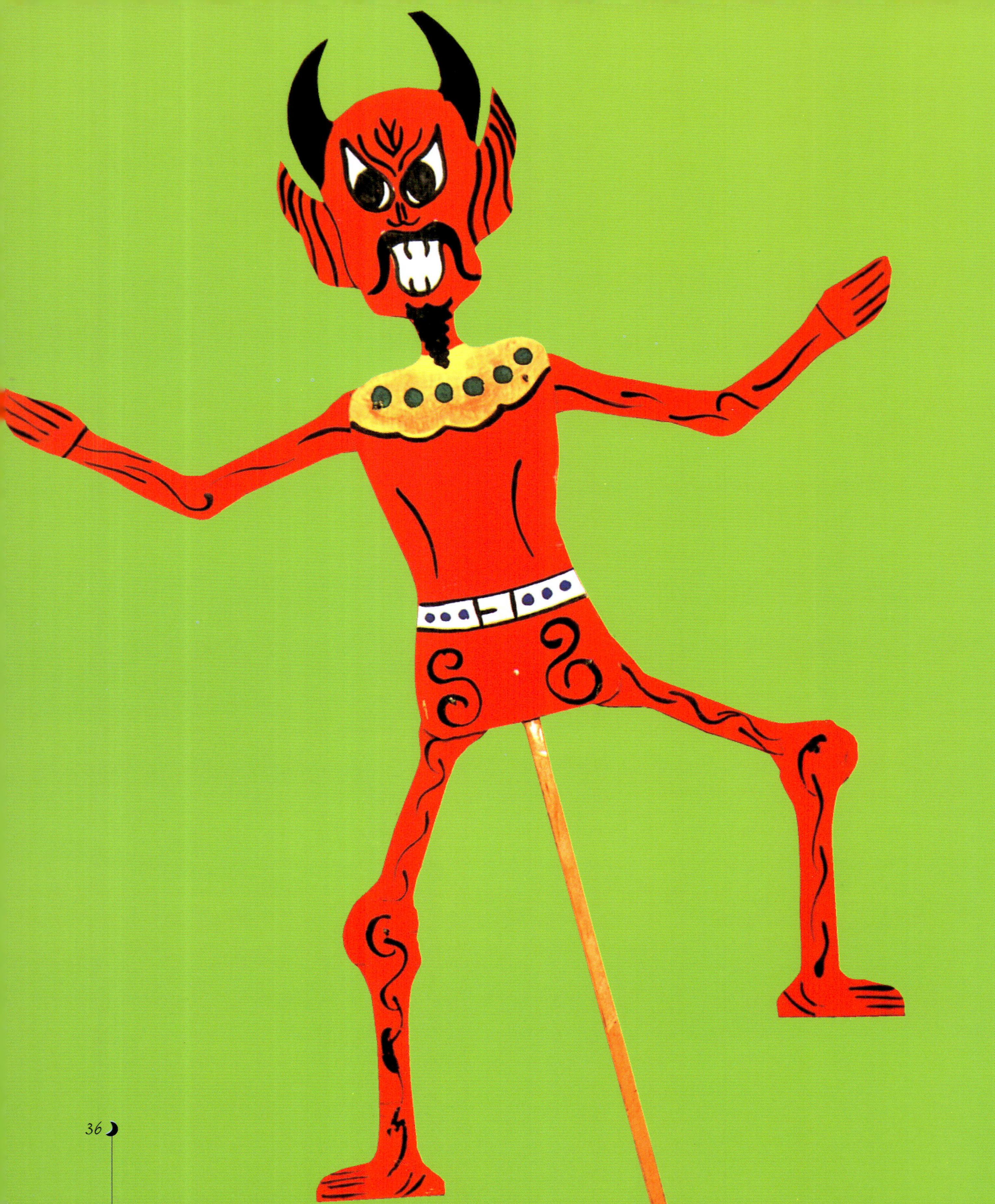

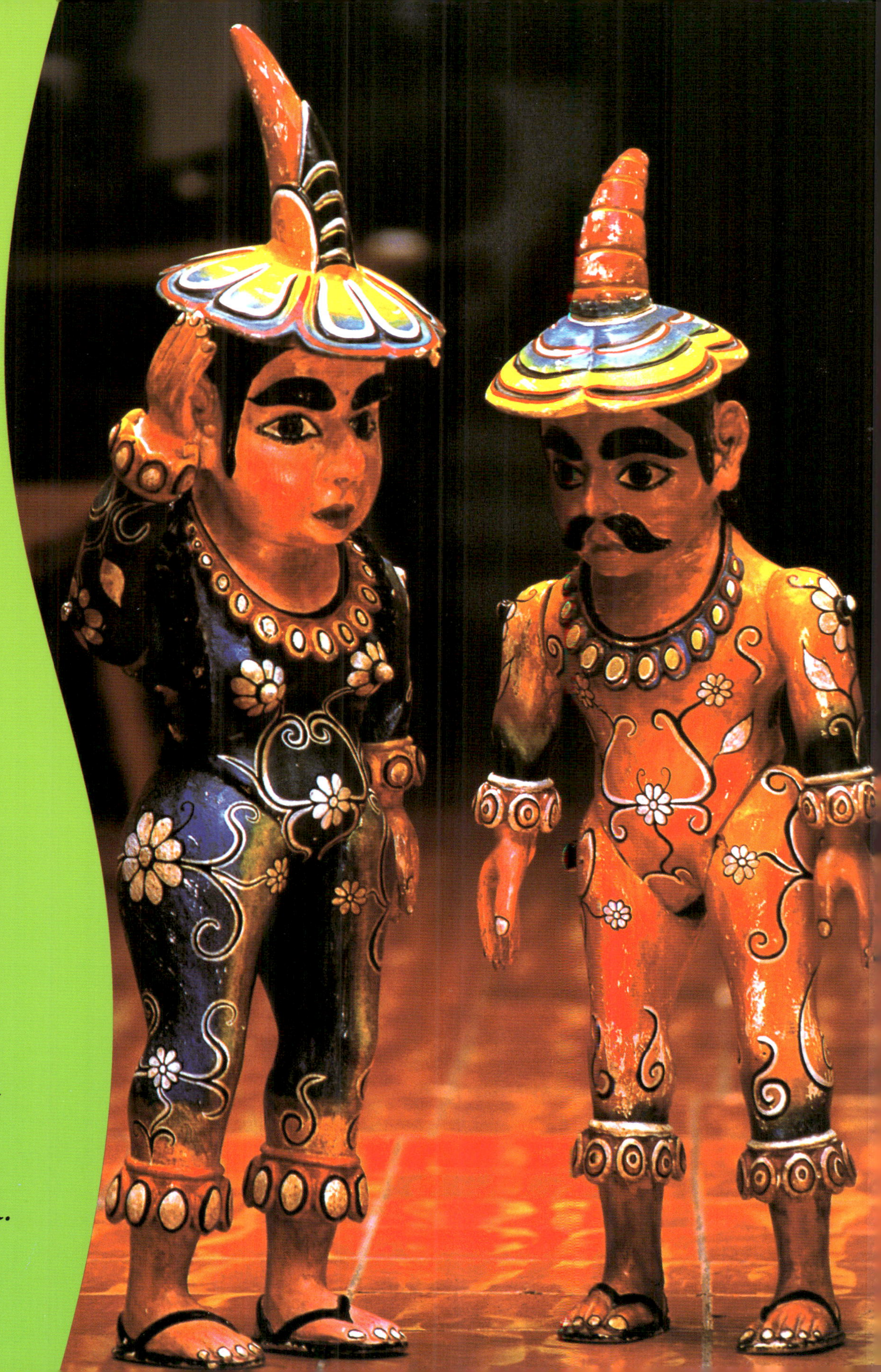

Imaginary worlds,
creatures from fantastic
menageries
and creatures from forests
   still found in nature…

flowers uprooted
by hands that deliver them
to the gentle surface
   of the burnished garden.

A jungle of glowing creatures
that have never been seen in the mirrors of other eyes.

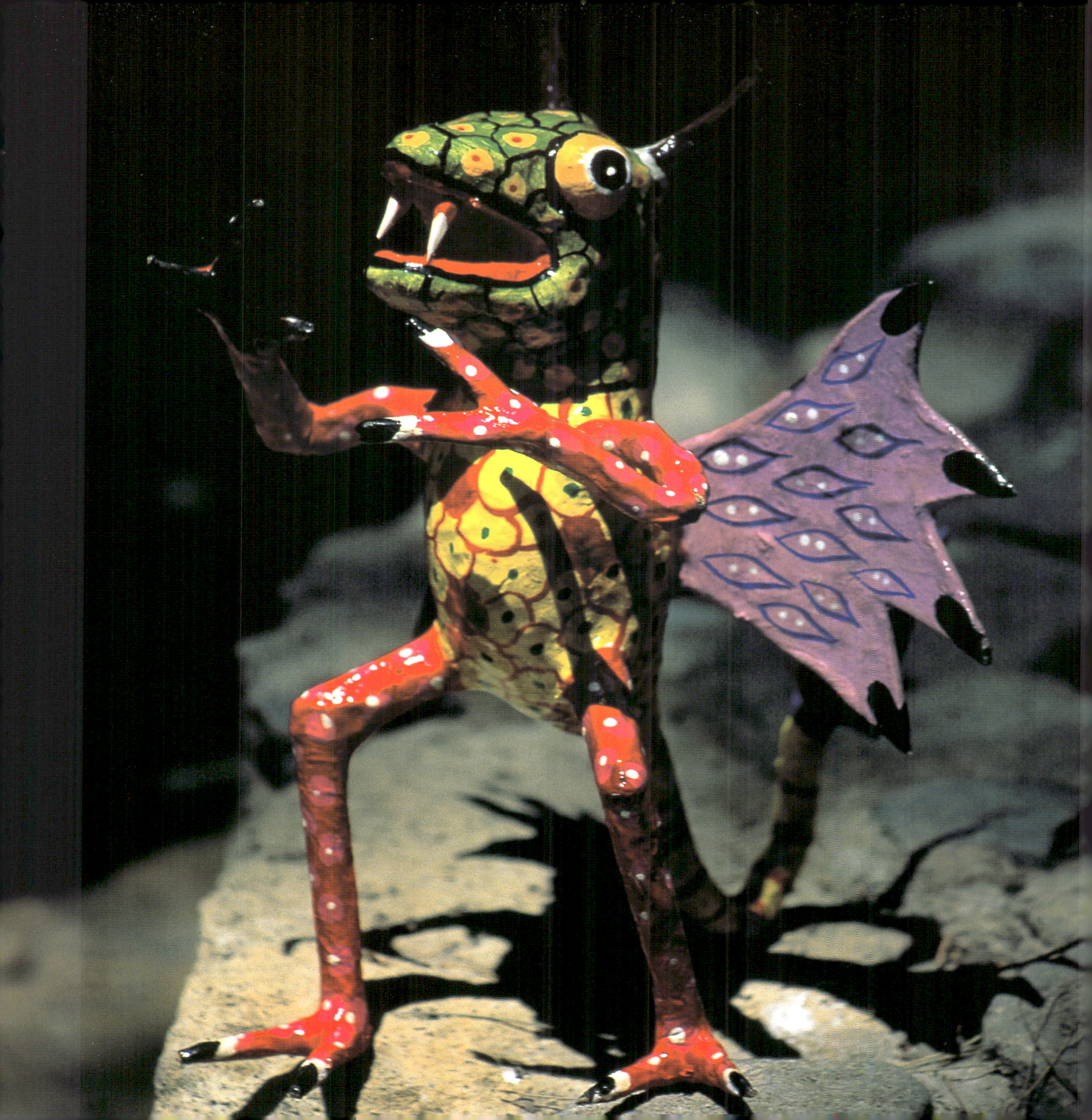

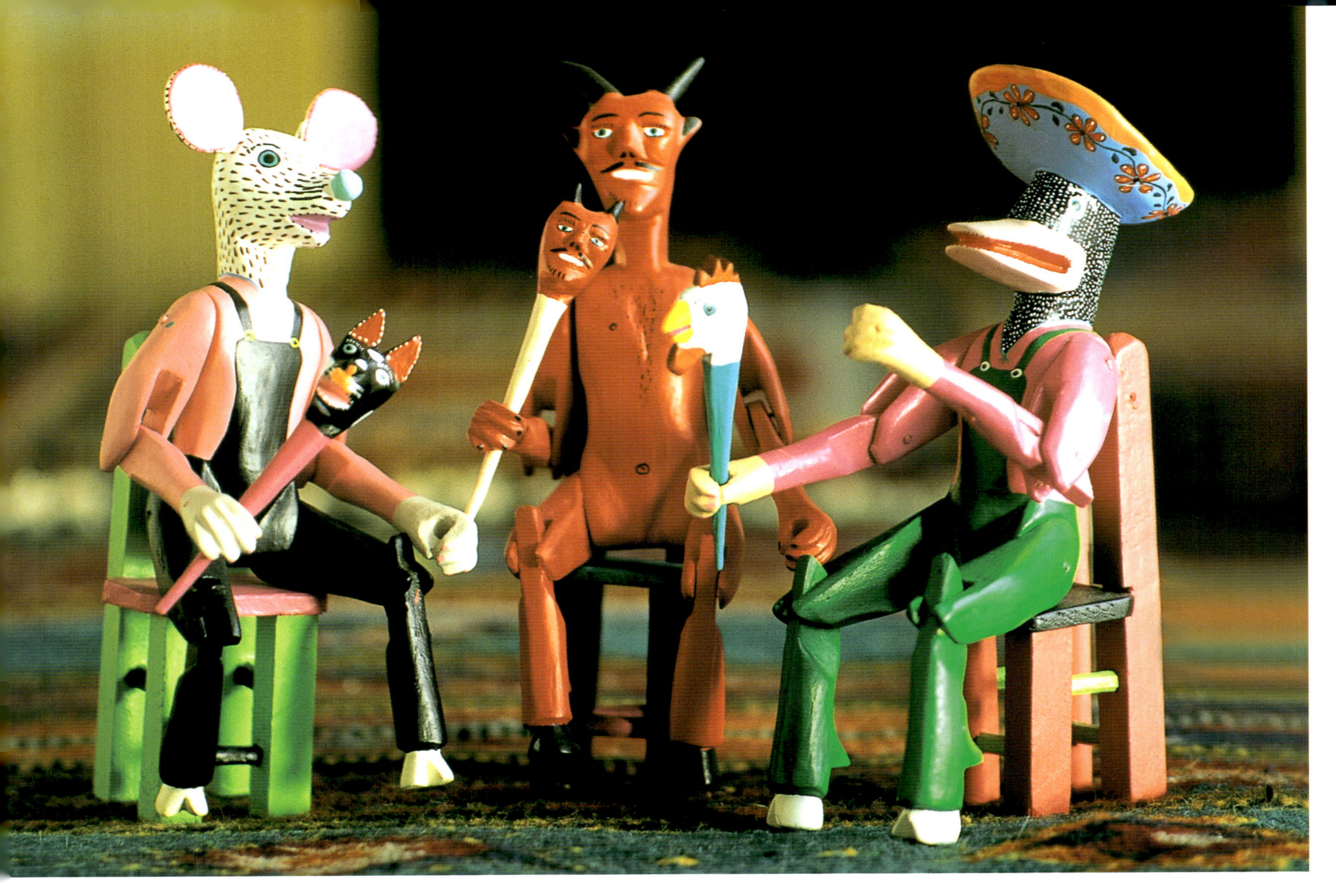

In the magical zoo
    they exhibit the best reveries,
        but also the weirdest nightmares
            of star-struck artisans.

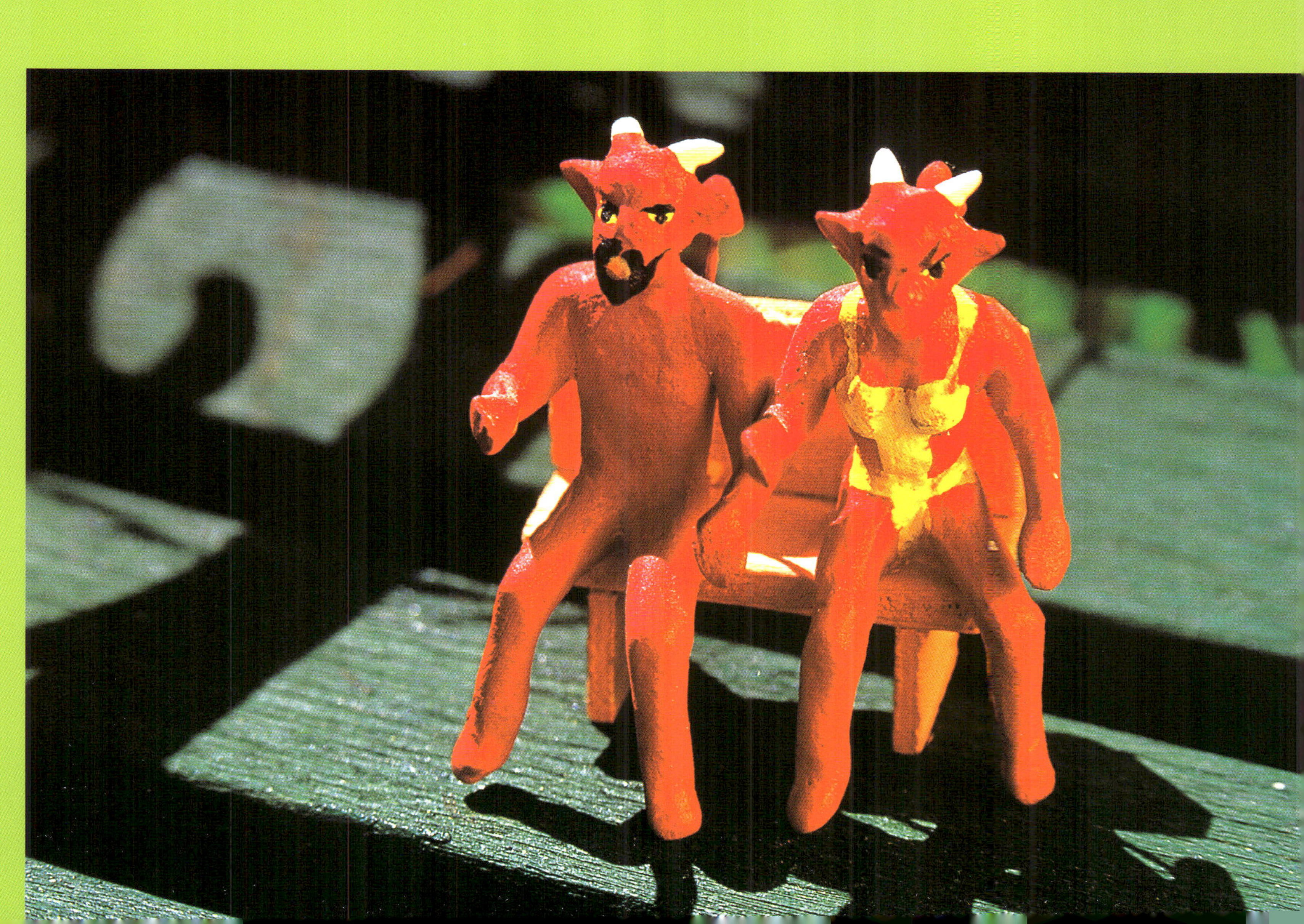

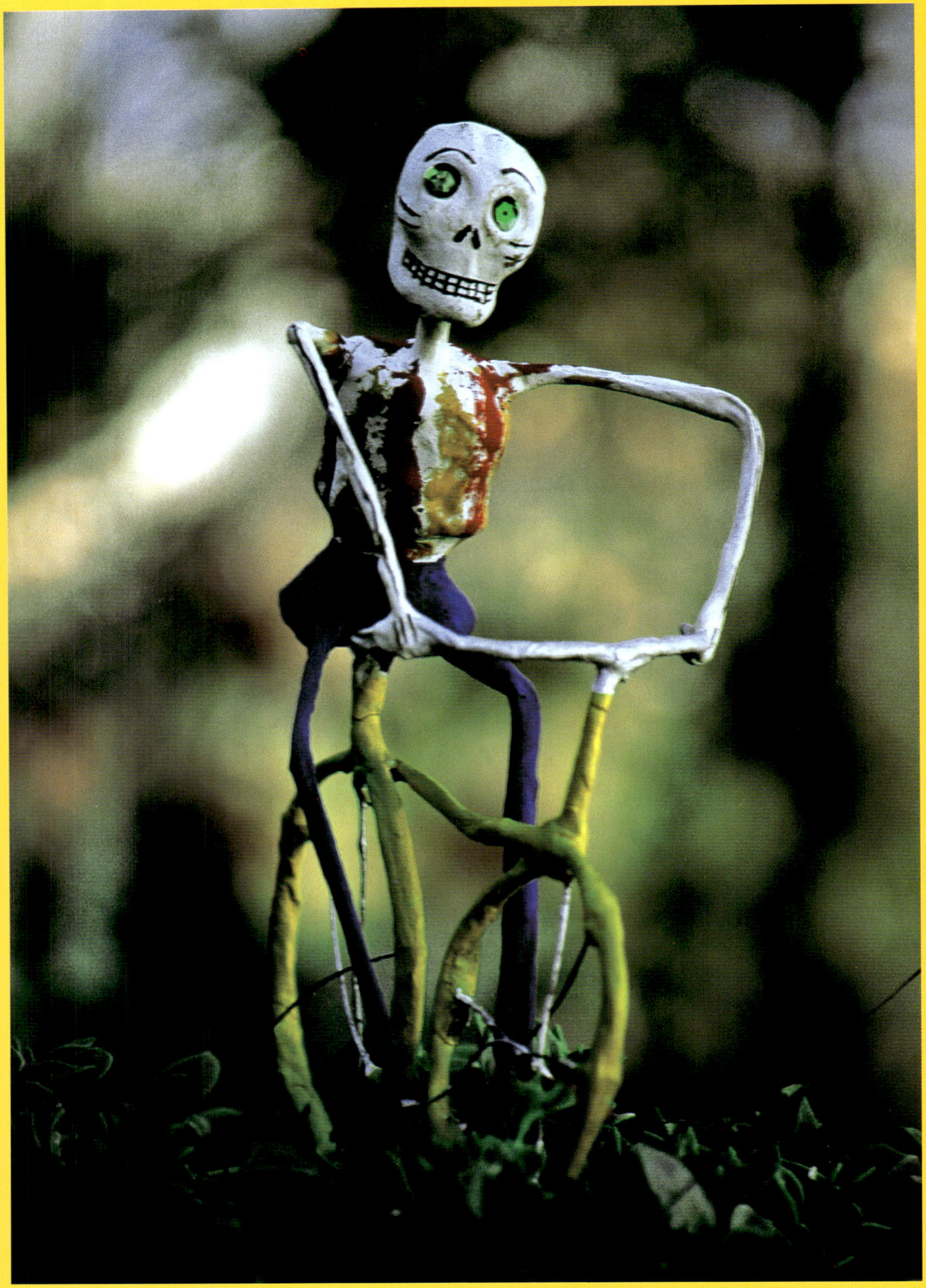

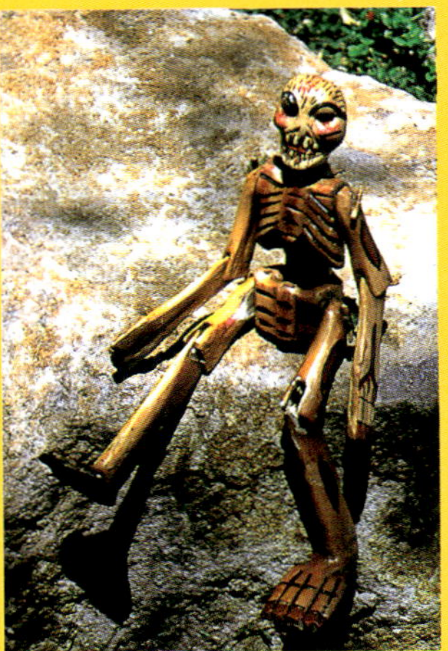

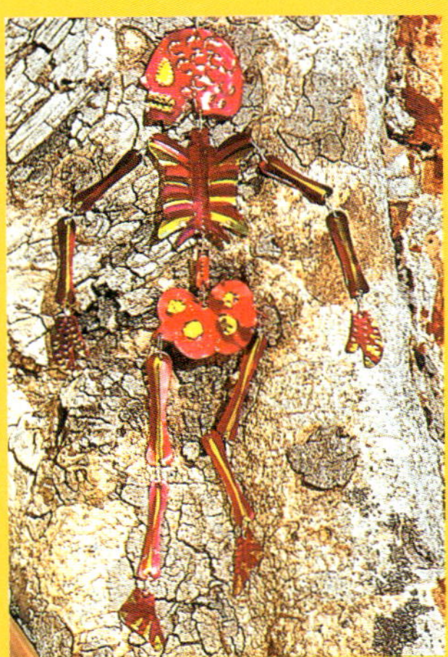

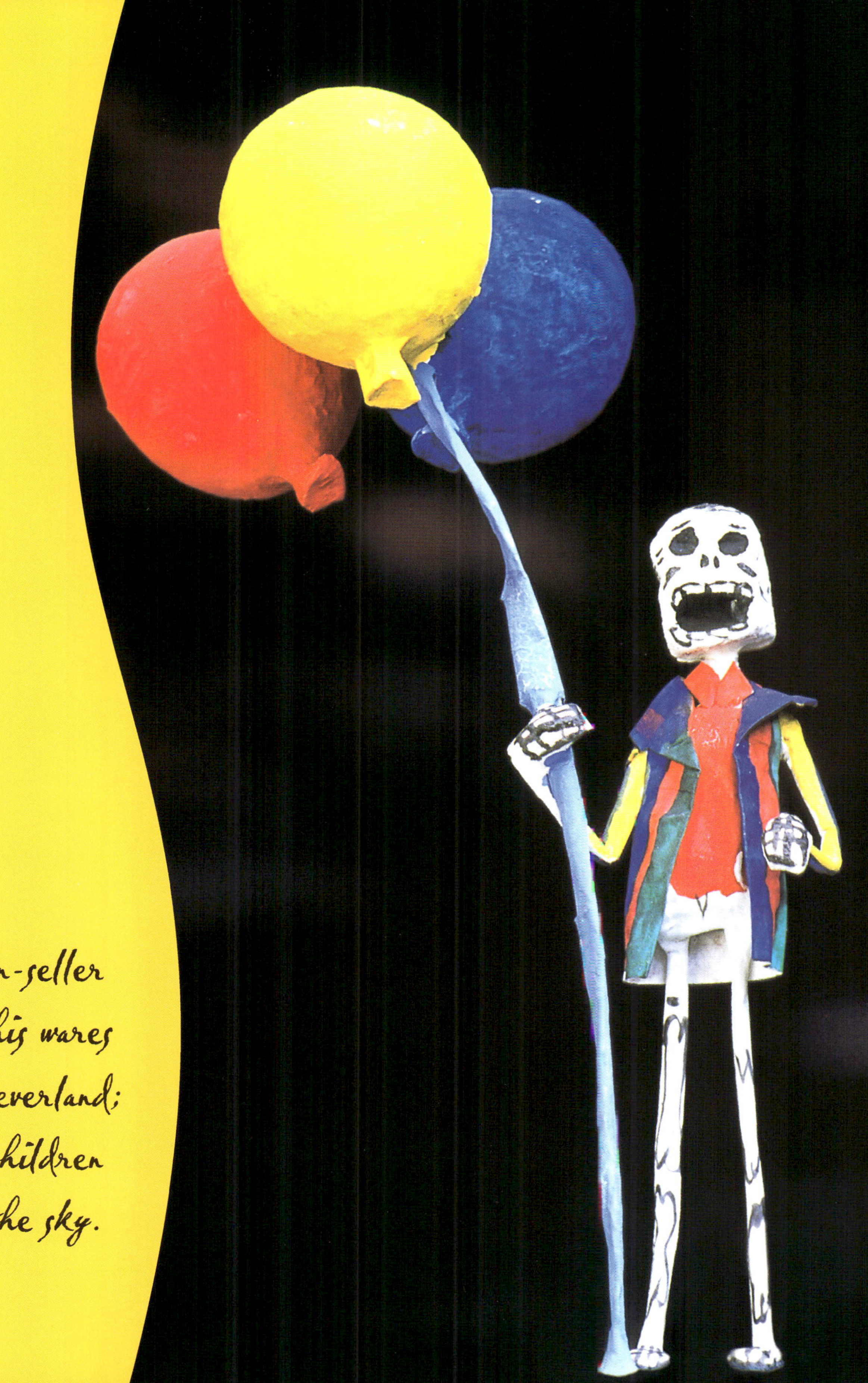

Skeleton balloon-seller
announces his wares
on a corner in neverland;
a sign that heaven's children
also keep playing in the sky.

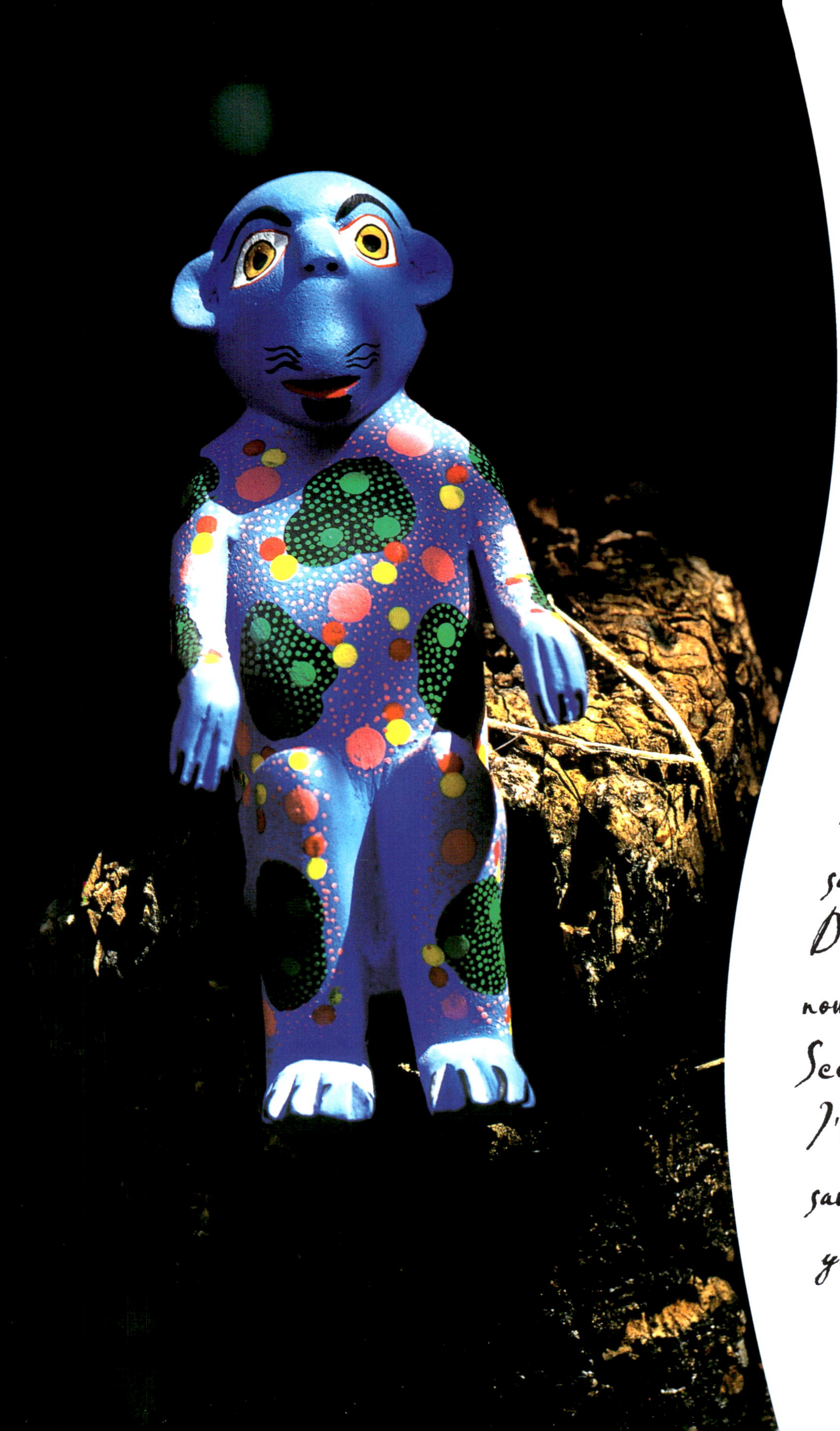

Matanga,
said the monkey bold
Devil said,
now you're really too old,
Scorpion said,
I'll finish you off,
said Pelican,
you think you're so tough!

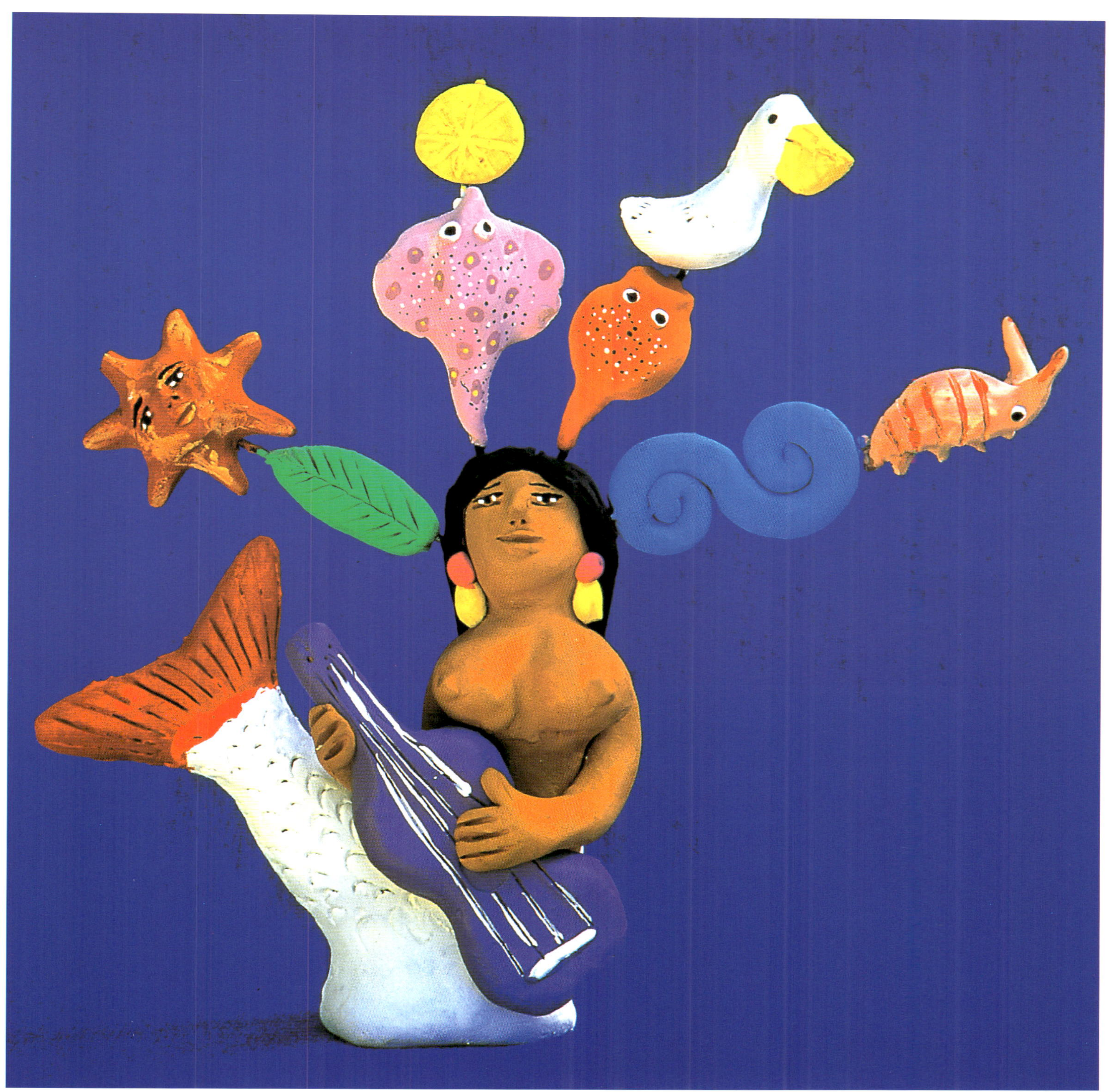

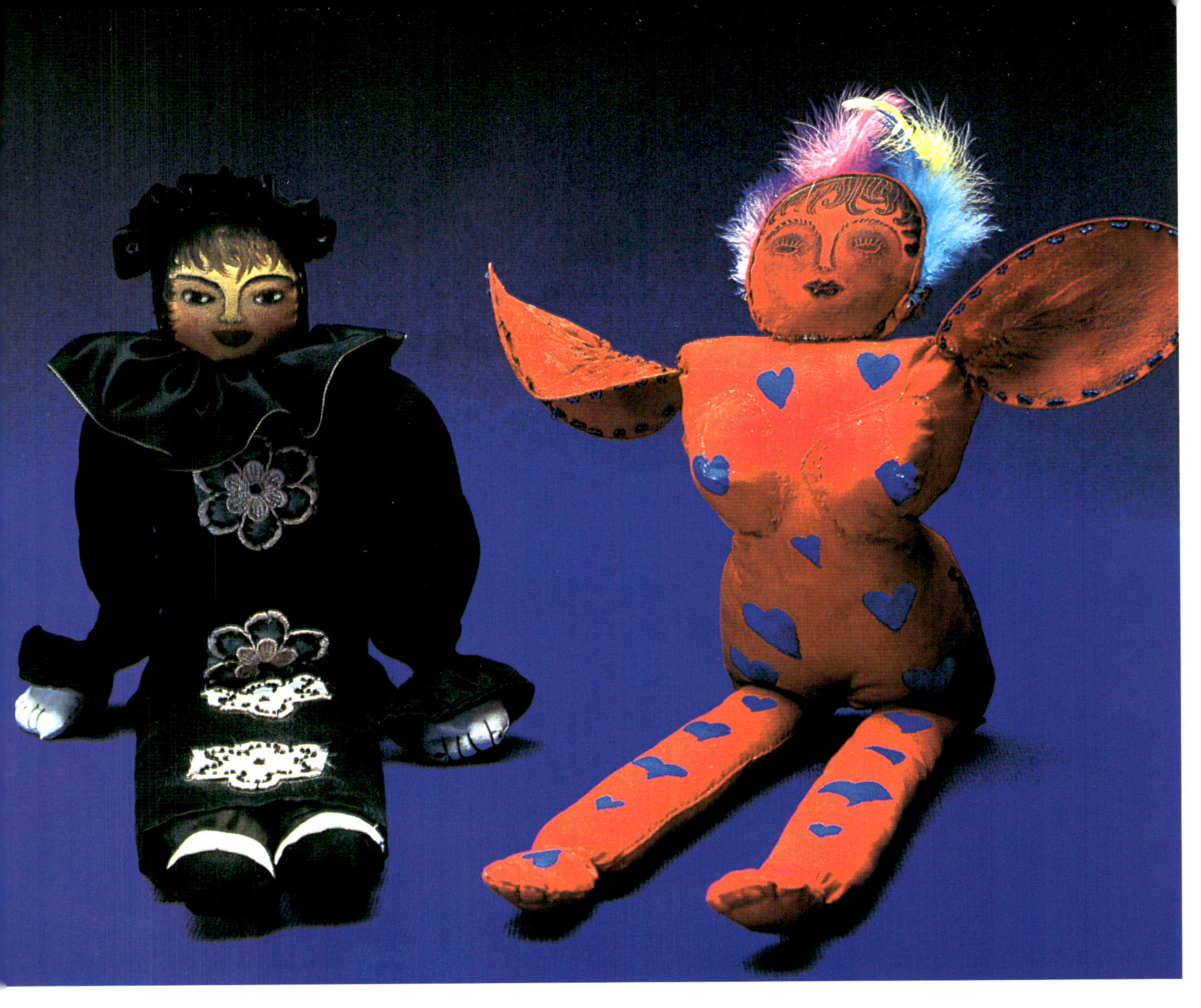

With your arms as wings
      you want to fly to your jungle-heaven,
but how unsettling, not to know if you are night-bird,
      wild-girl or fruit from a spell-cast tree.

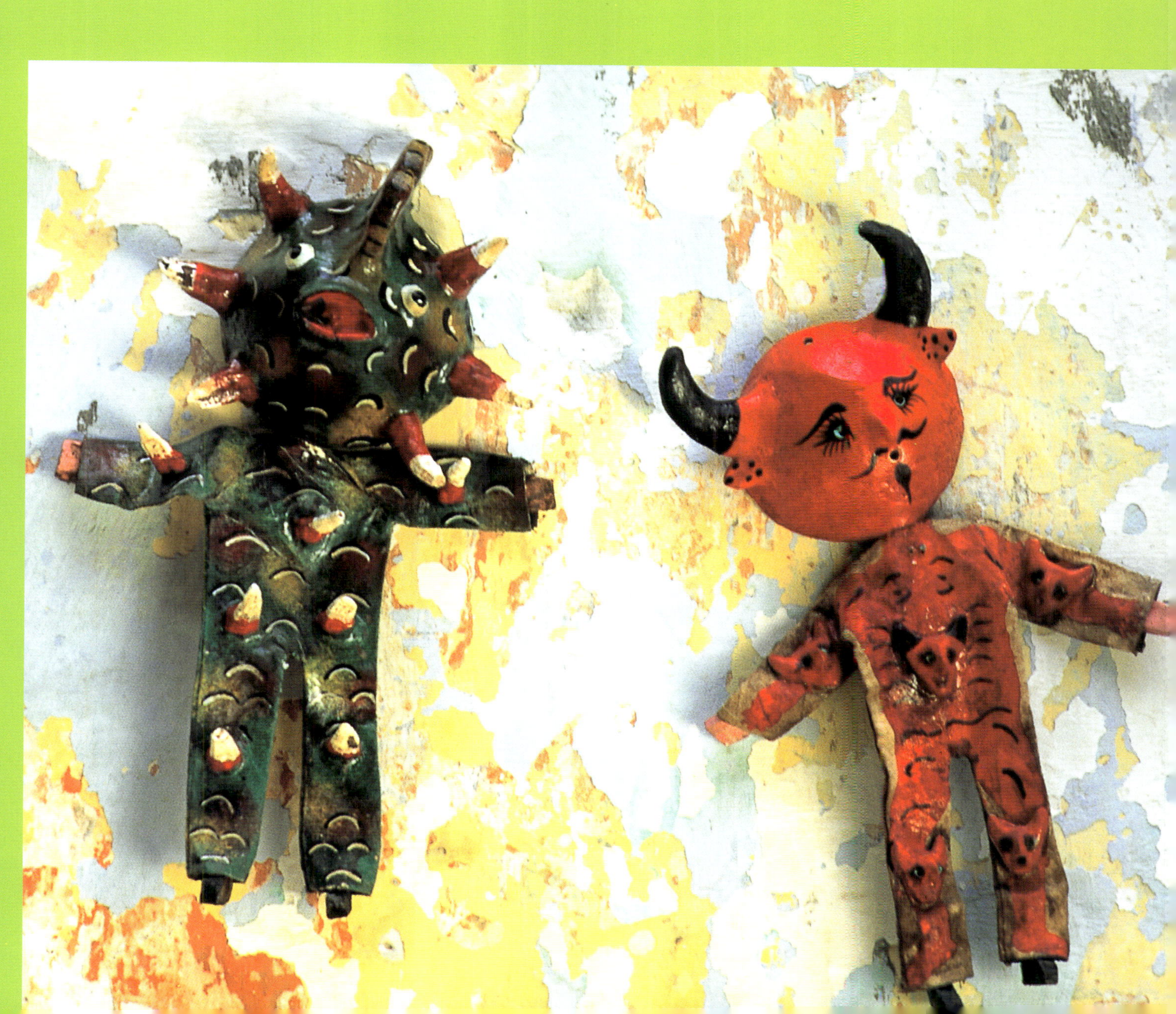

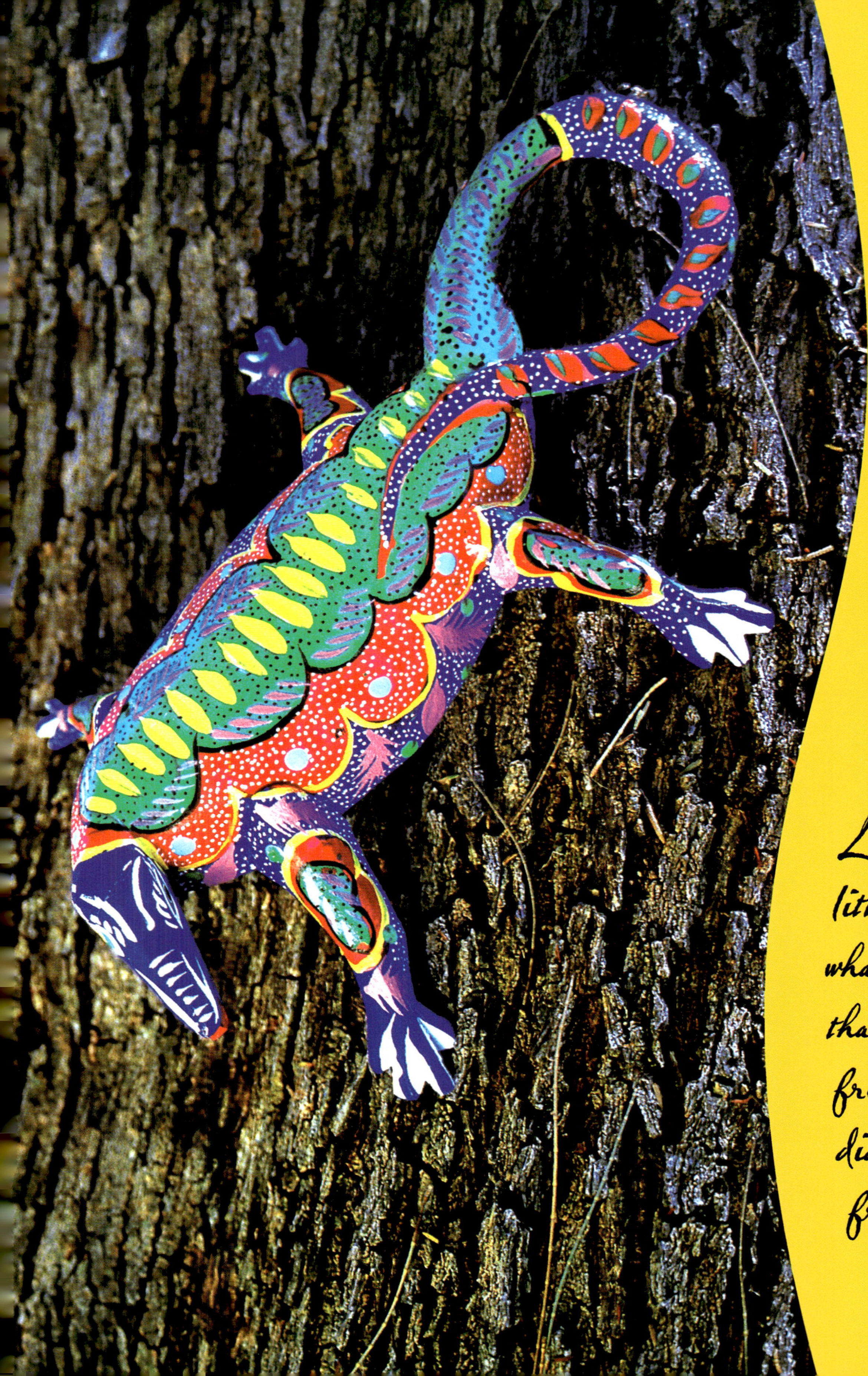

Lizard from another world
little reptile I've hallucinated
what are you seeking here
that you don't have there?
from which dream
did you break away,
from which starry zoo?

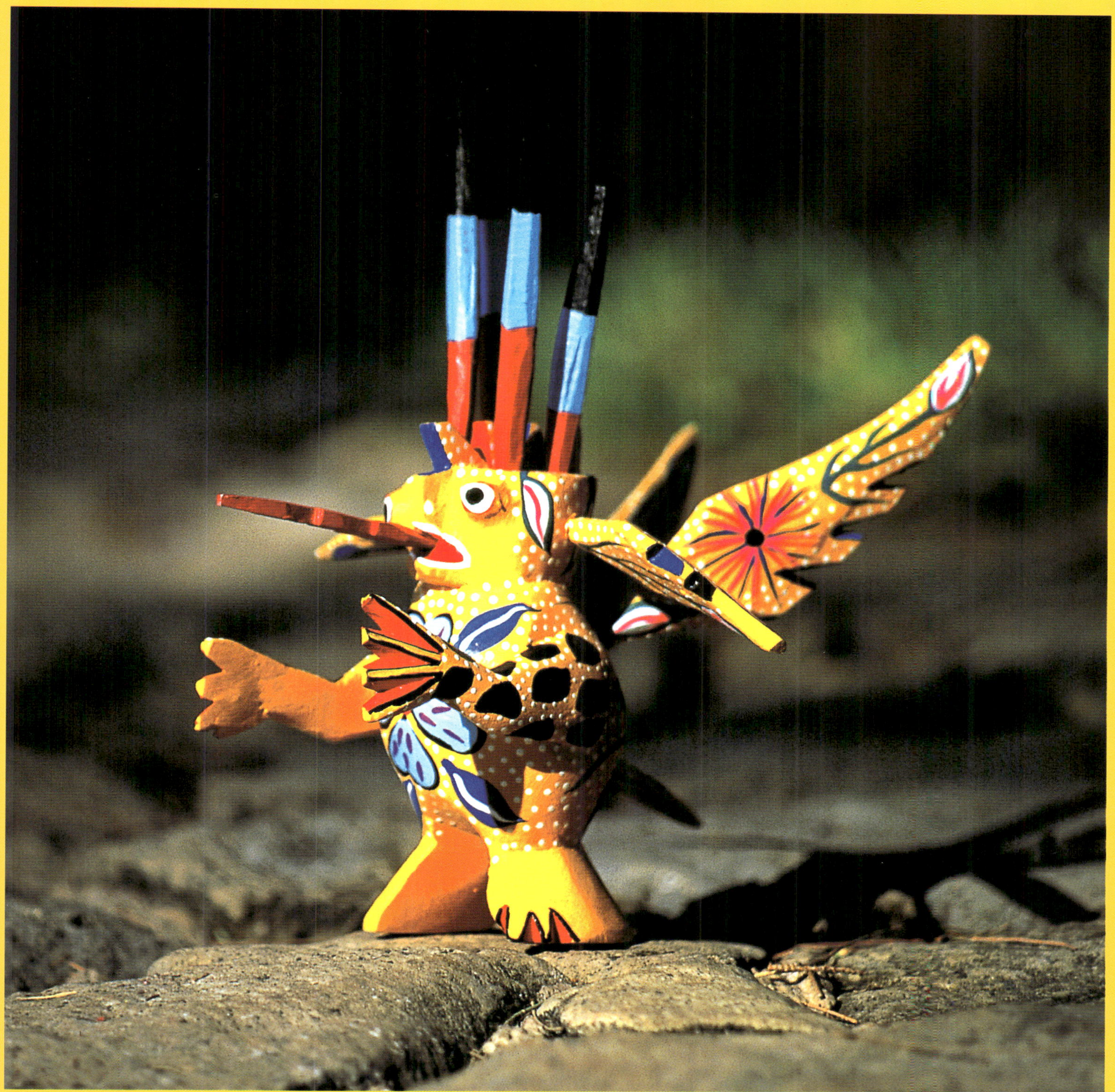

They look too much like us,
despite their outlandish shapes,

because toys, I must tell you,
make-believe they're people.

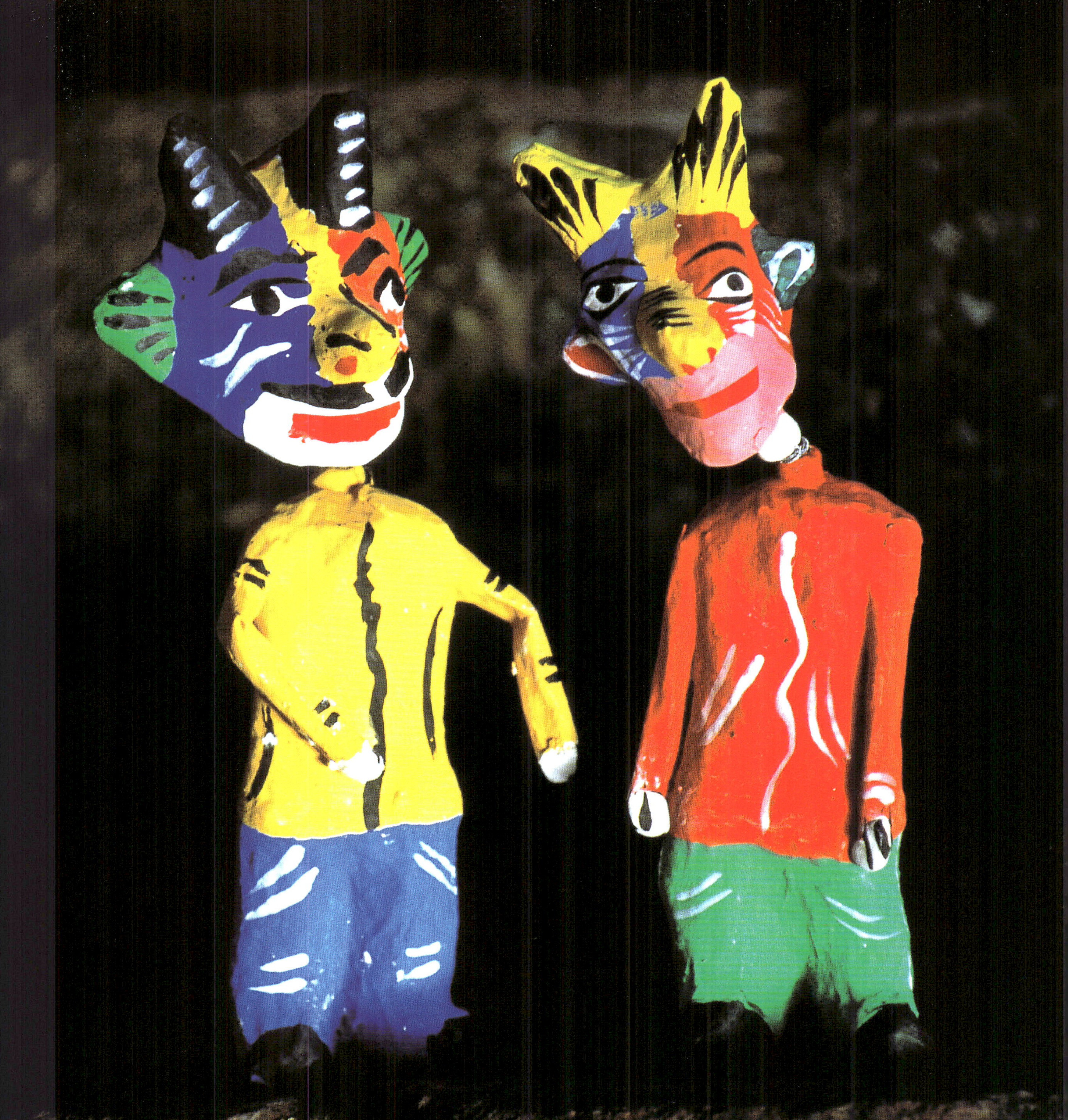

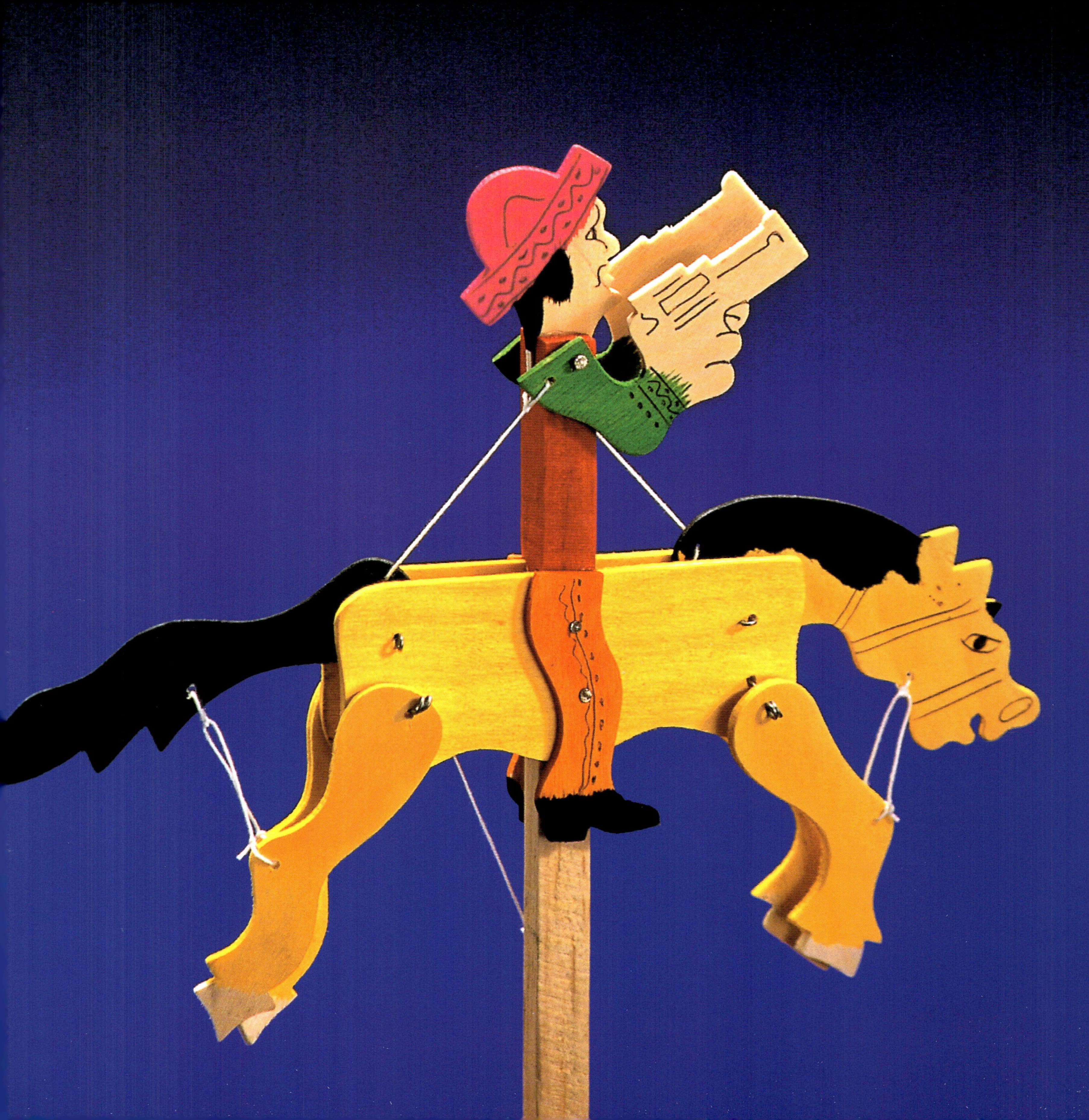

Famous for the ingenuity of their designs, their variety and strong colors, toys brought forth by the diligent hands of traditional artisans capture the spirit of childhood with their simple and clever mechanisms.

Hobby-horses, woven reed snakes, fighting roosters, boxers, puppets and marionettes are converted into true mascots which — whether through human know-how or mechanical gadgetry — come alive or remain spiritless, depending on their owners' will.

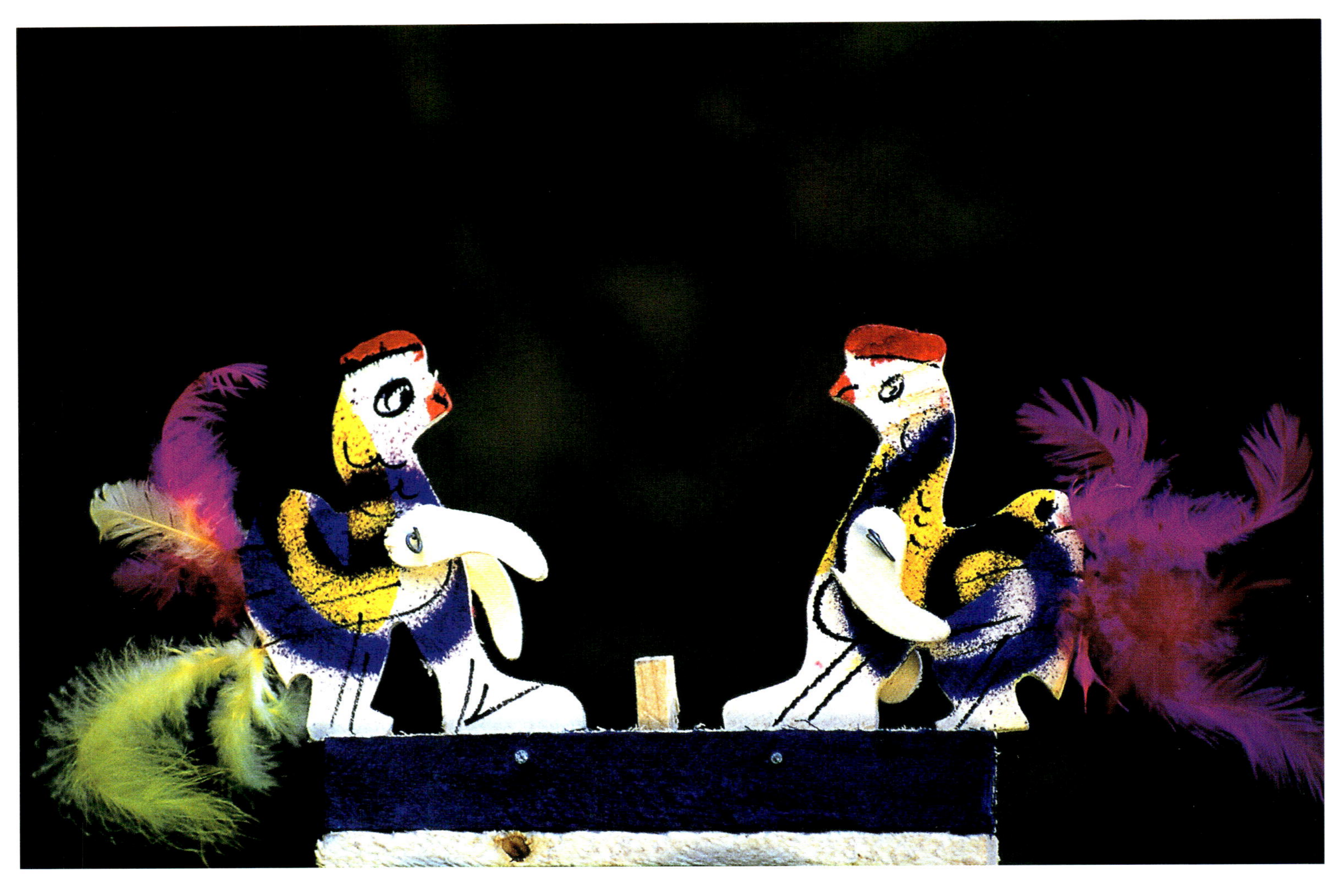

They fight to the death
thrown together in the toy arena
pecking each other with maddened feathers.

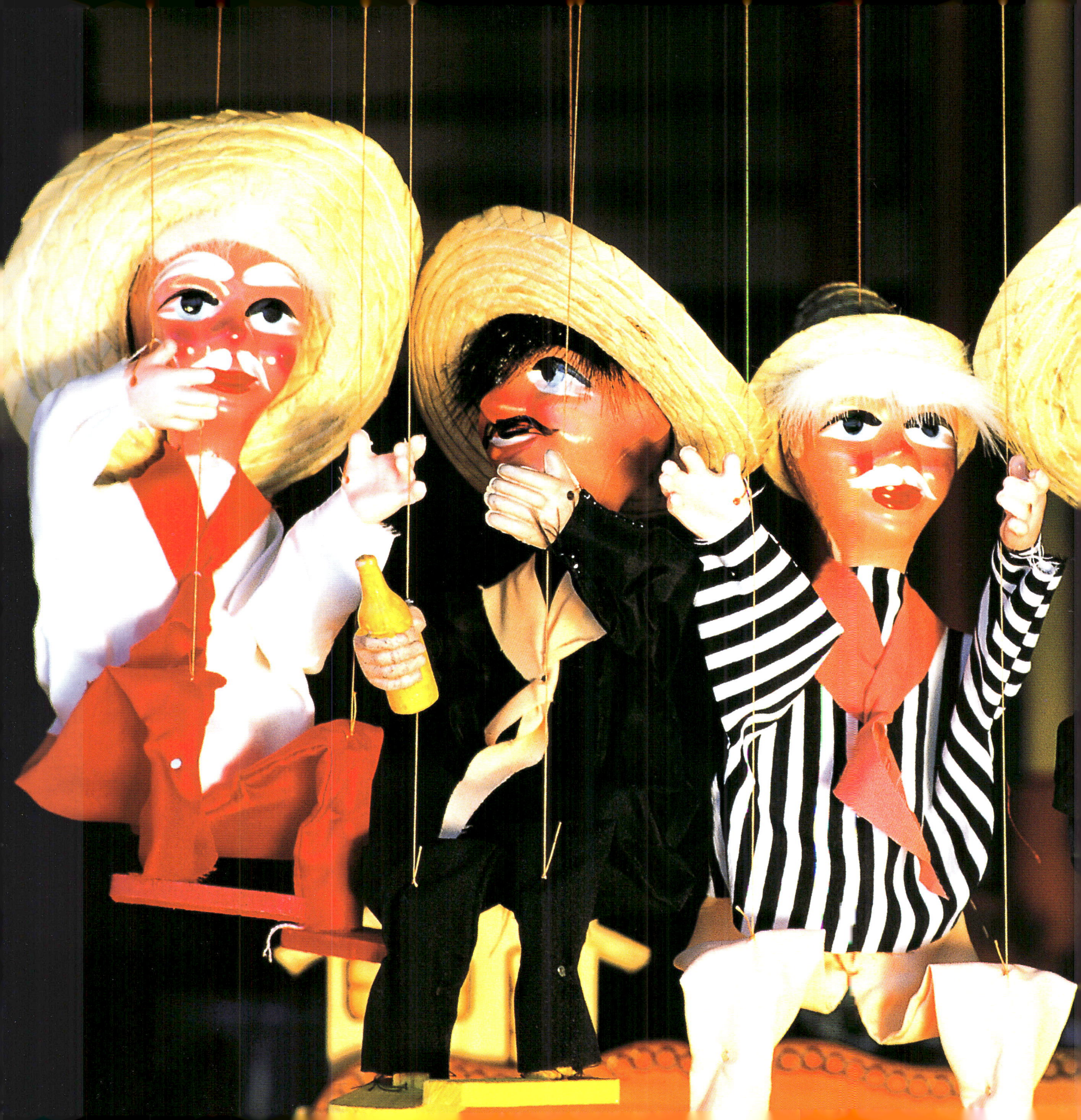

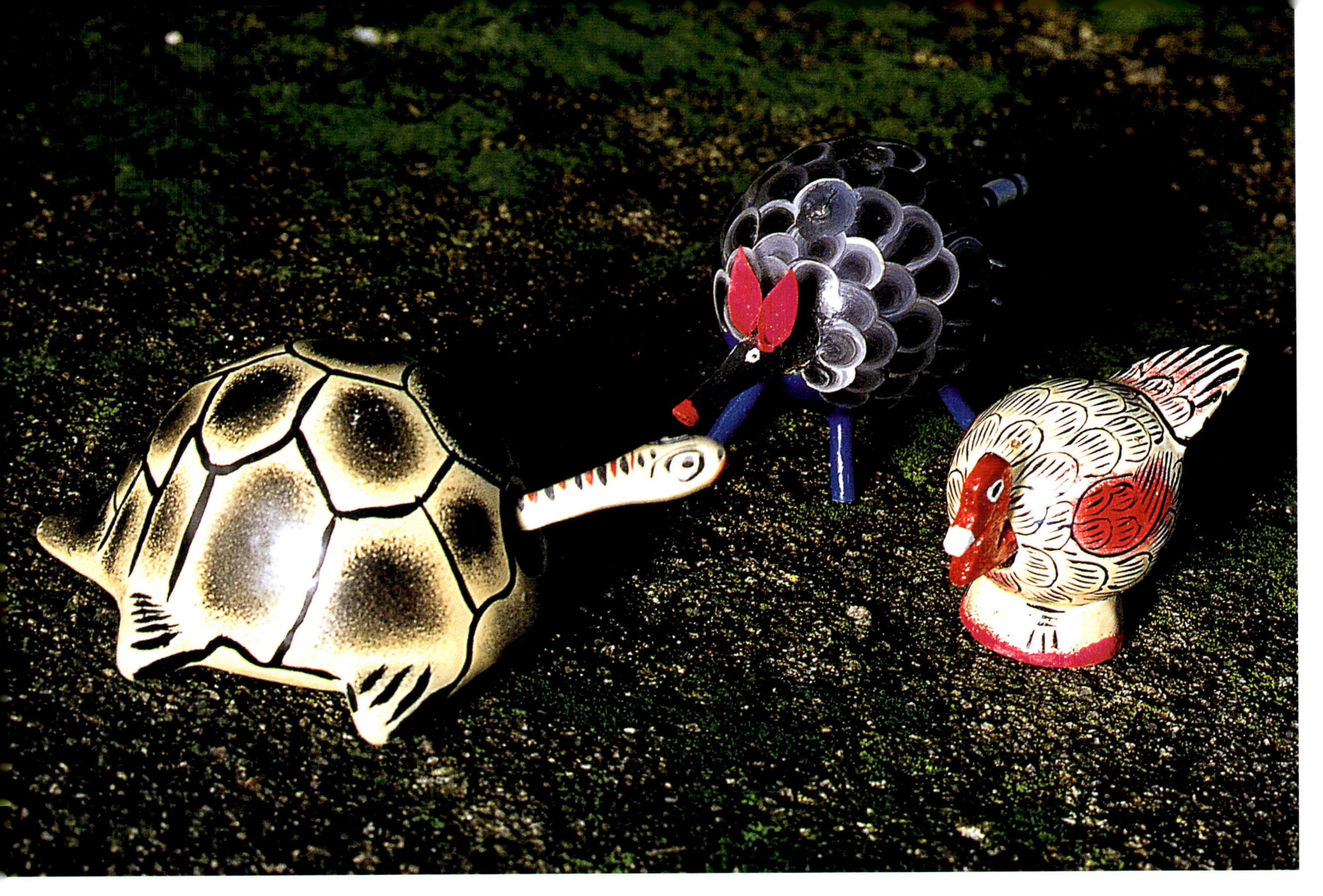

Toys from every walk of life,
  A movable zoo, of clay or wood
for improvising a jungle or farmyard
  in the flowerbox.

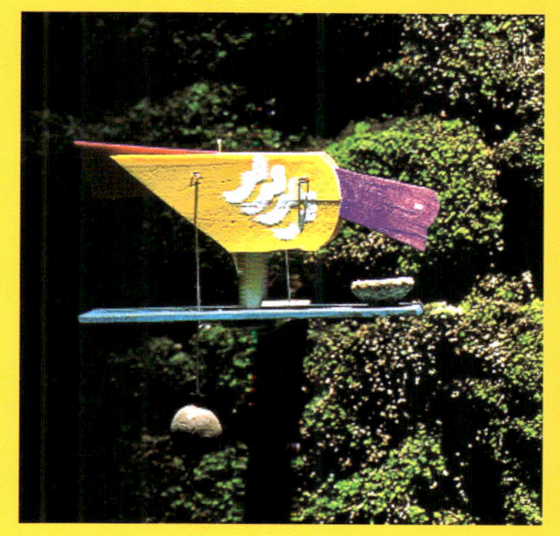

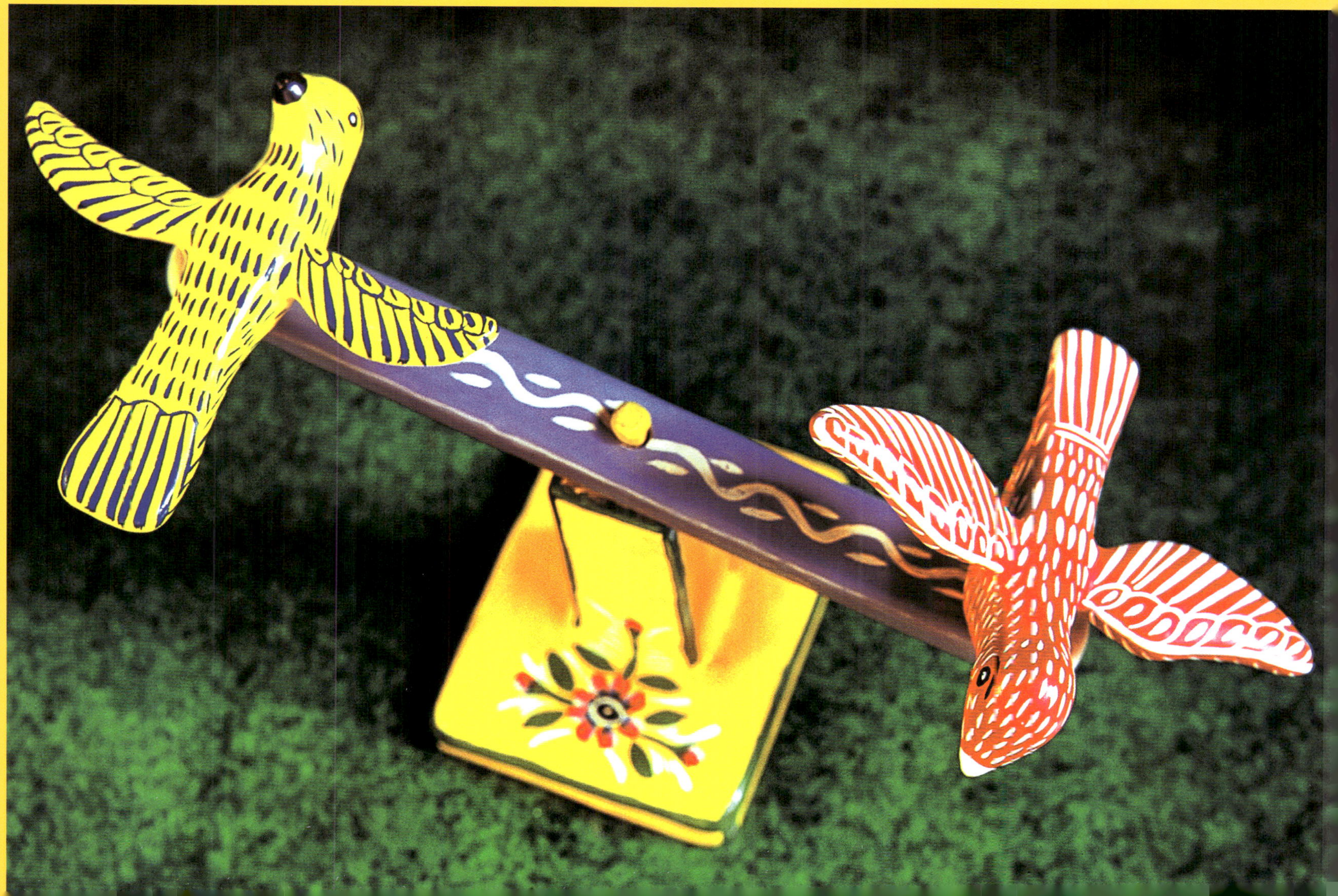

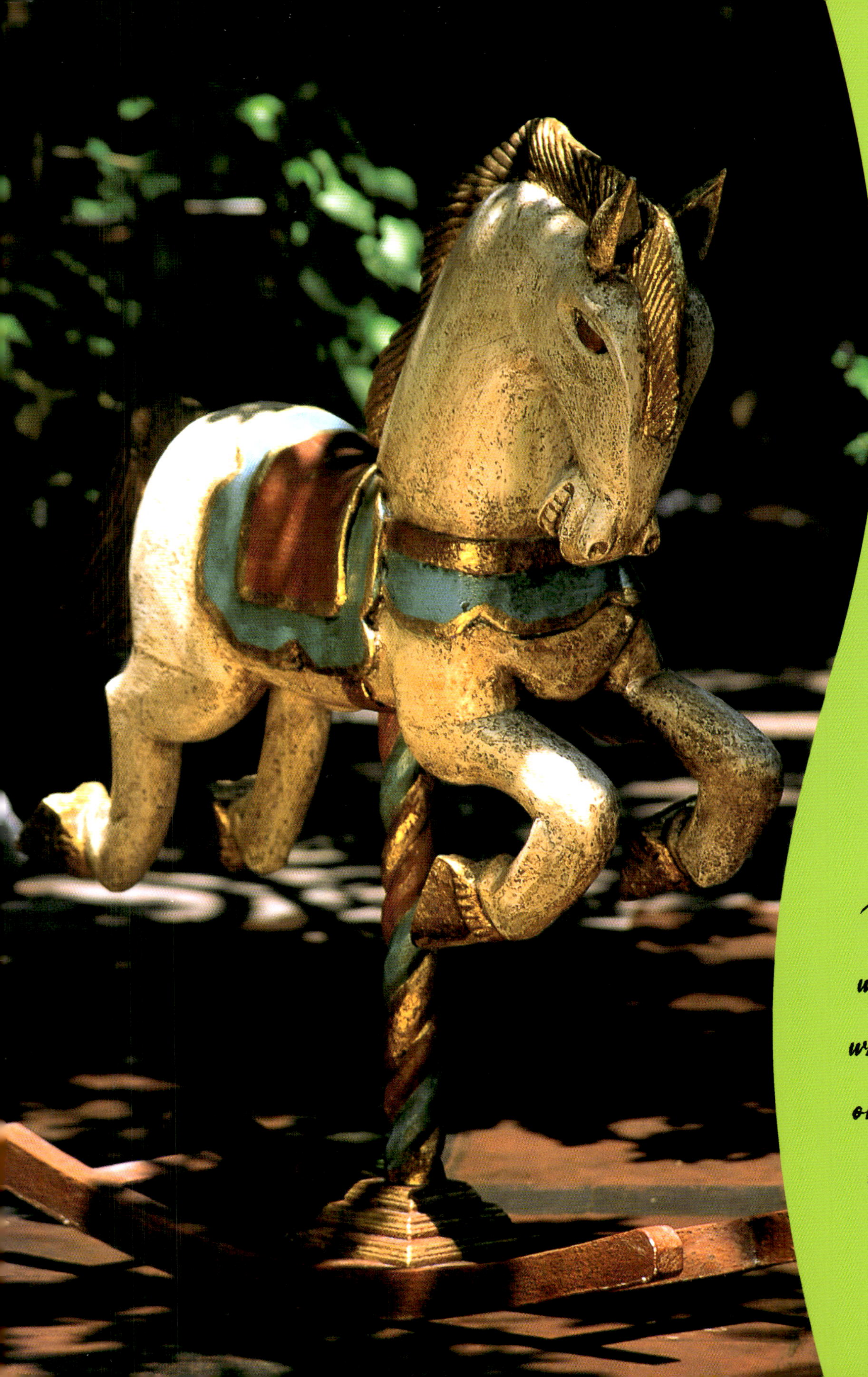

Wandering horse,
who cannot run,
who only rocks,
only sketches
half its journey.

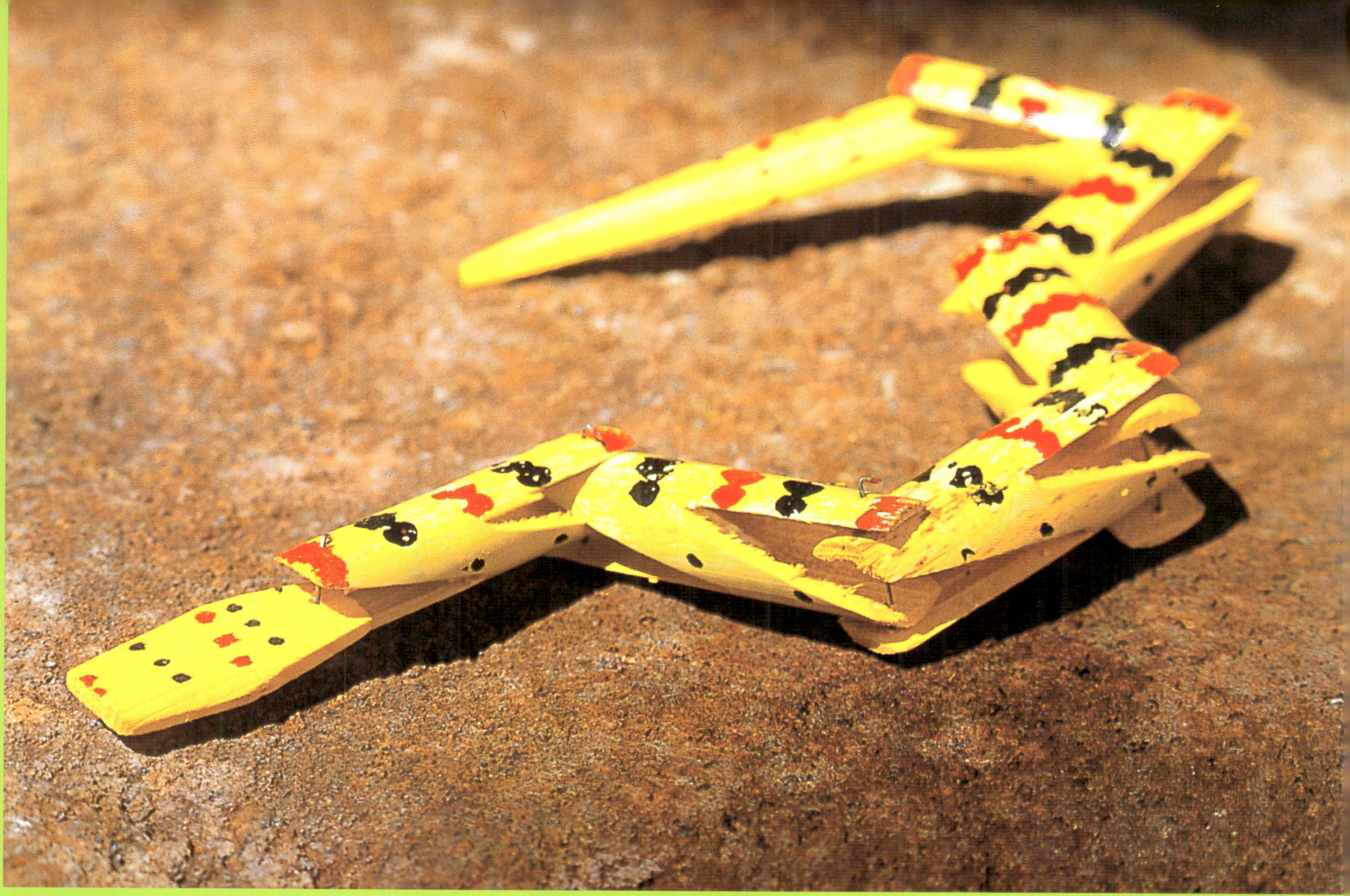

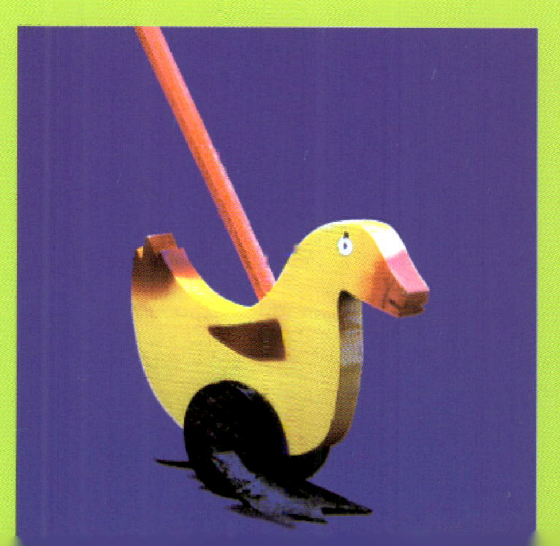

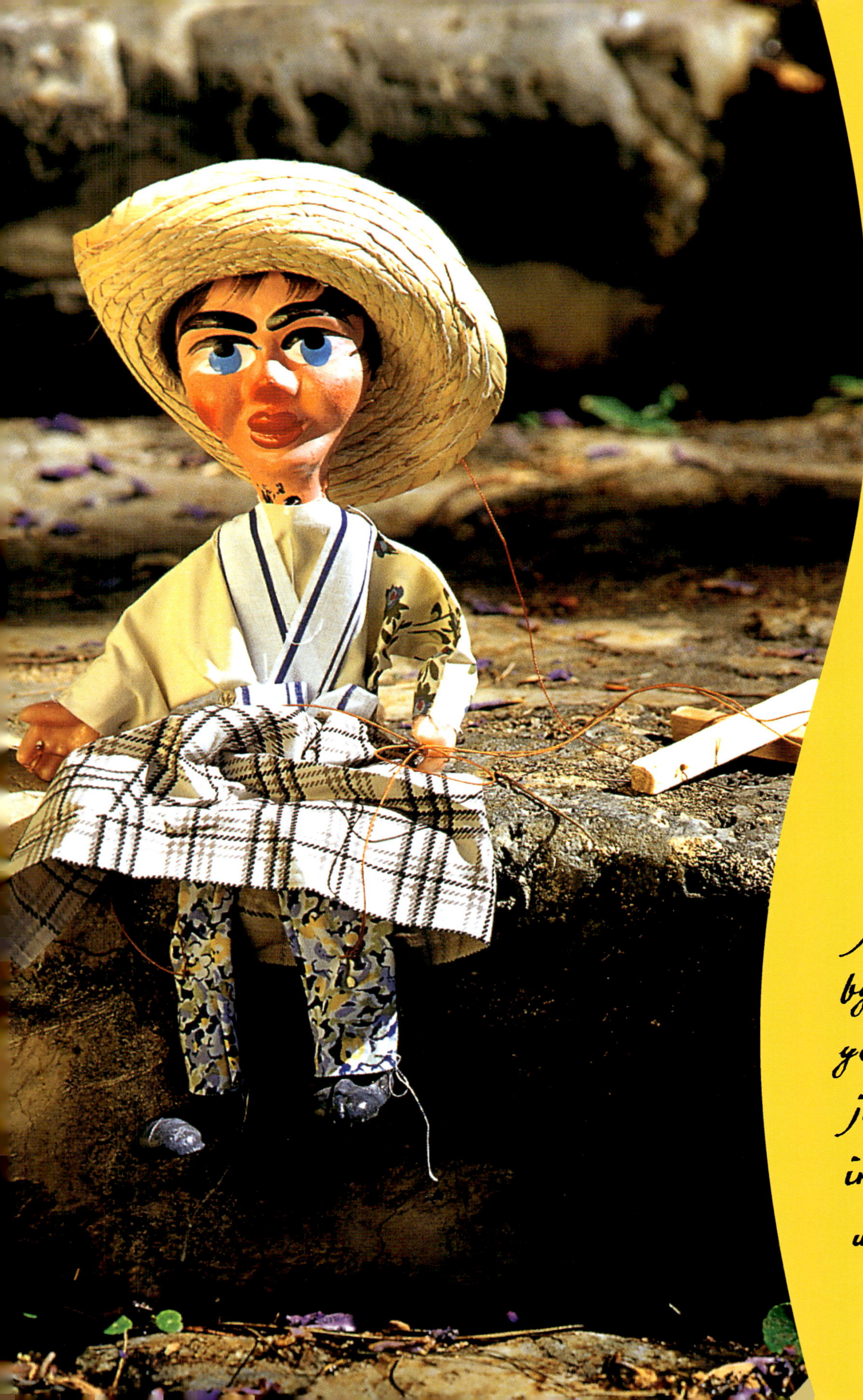

Just hanging
by a few strands
your life is
just barely
in fate's
unseen hands.

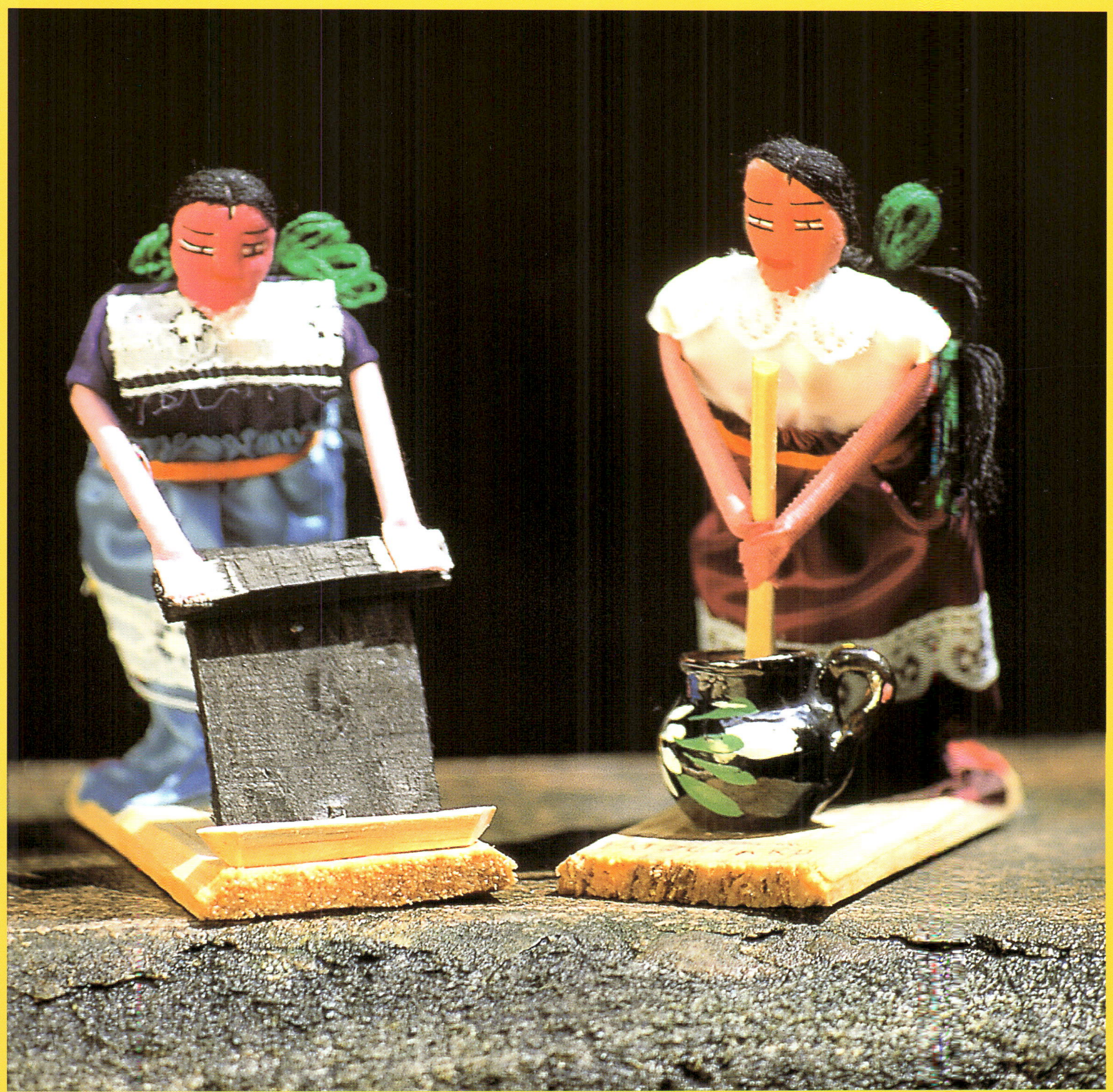

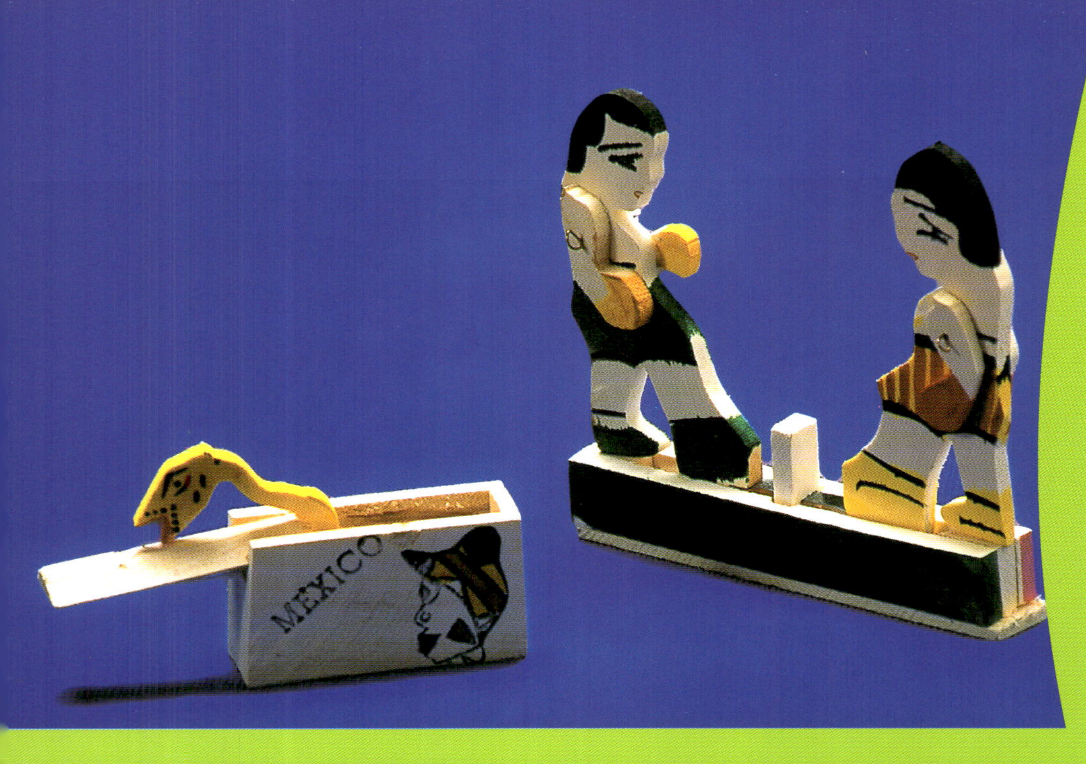

Forced into action
by a relentless spring,
they dance and dance
with their own shadows
in the hand-held boxing ring.

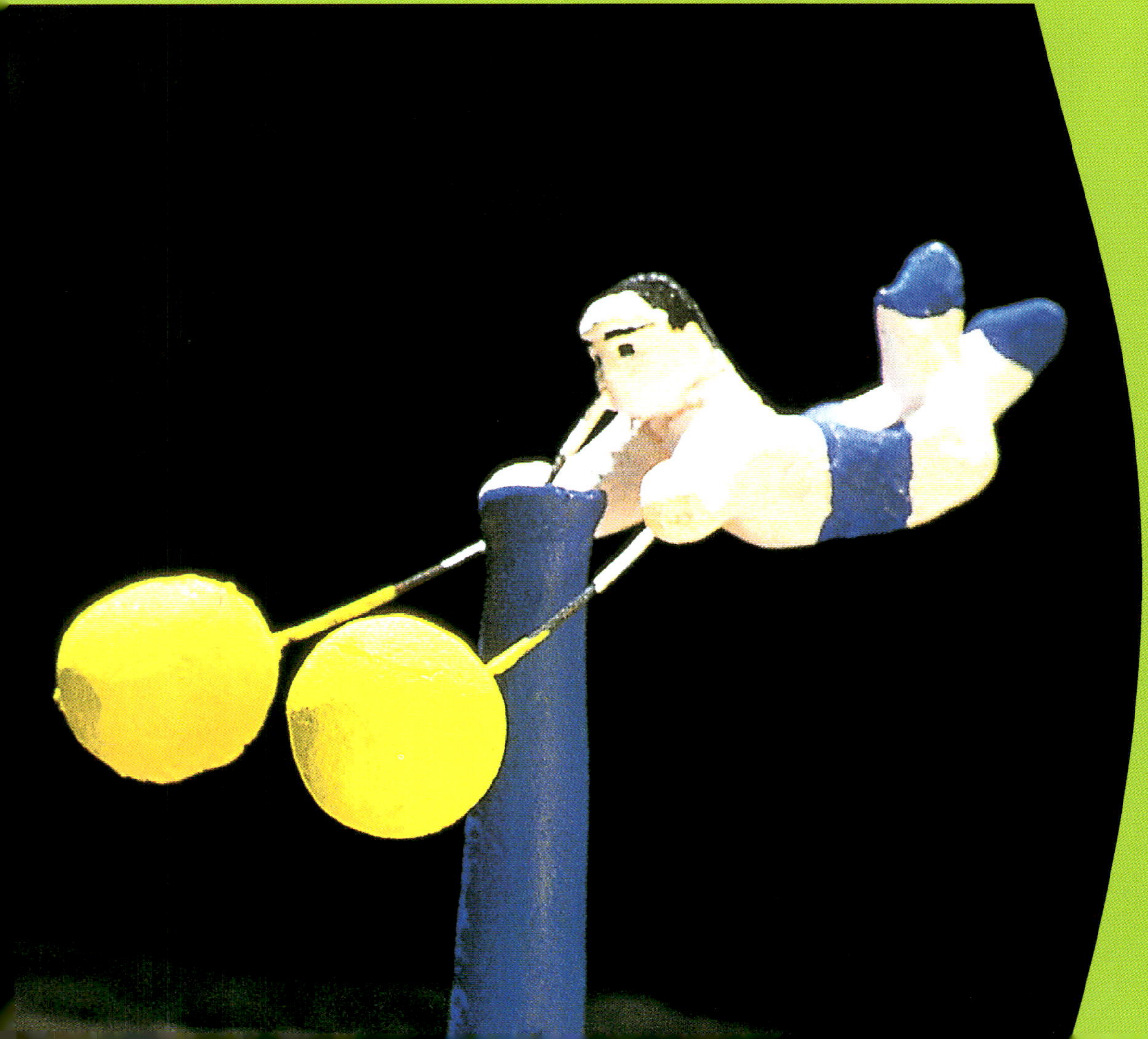

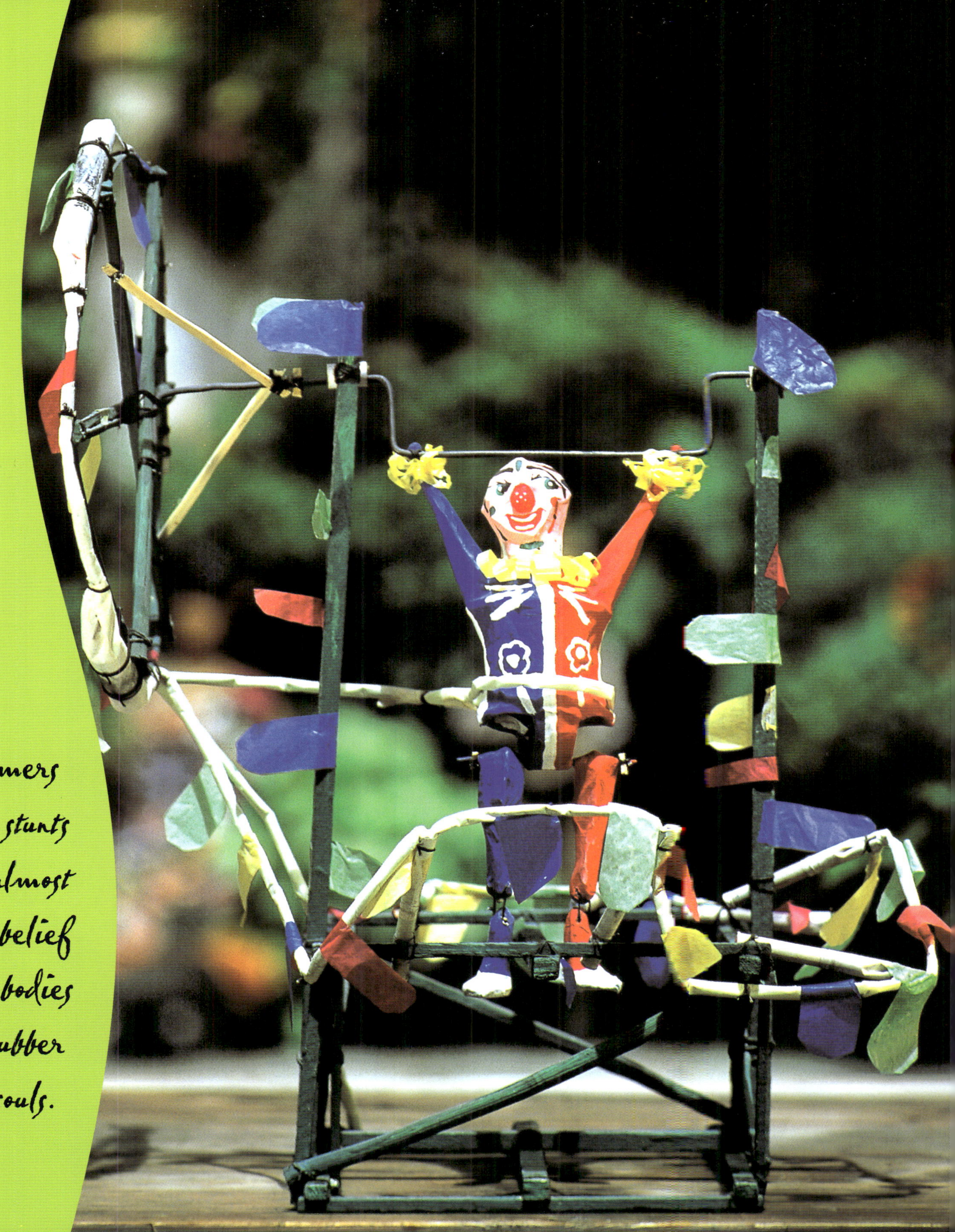

Circus performers
can do stunts
that are almost
beyond belief
with their bodies
of rubber
and harlequin souls.

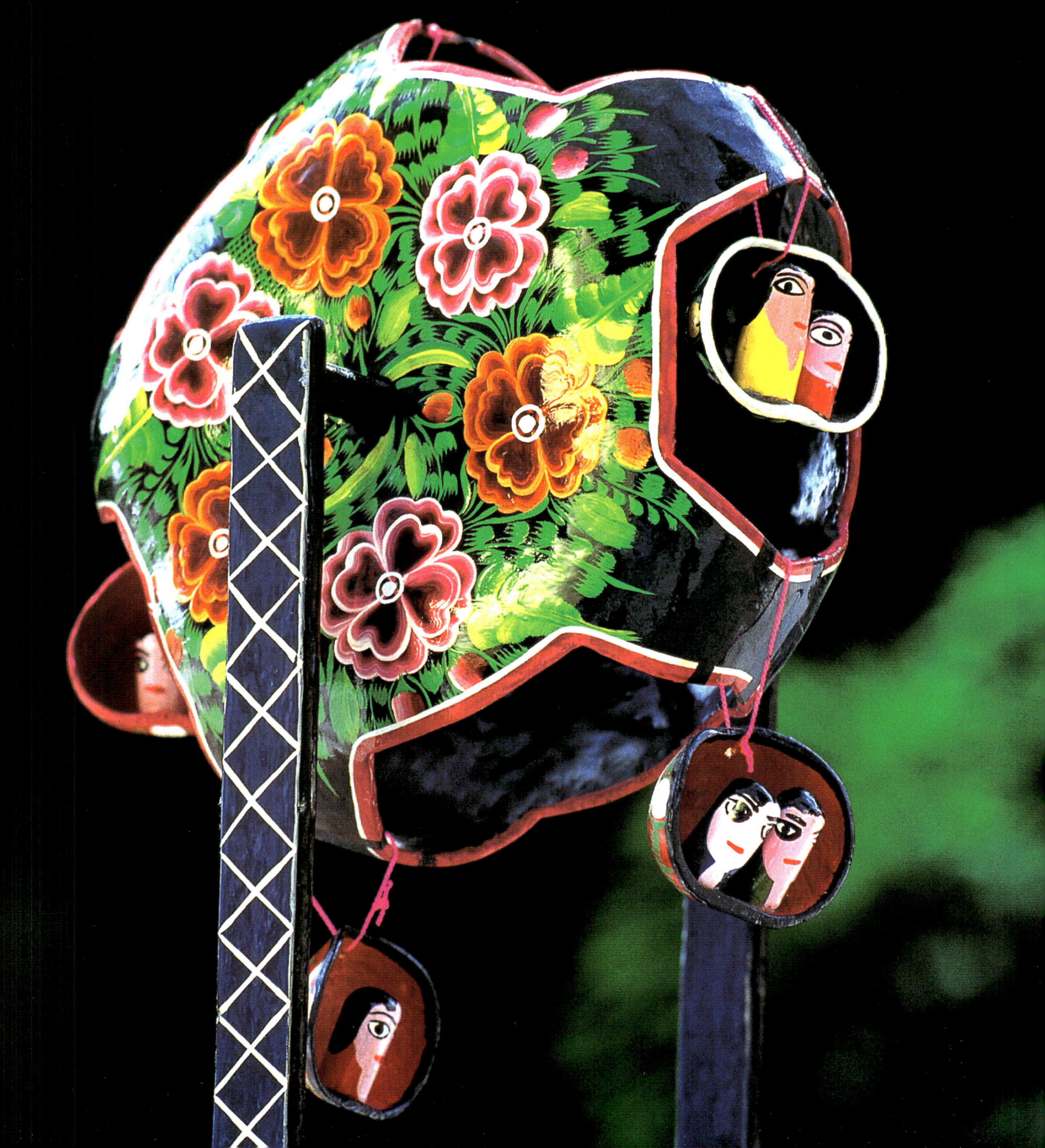

It is well known that movement exerts a special attraction in play. For this reason, there is a special place in the world of traditional toys for those that thrive on dizziness, on spinning, on bouncing.

All year round, whether in the form of balls or marbles, spheres win children's hearts. The seasons of playing with tops, yo-yos or baleros, *follow each other as well, through an annual cycle that is in strict compliance with childhood customs.*

Carousels and ferris wheels, roundabouts of all shapes and sizes, tight-rope walkers and trapeze artists, all are blessed by their artisans with the charm of motion: so that they may capture boys and girls, and get them to show off their skills.

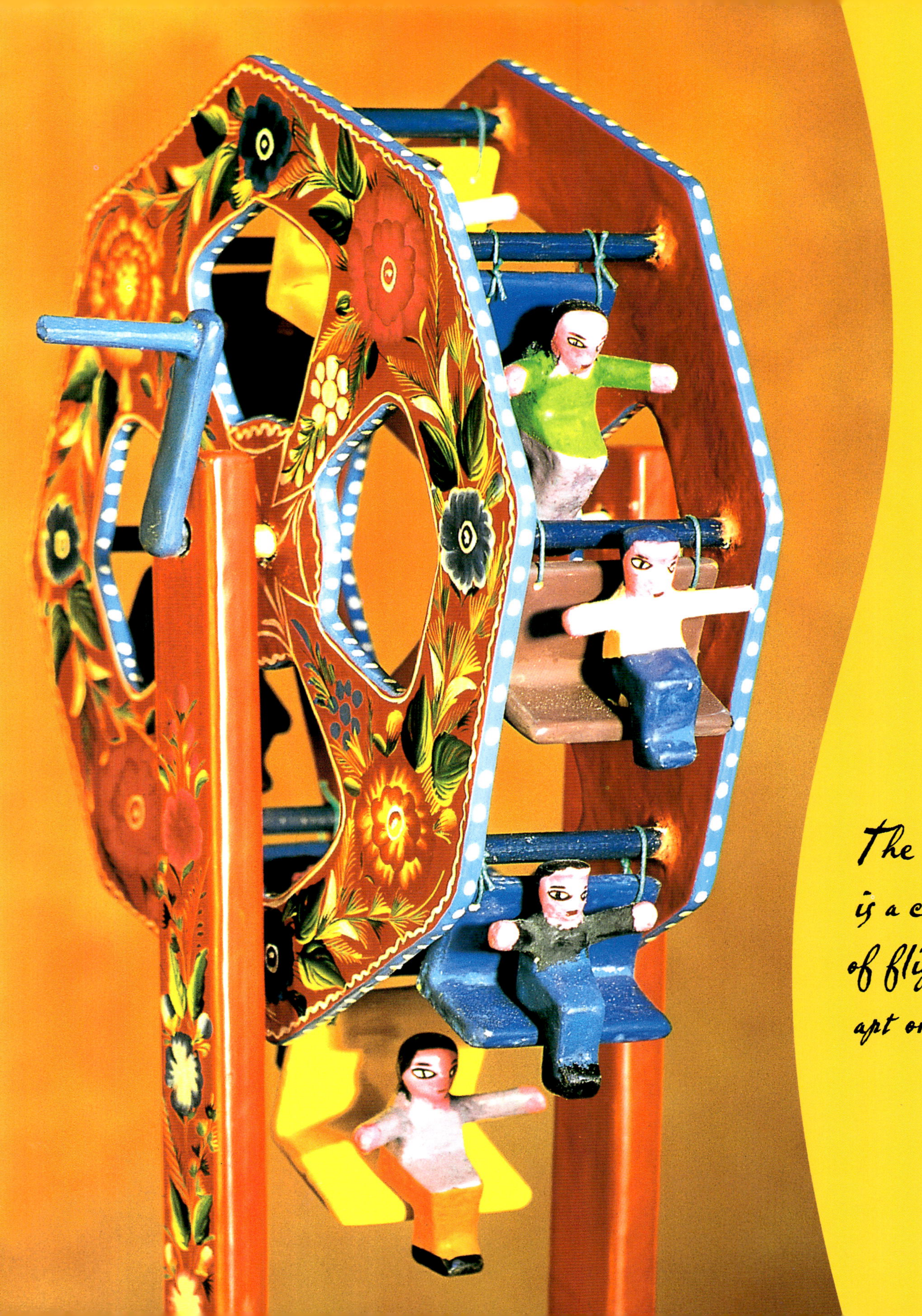

The ferris wheel
is a celestial device
of flights and heights
apt only for angels…

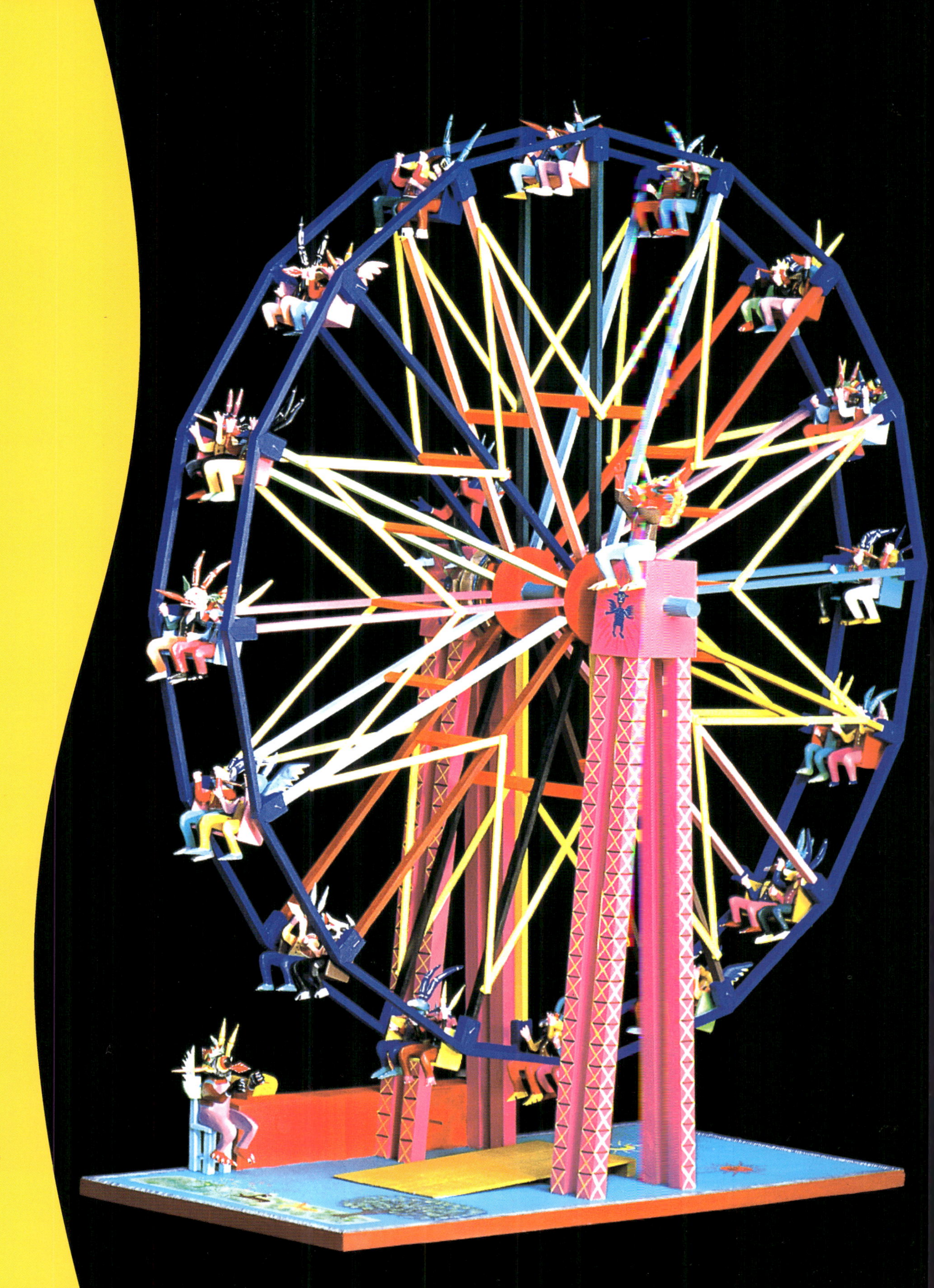

...and little devils.

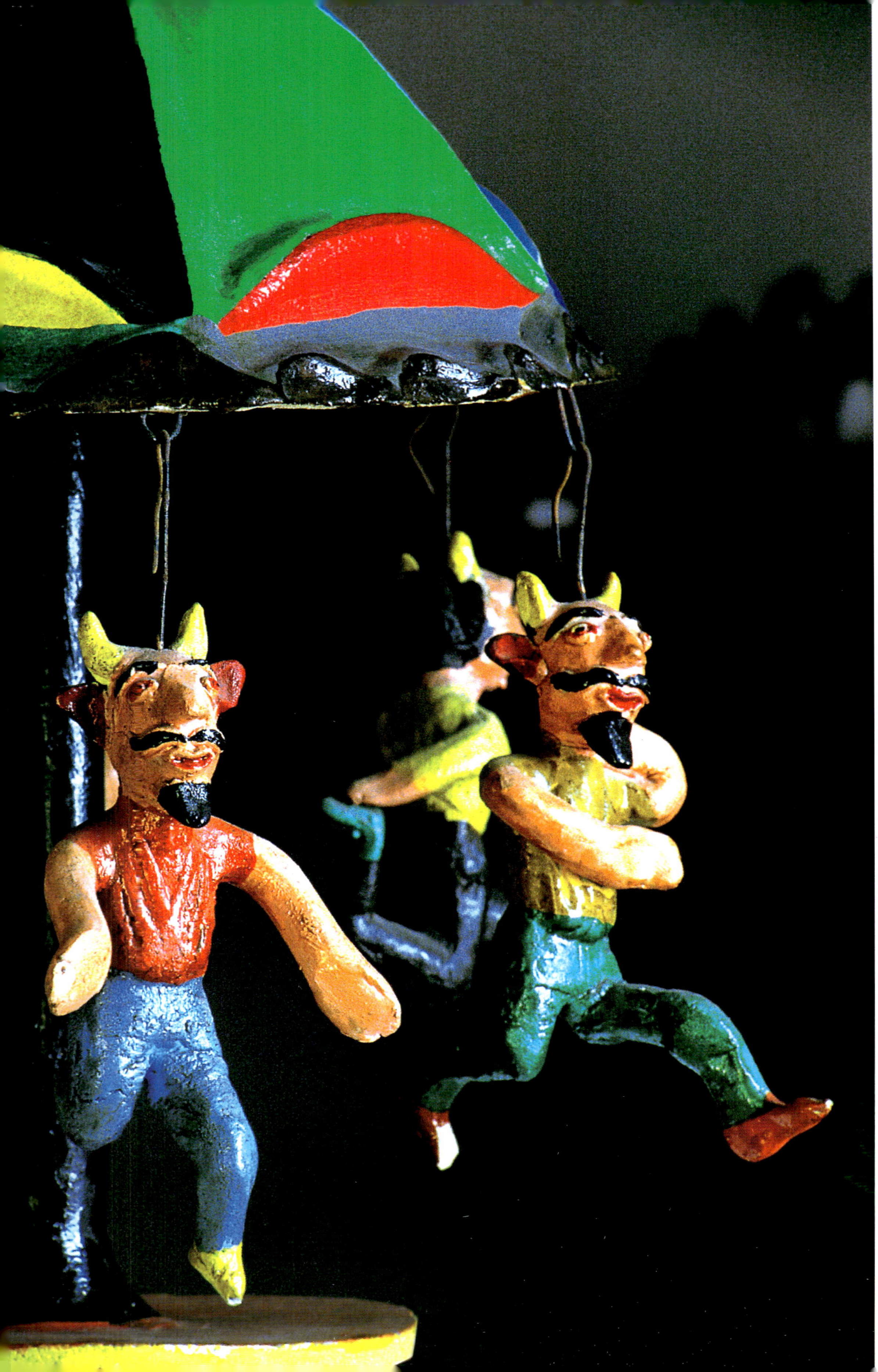

Volantín,

fiendish tree,
hung from the air,
spinning with the sky
toward every compass
point of the soul.

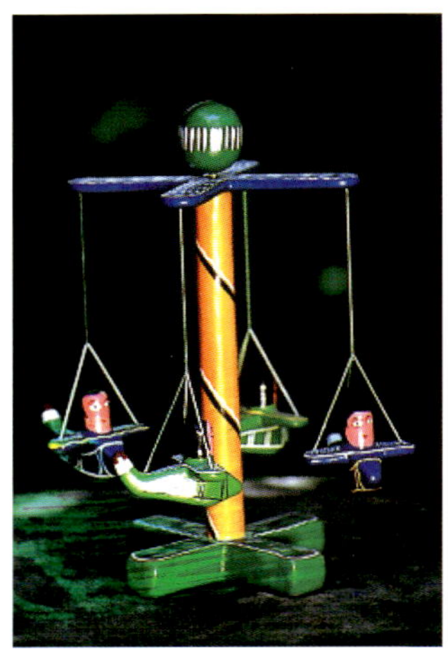

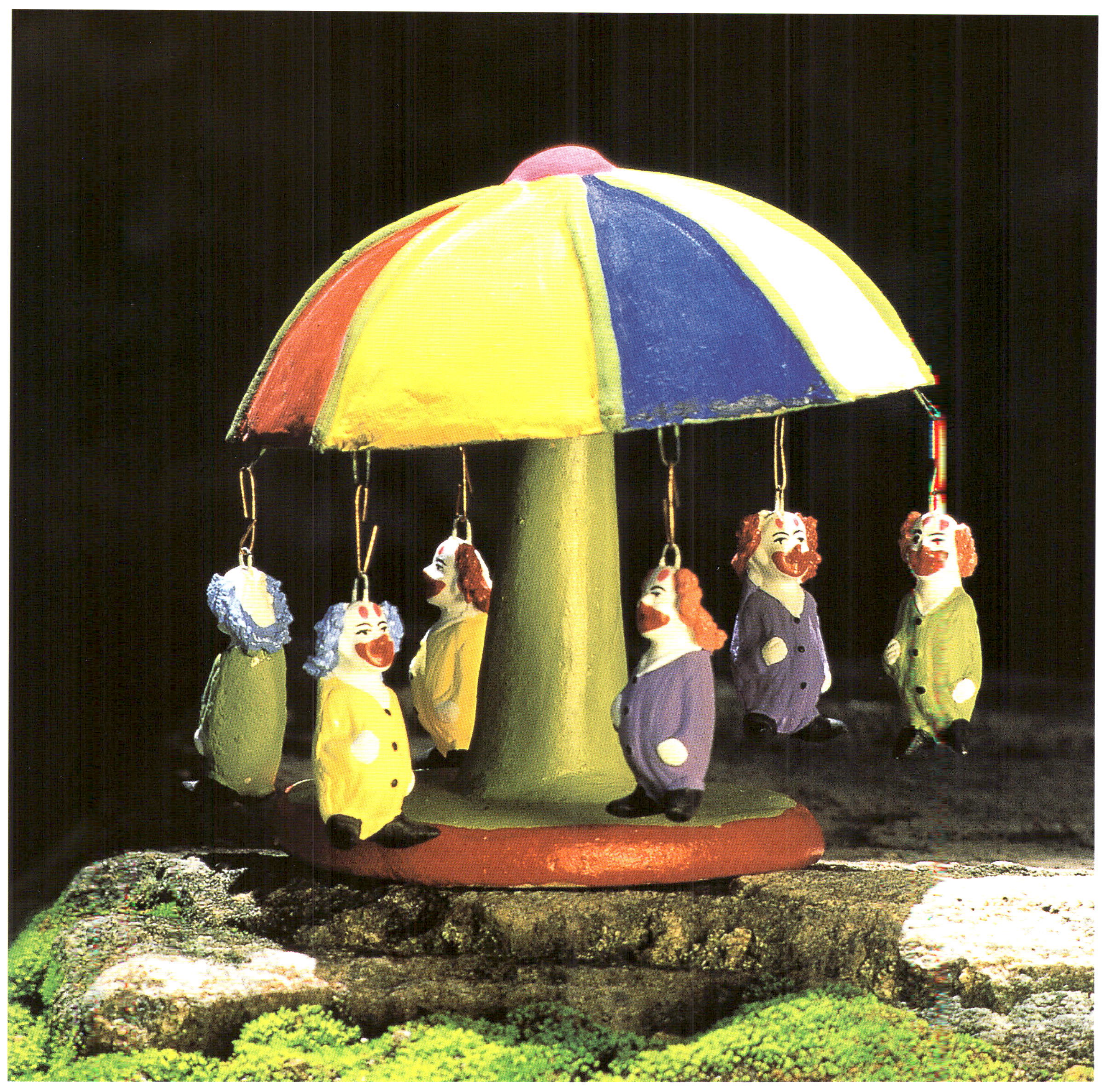

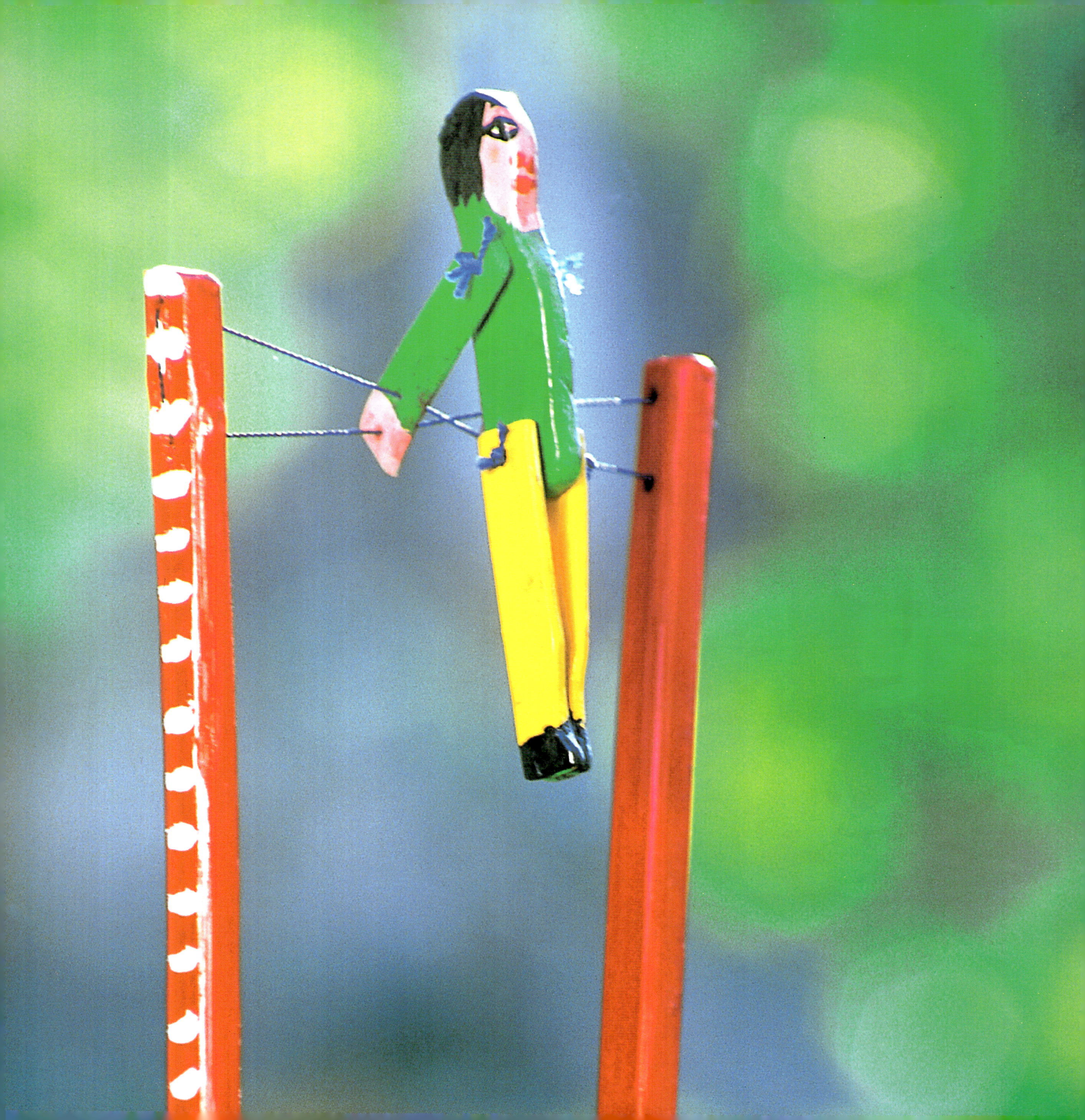

*Juggler of lights
weaving the air
into fantastic images*

of impossible worlds.

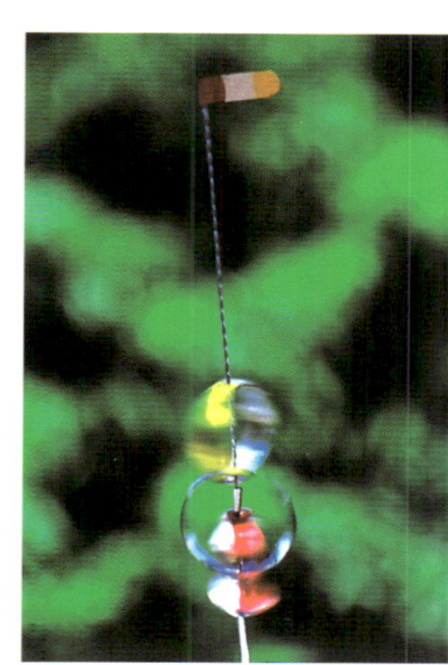

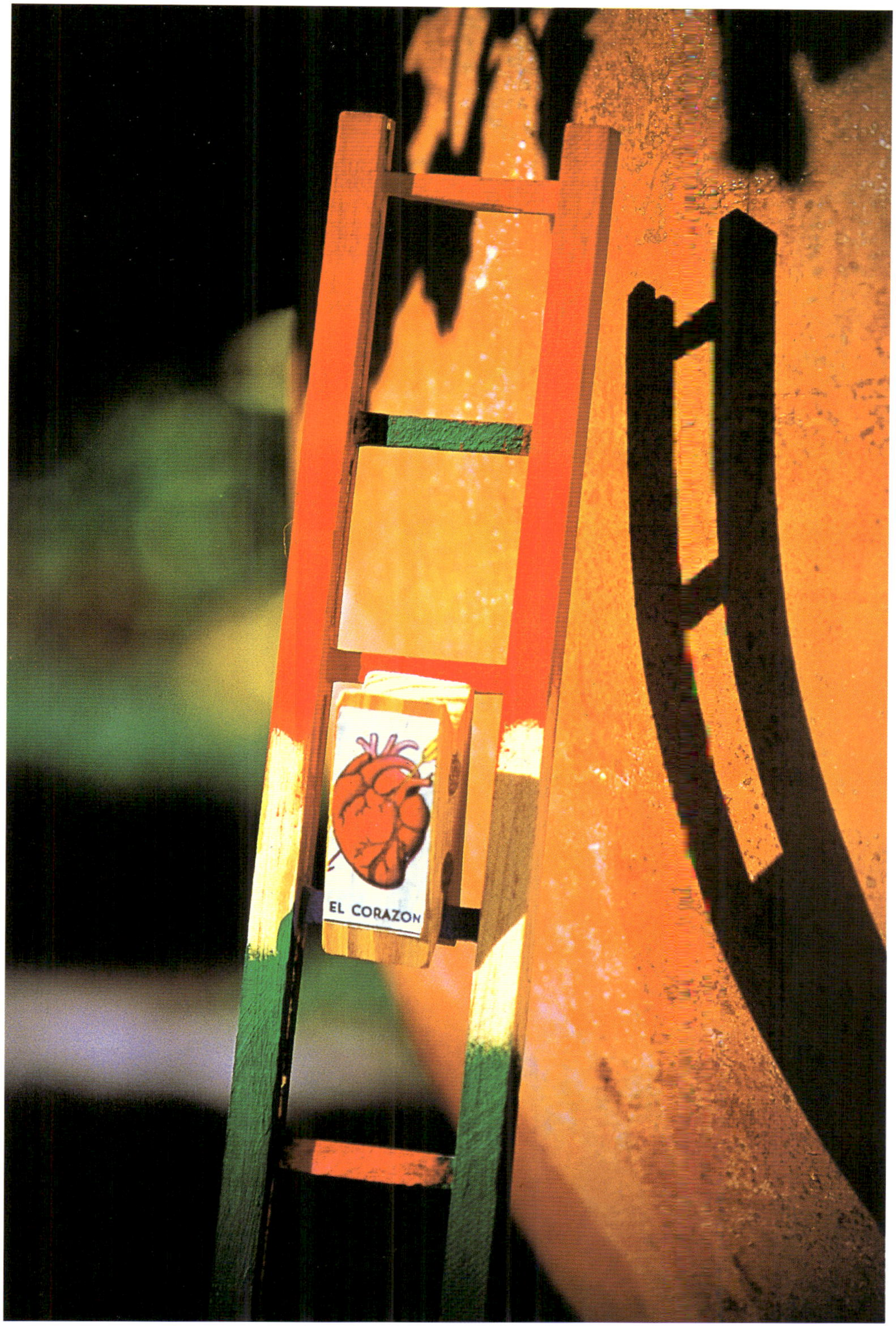

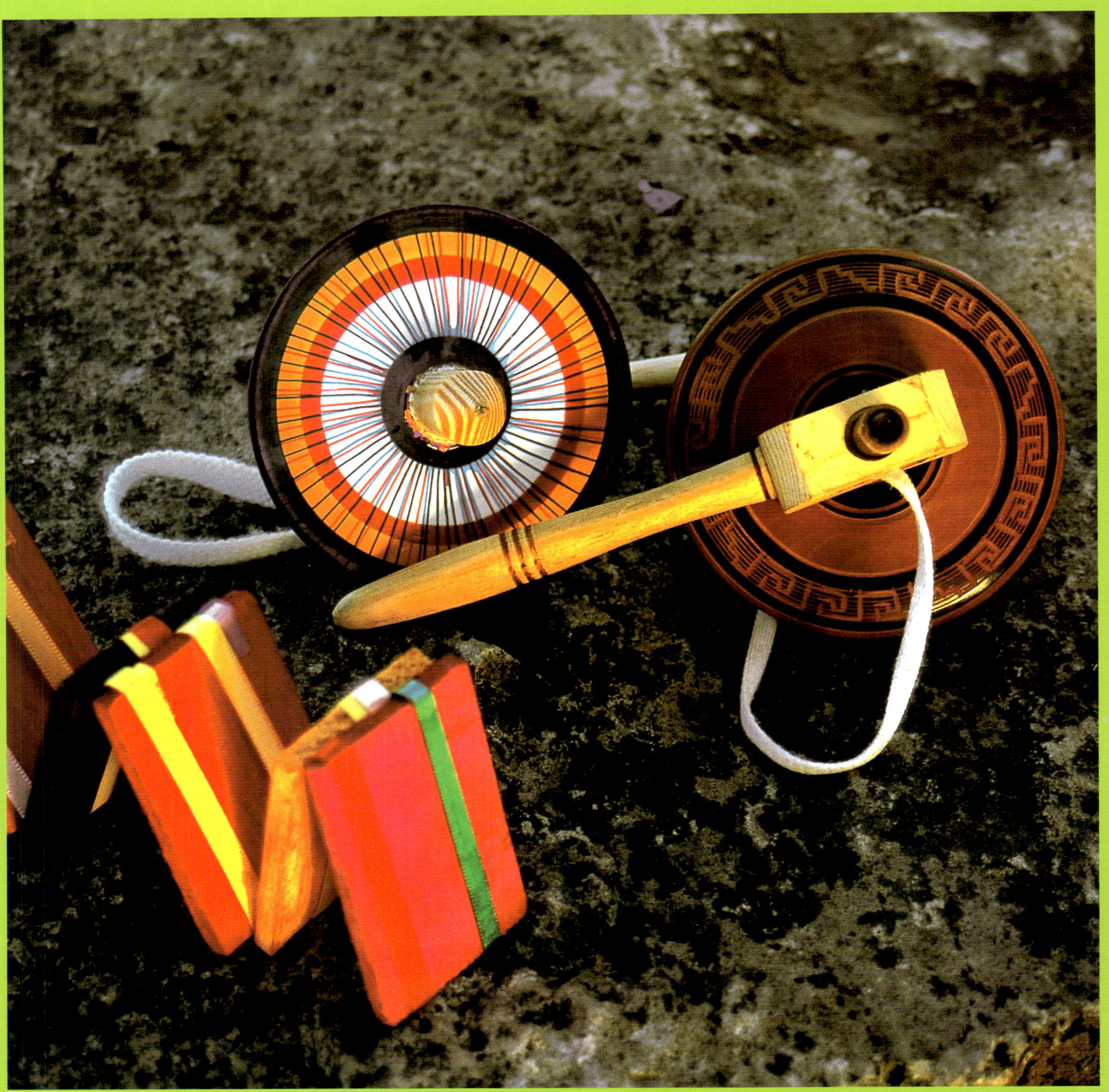

Acrobats and dancers,
the top, balero and yoyo,
improvise poetic turns and leaps
that outshine the sun's circus.

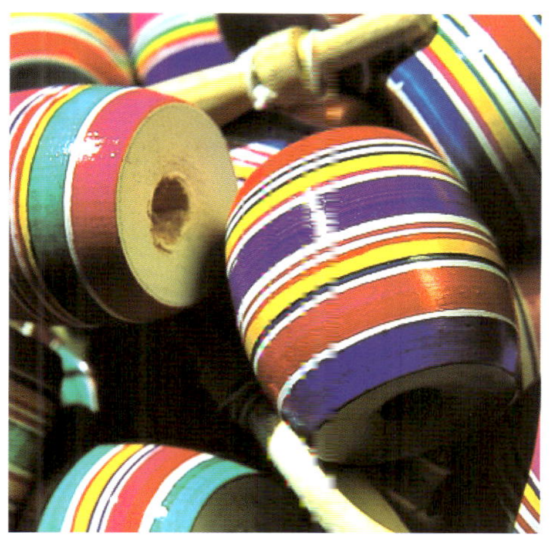

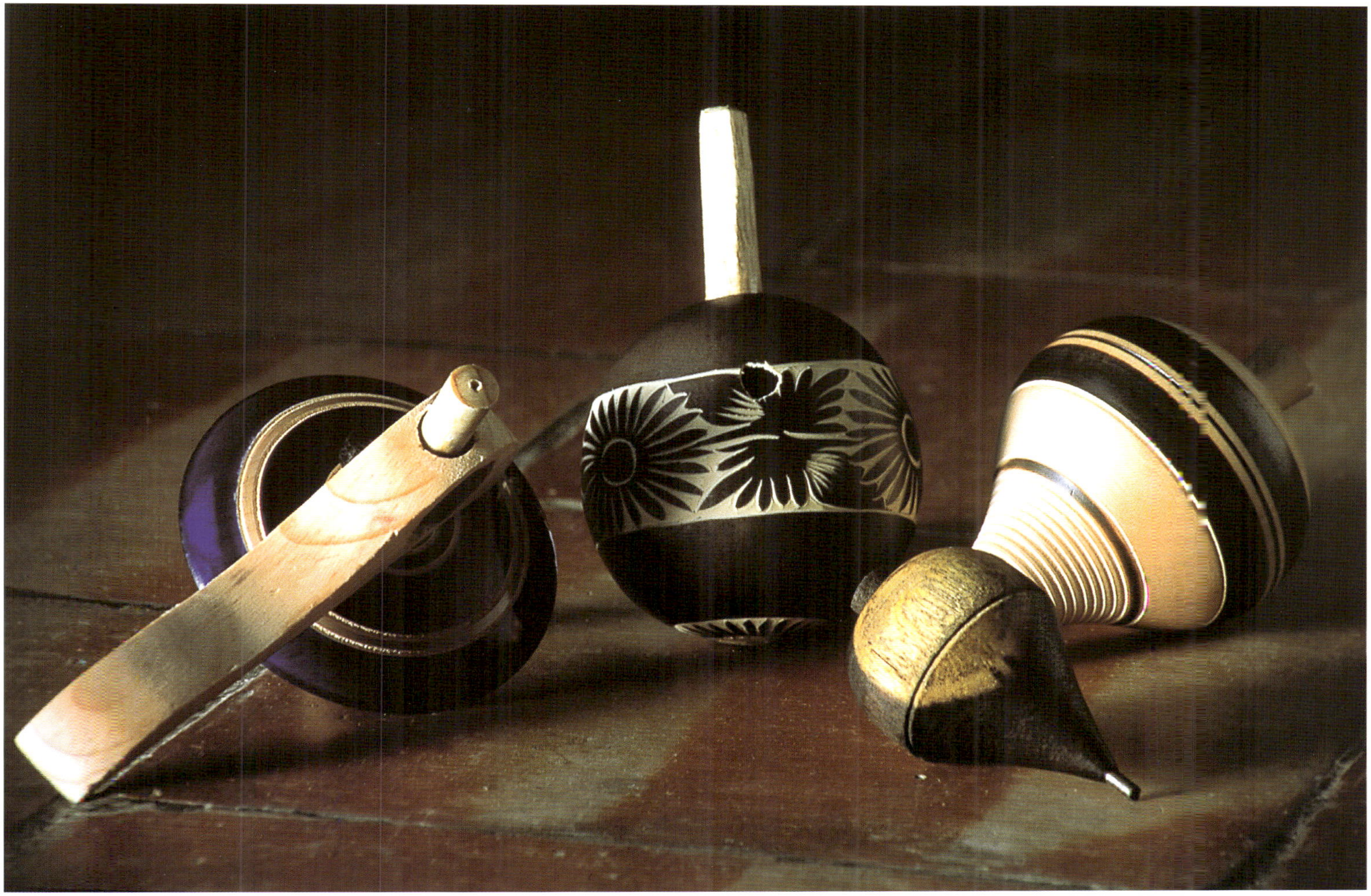

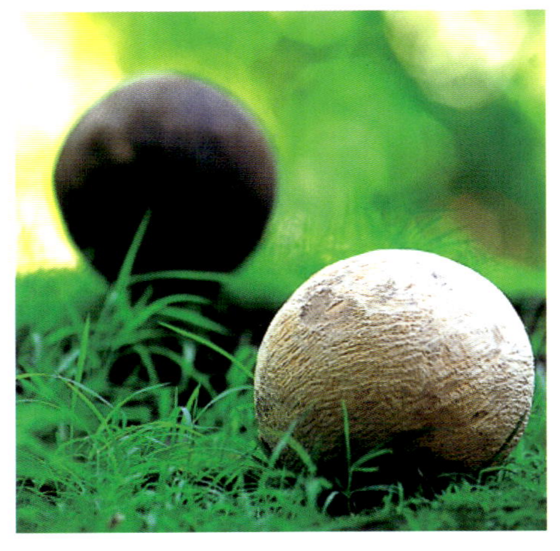

The colors spin
and beget stars
in perfect spheres,
God's marbles
for angel children.

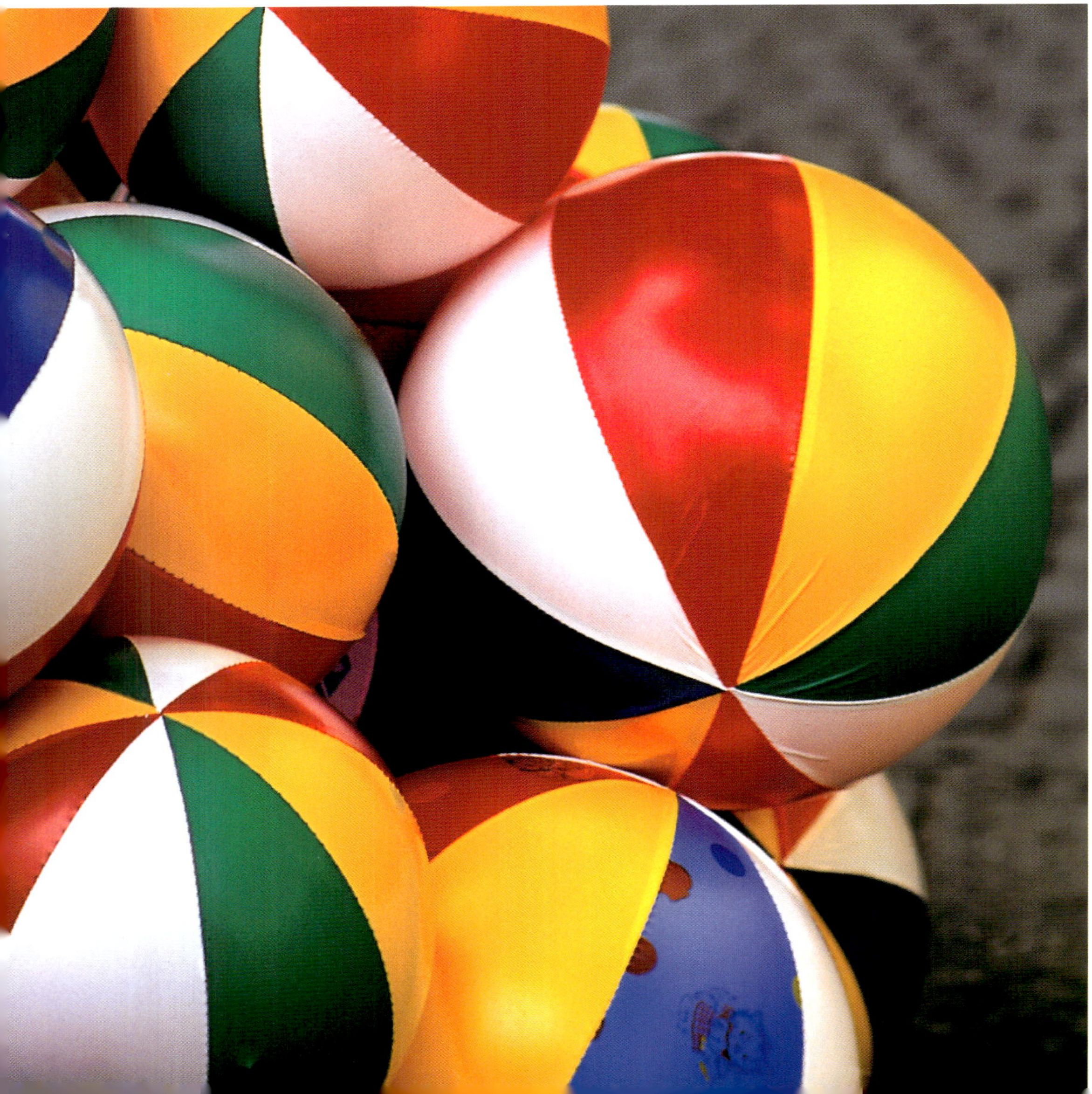

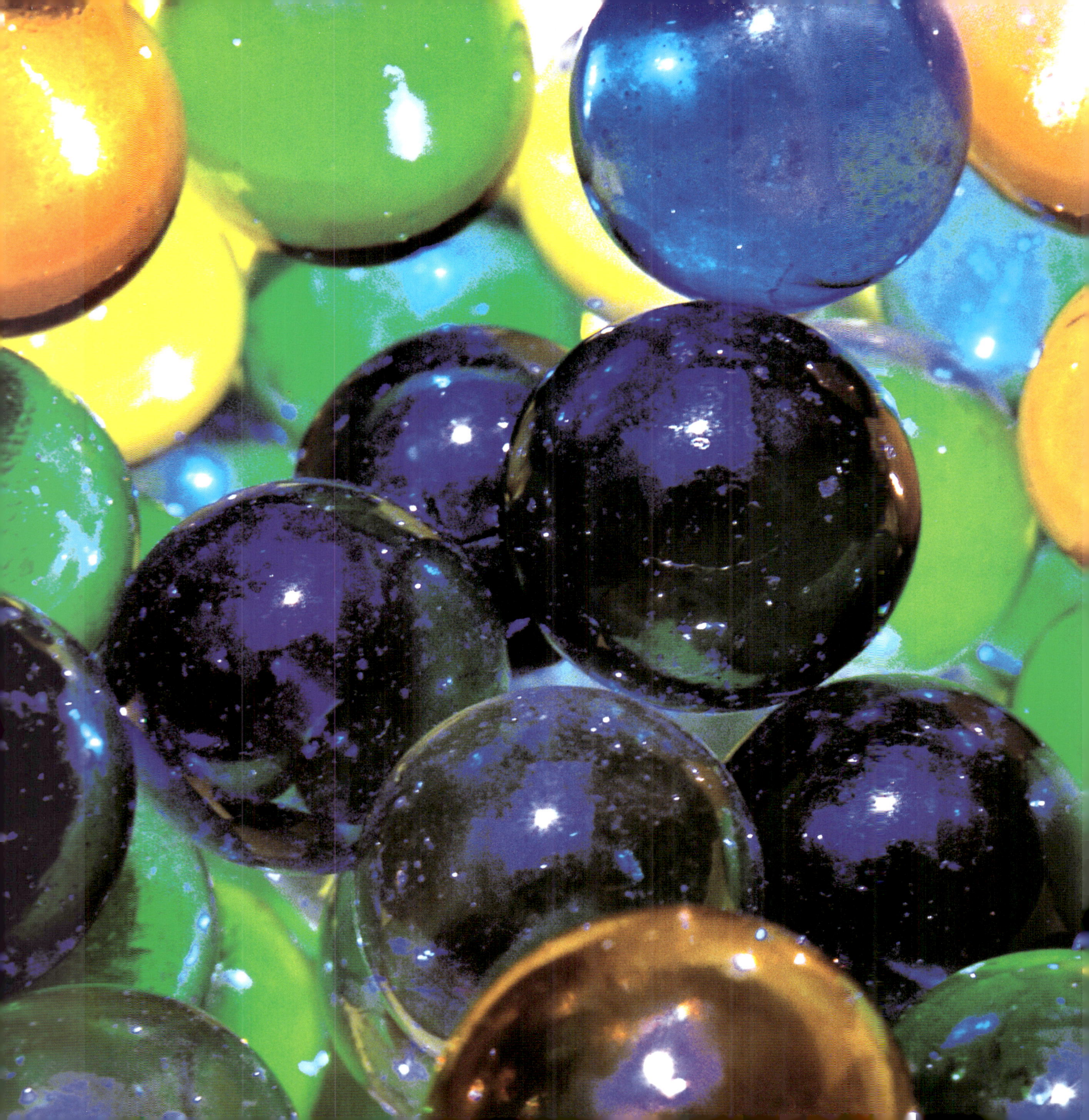

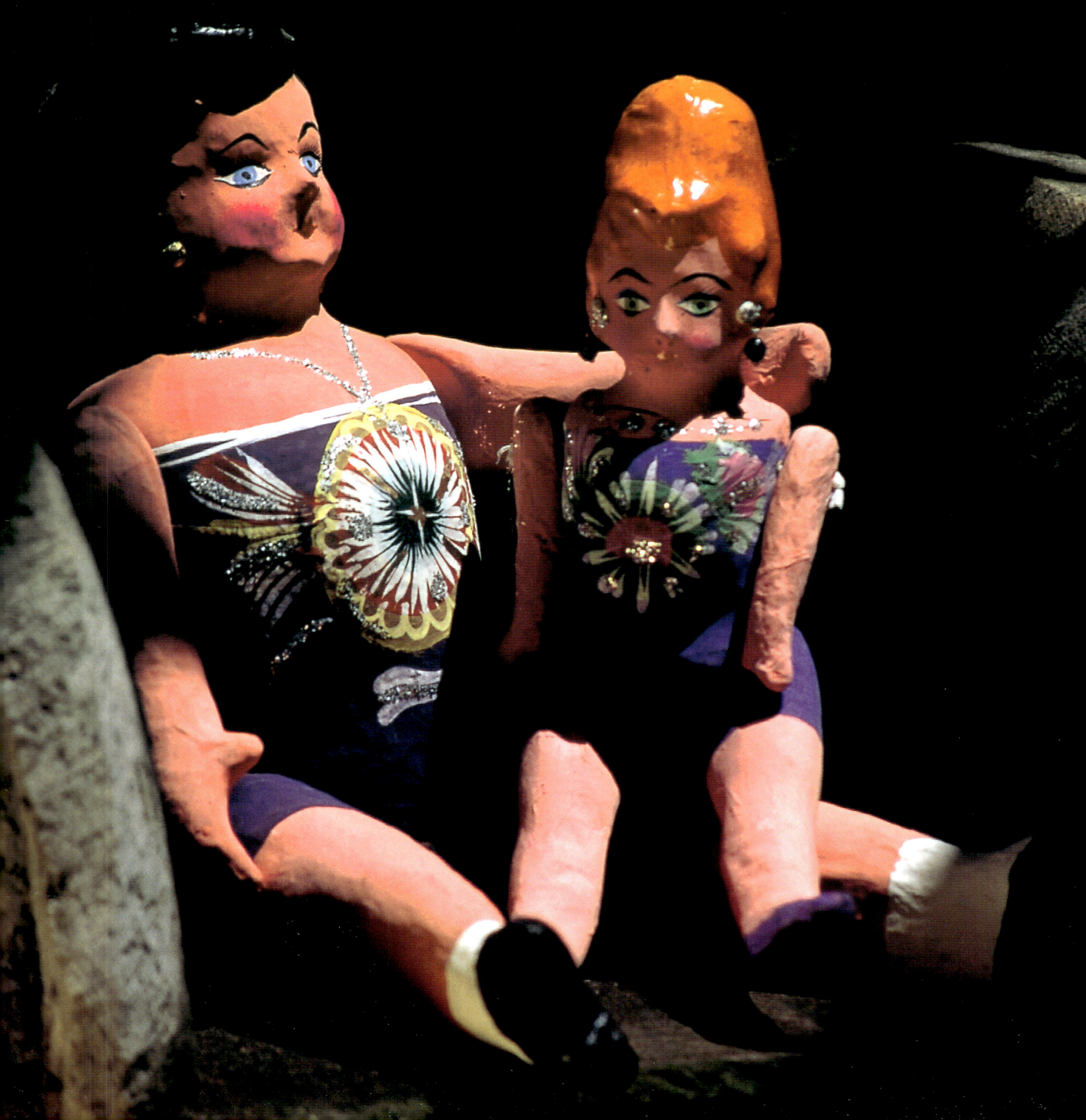

Children have the capacity to turn anything into a toy just by playing with it. There are, nevertheless, an infinite number of objects that take on the special role of "being useful" when children play at being grownups.

Once it's been decided to abstract from everyday life (that is to say, once play begins), children apply themselves to creating a world in miniature where dolls, household implements and tools for all sorts of work find their places.

This world of usefulness seems to play an important part in the formation of adults-to-be, as it allow little ones to practice jobs they'll have to do, soon enough. Playing with dolls, for example, girls undertake the illusion of being mothers, nurses, teachers; while boys apply themselves to learning strategy when they play at cowboys, Indians, pirates and soldiers.

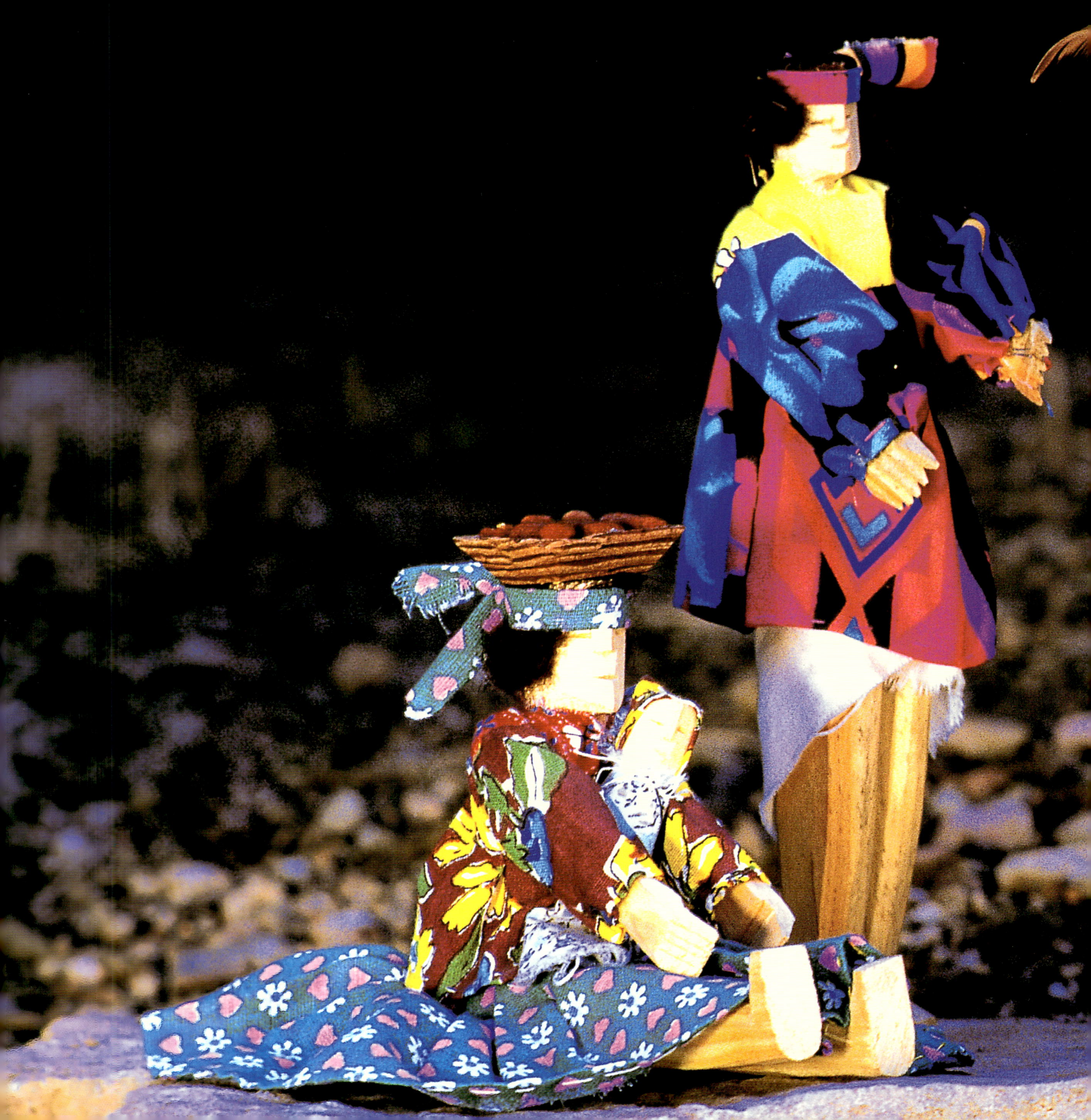

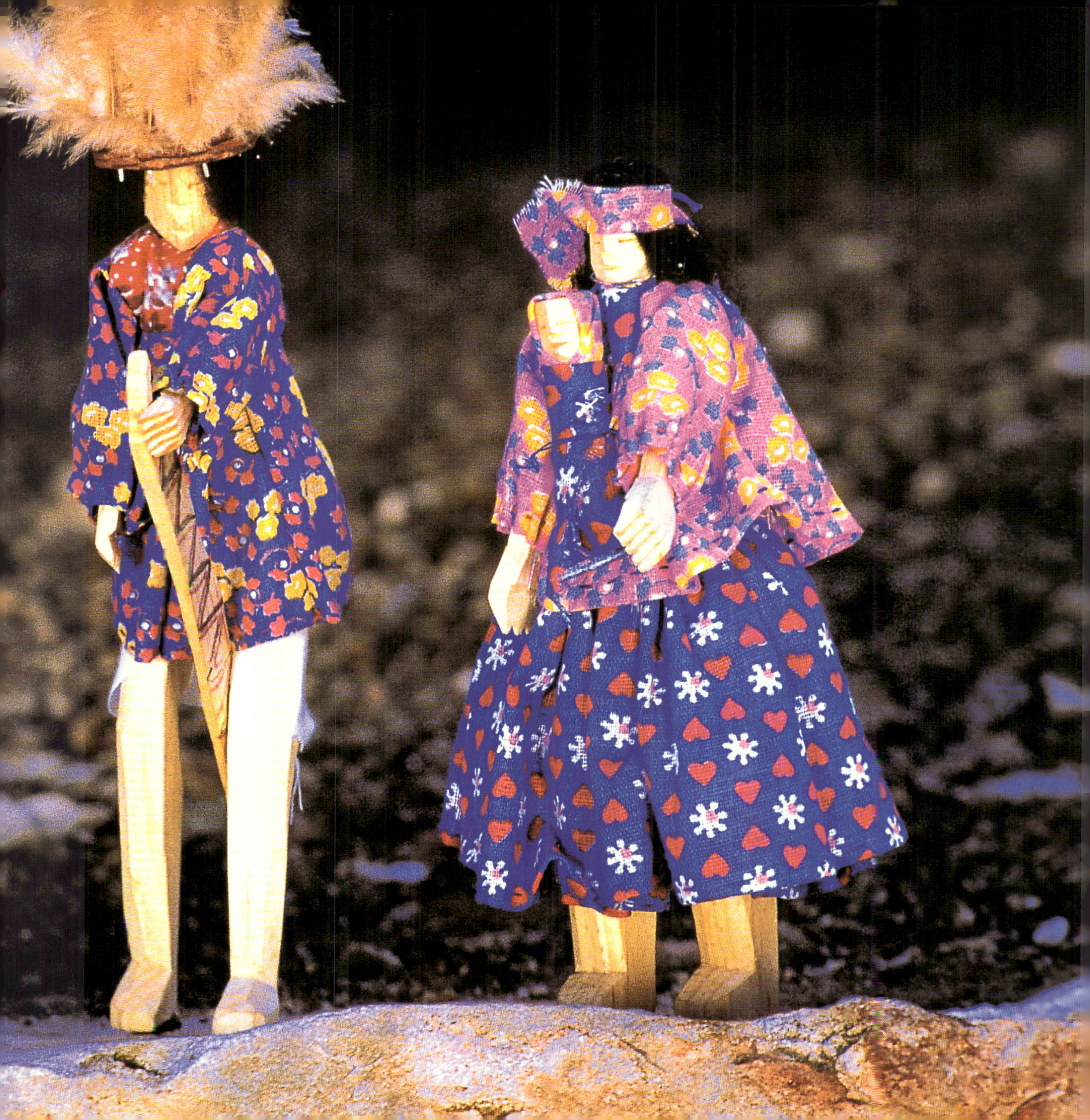

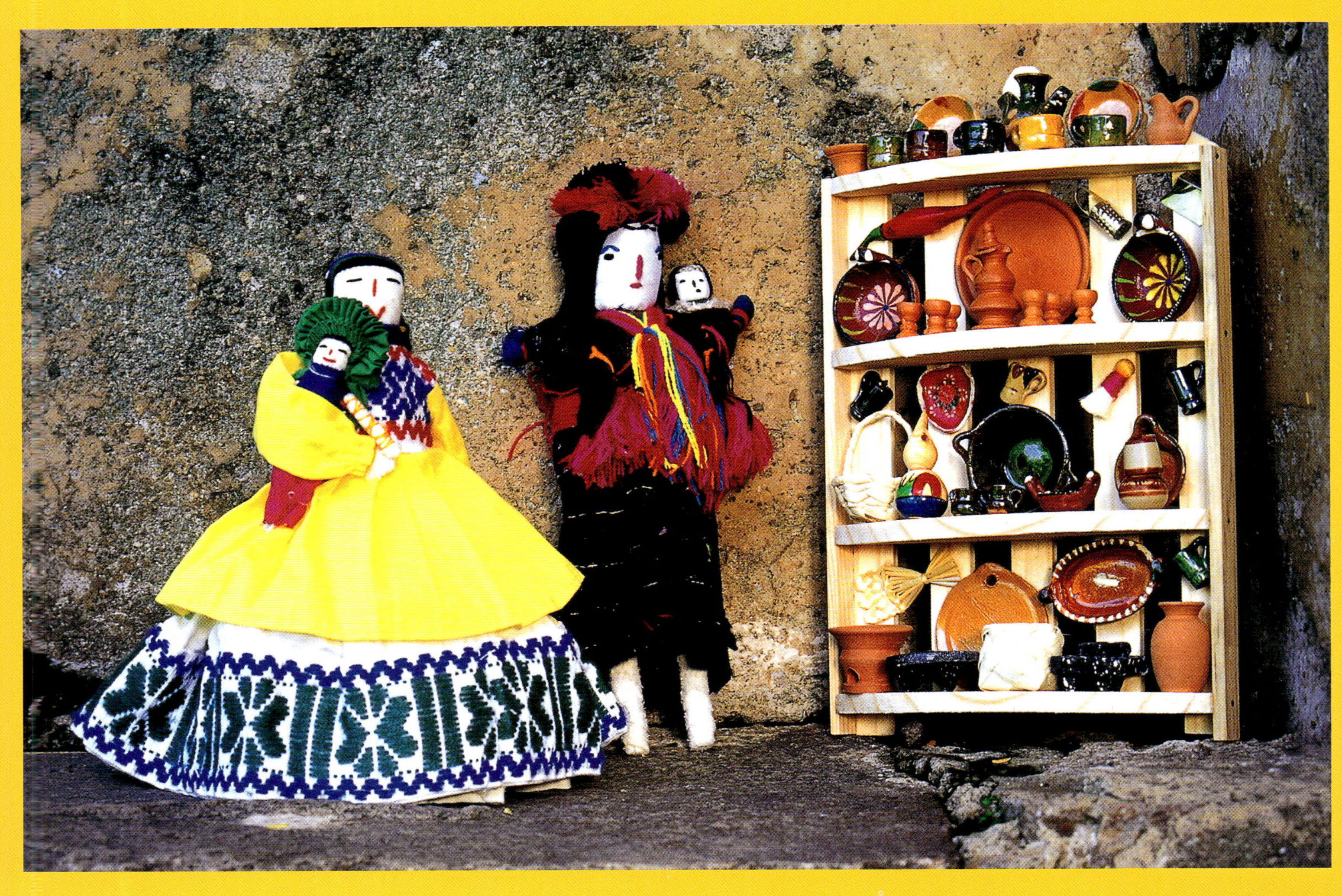

Dolls of rags and scraps
   wait with serene looks
      in Sunday dresses
         for brown-faced girls to come along
            and wake them from their daydreams.

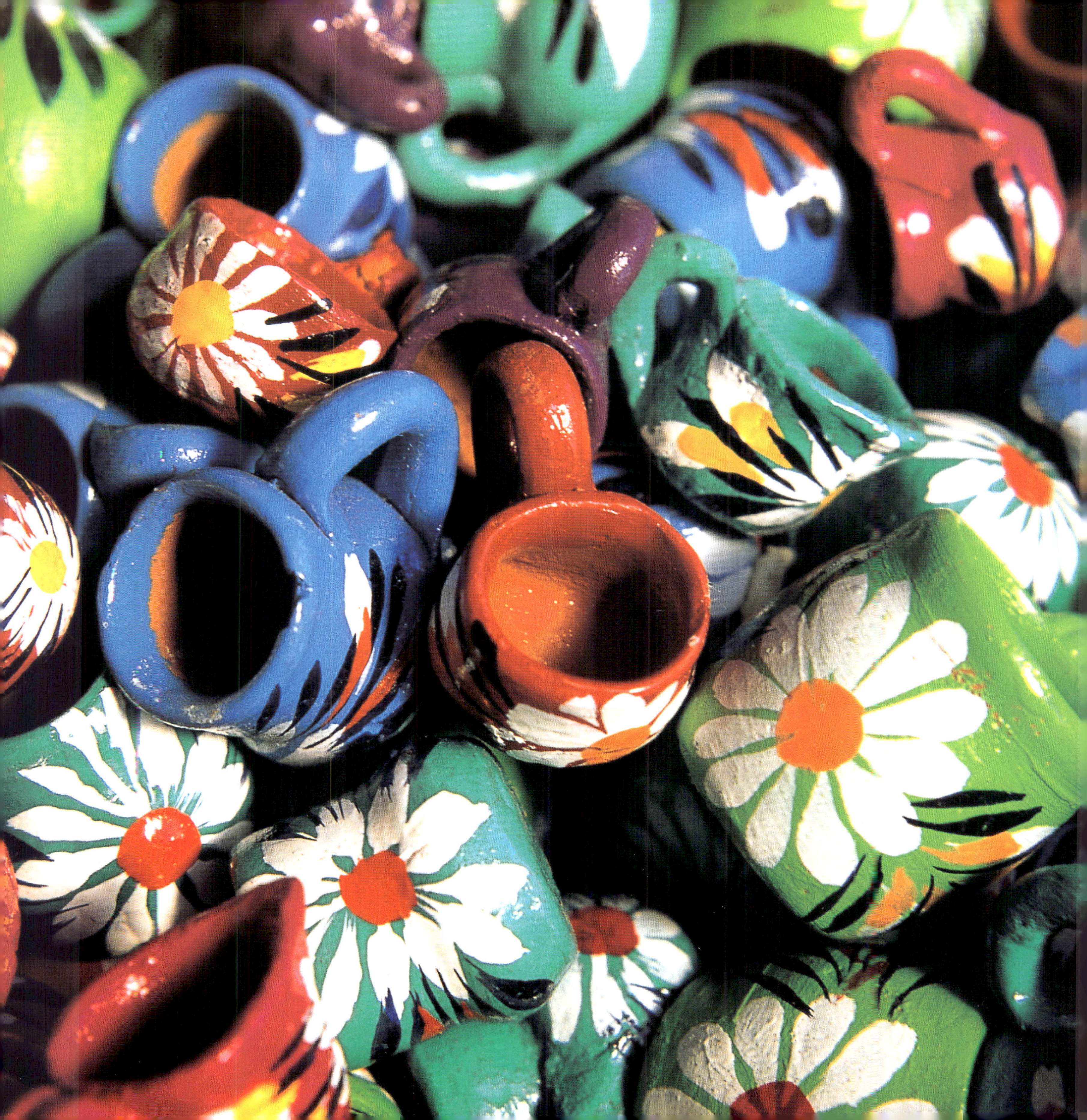

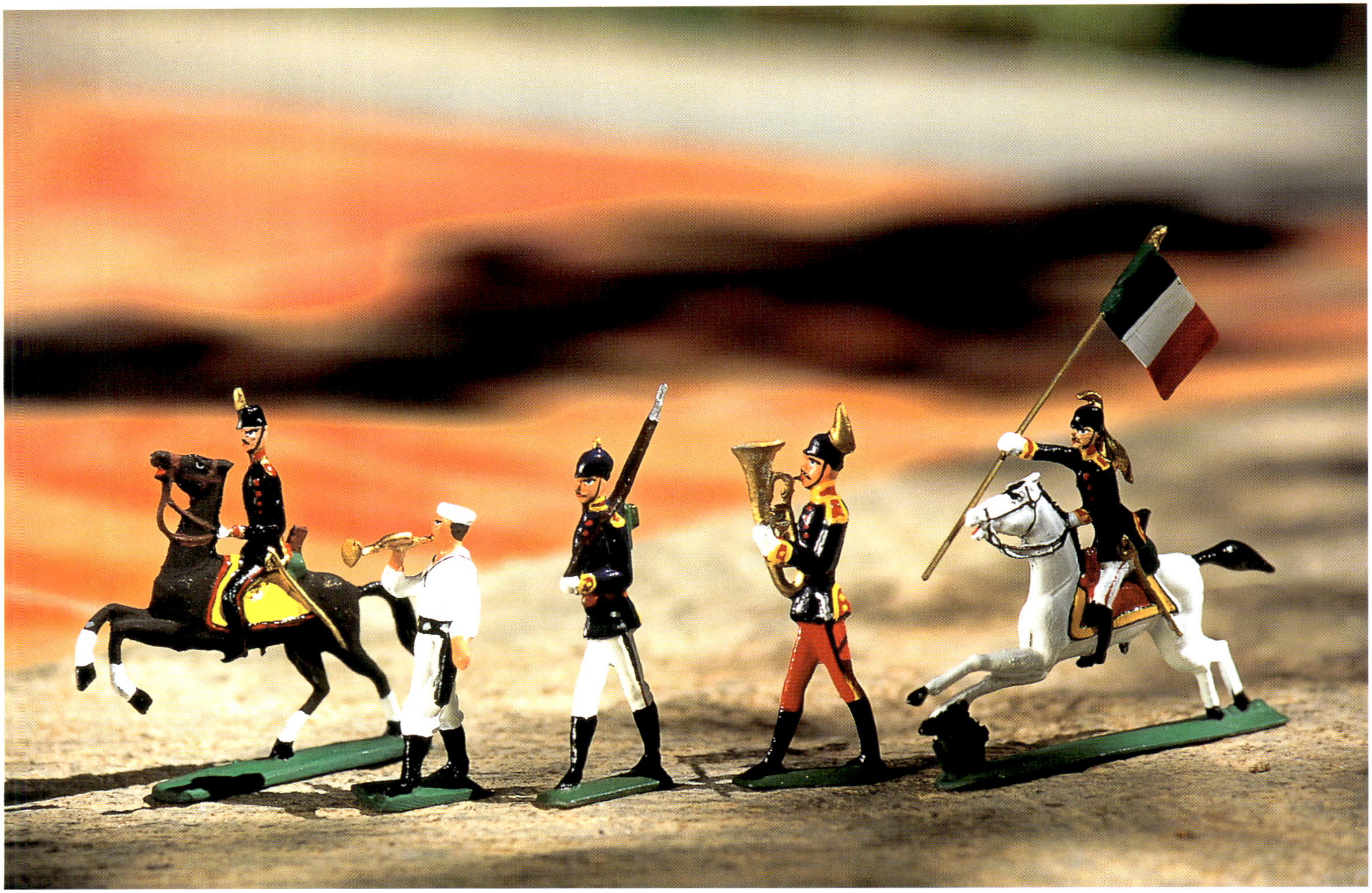

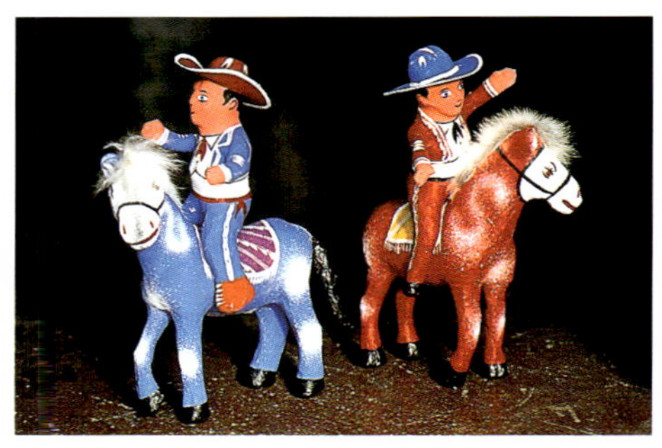

Playing their drums and cornets:
how bright their freshly-painted suits!
so all things shine
in their land of metal.

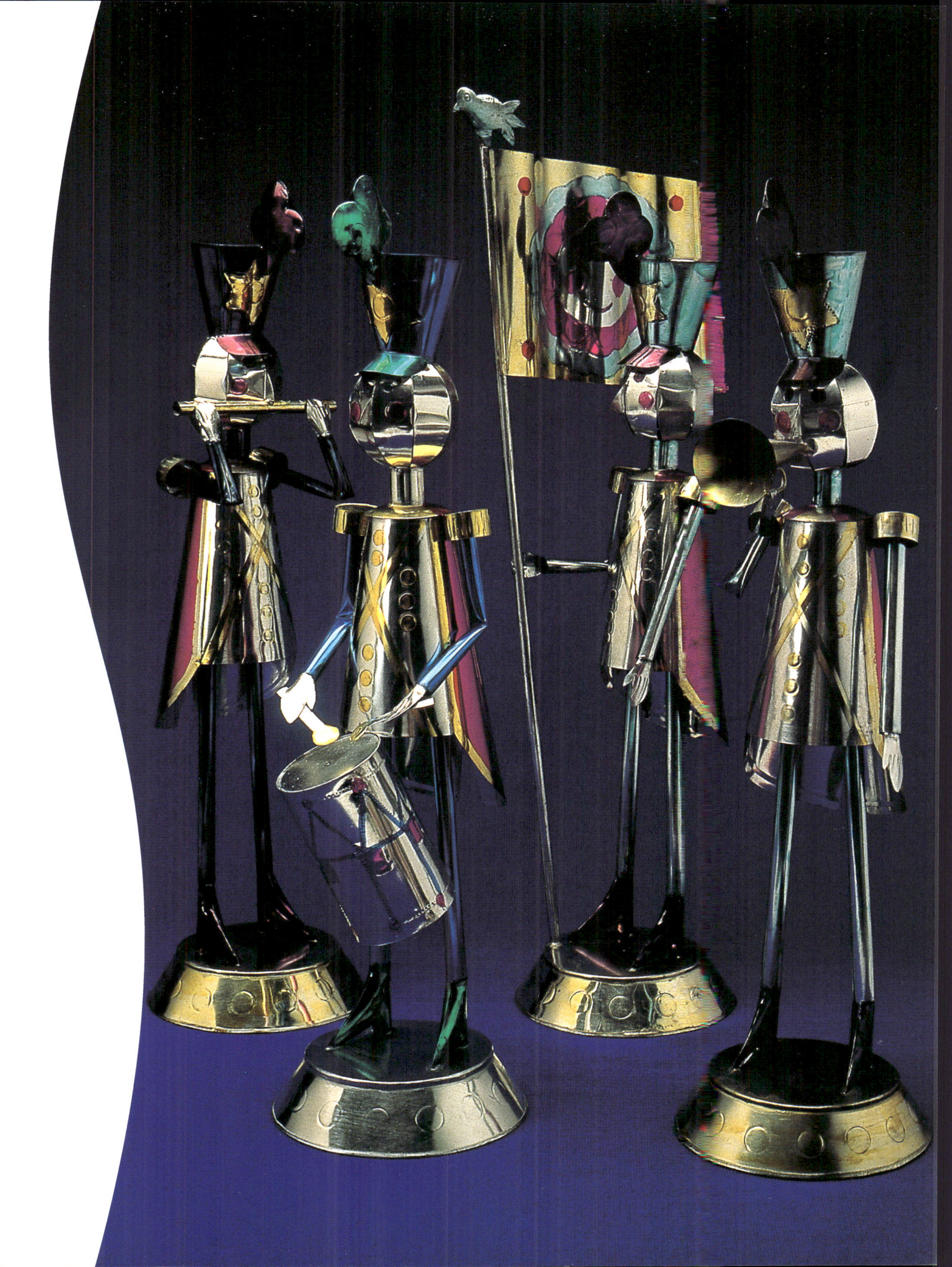

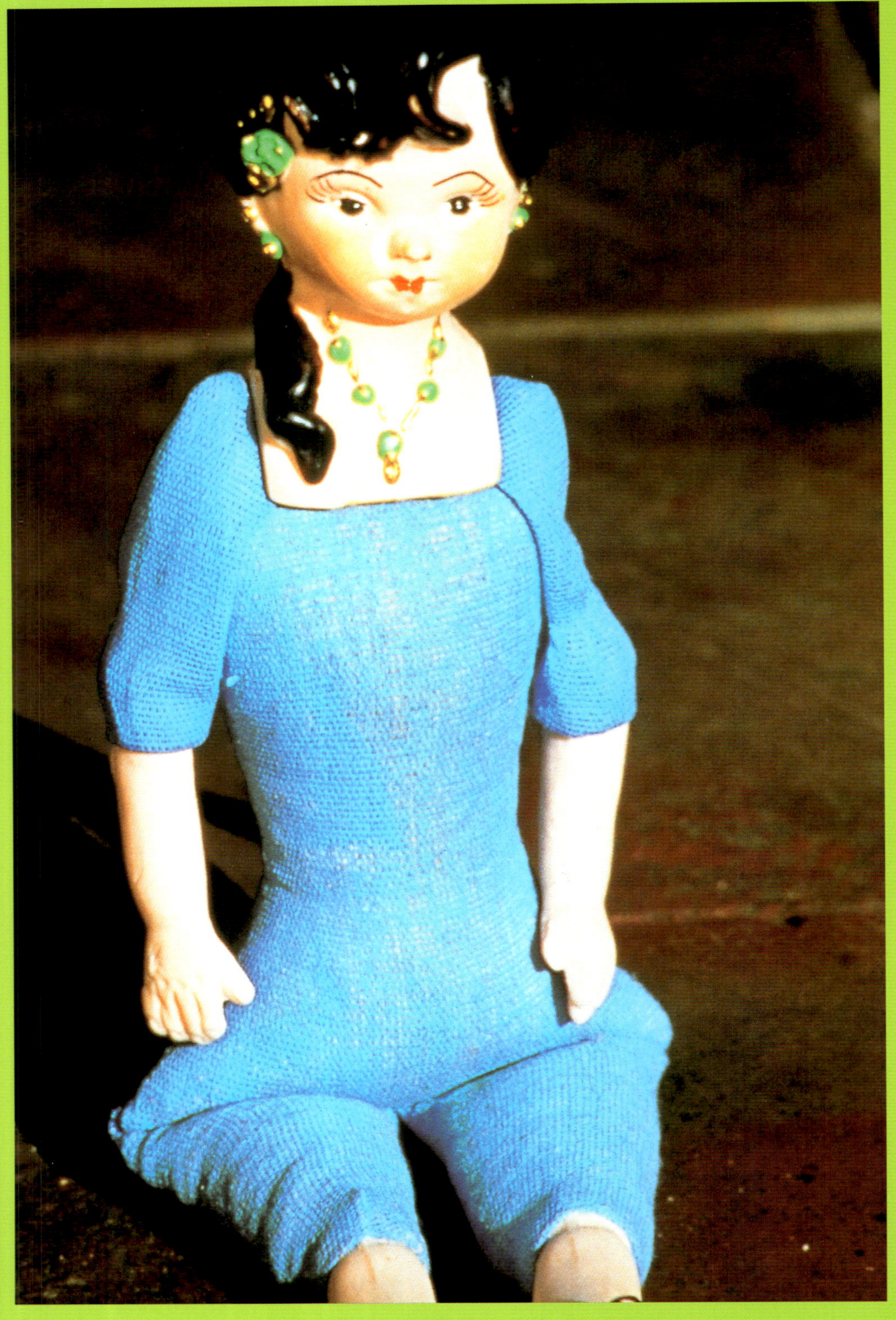

They are girls
who decided not to grow,
like certain dreams,
certain glances,
certain corners we know.

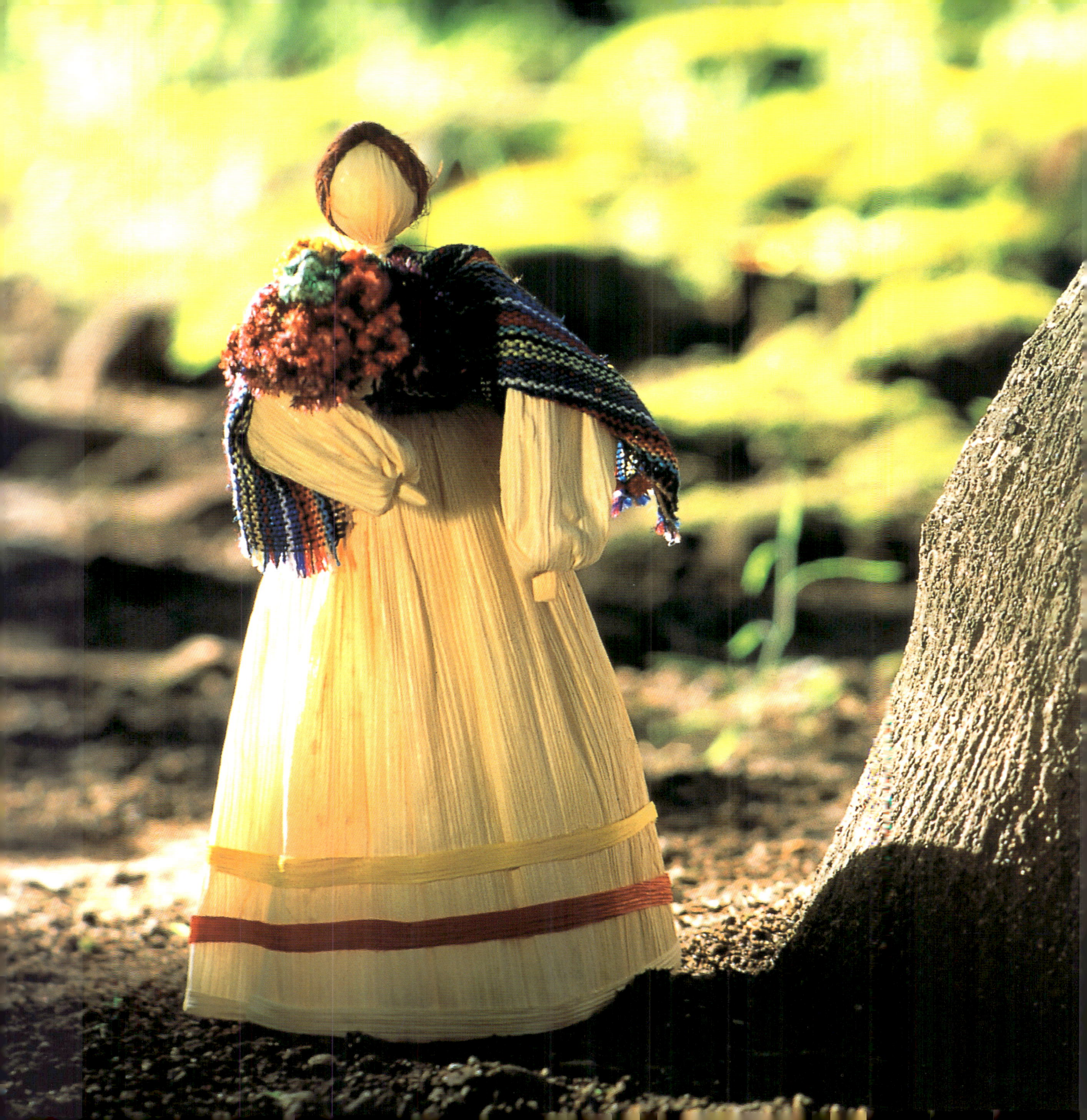

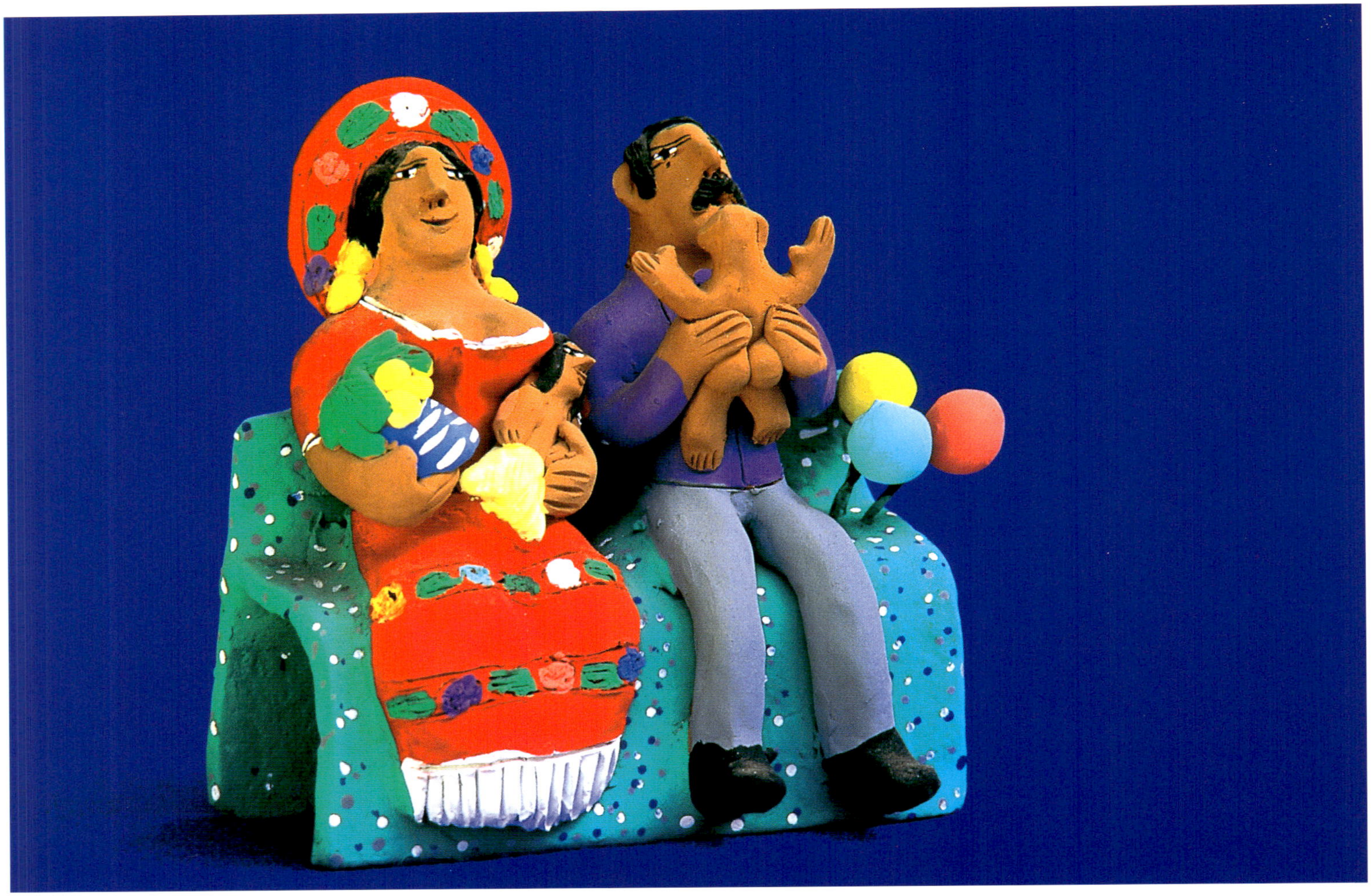

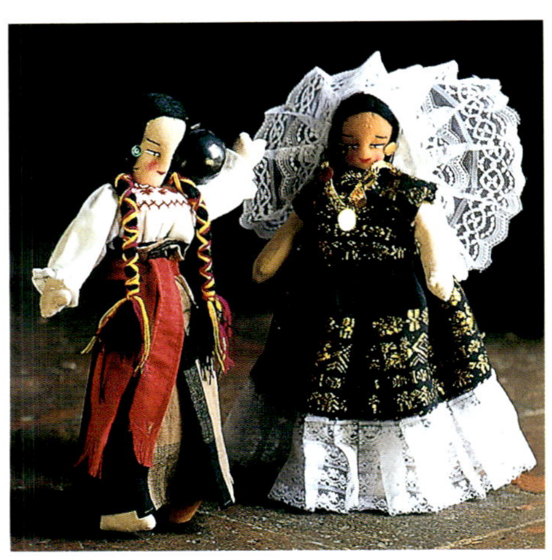

Dolls also fall in love
and live waiting for prince charming
or not so charming.

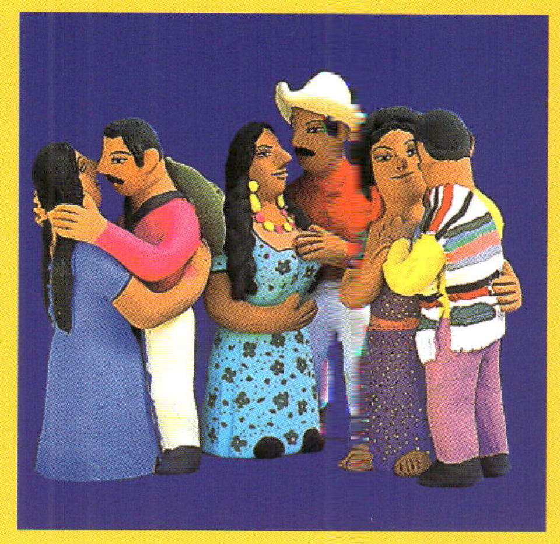

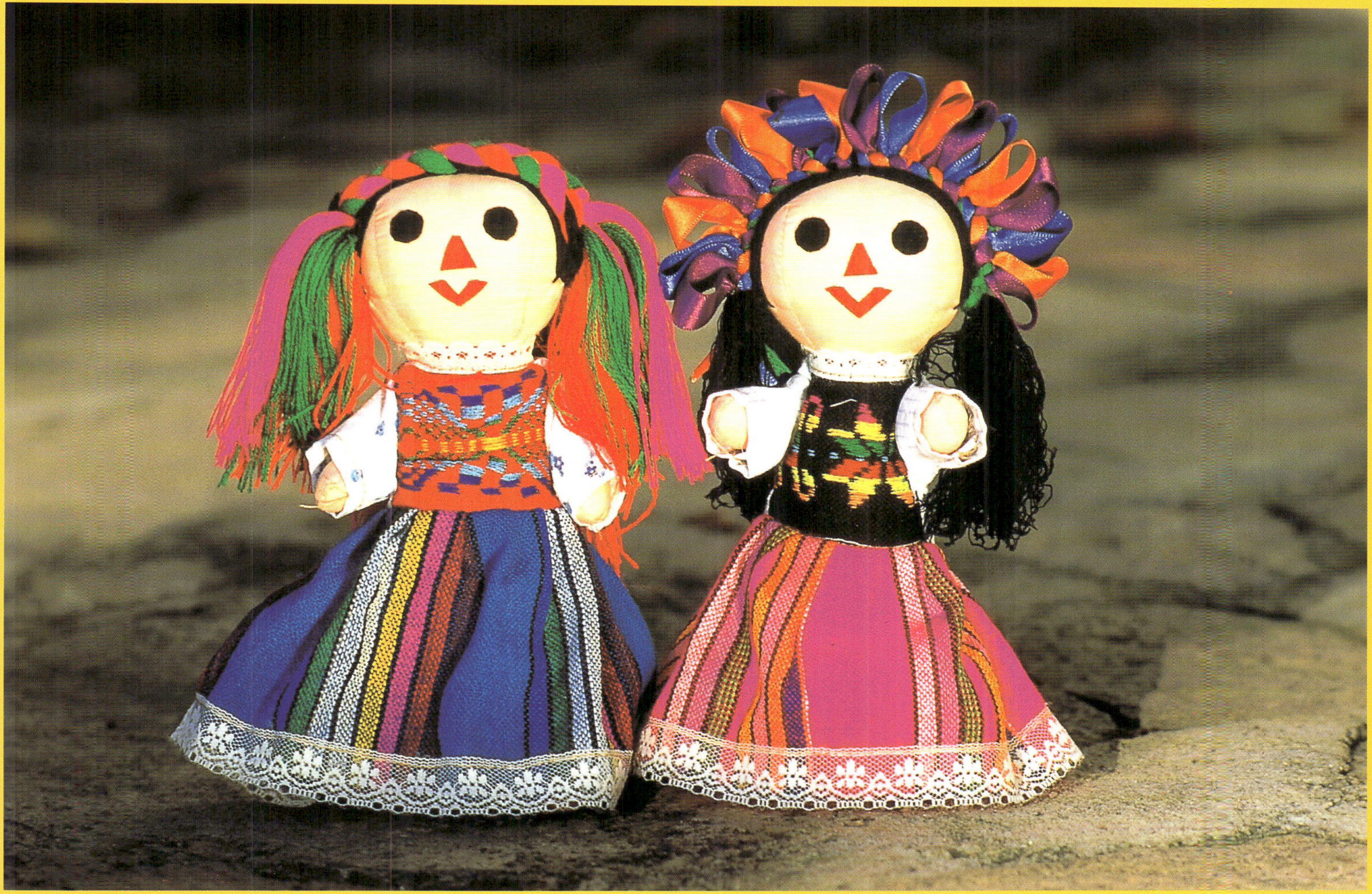

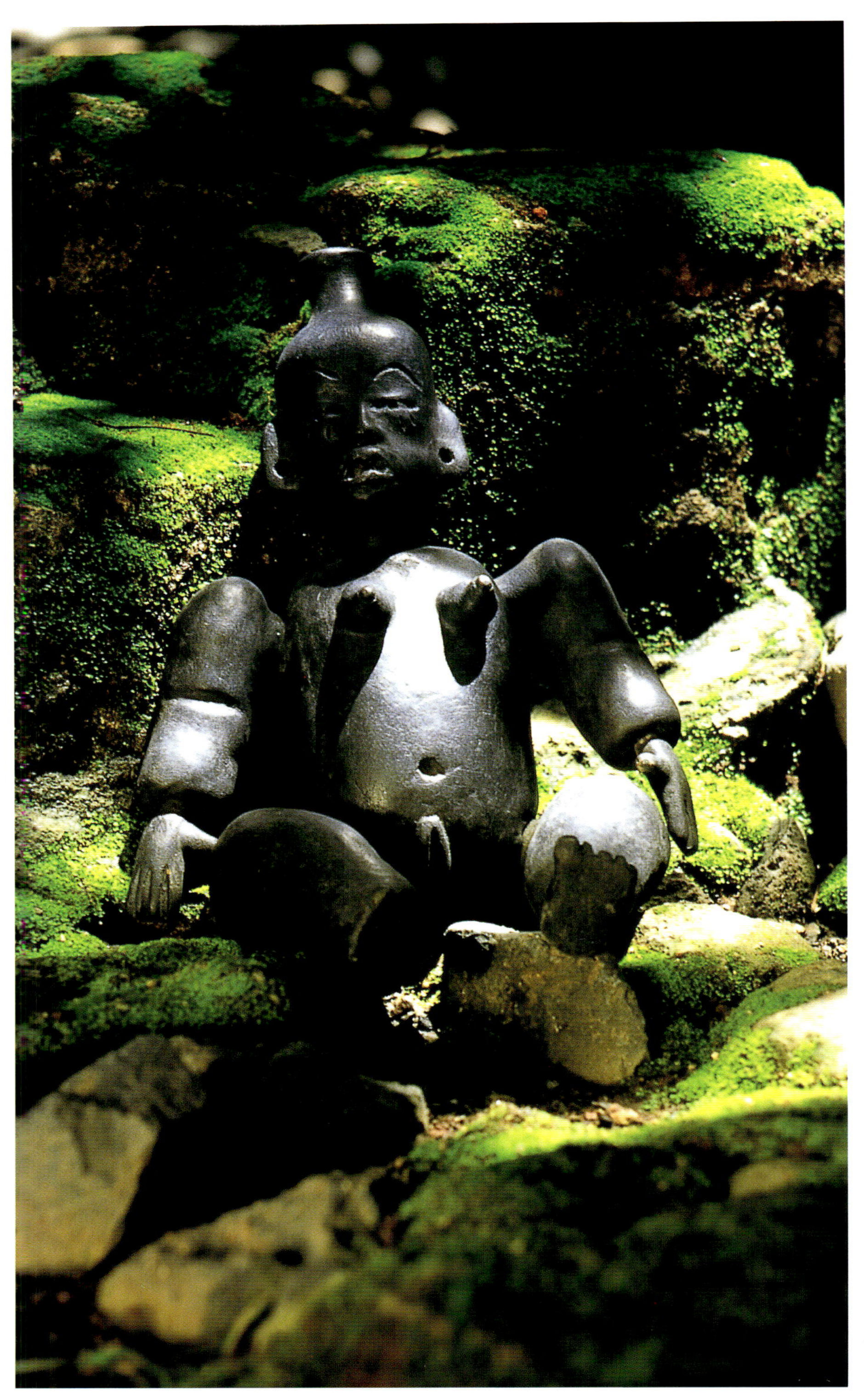

Shadowy doll,
other-world girl,
for you to travel
in this realm of light
is mossy green pleasure,
like that felt

by sprites
who live under rocks.

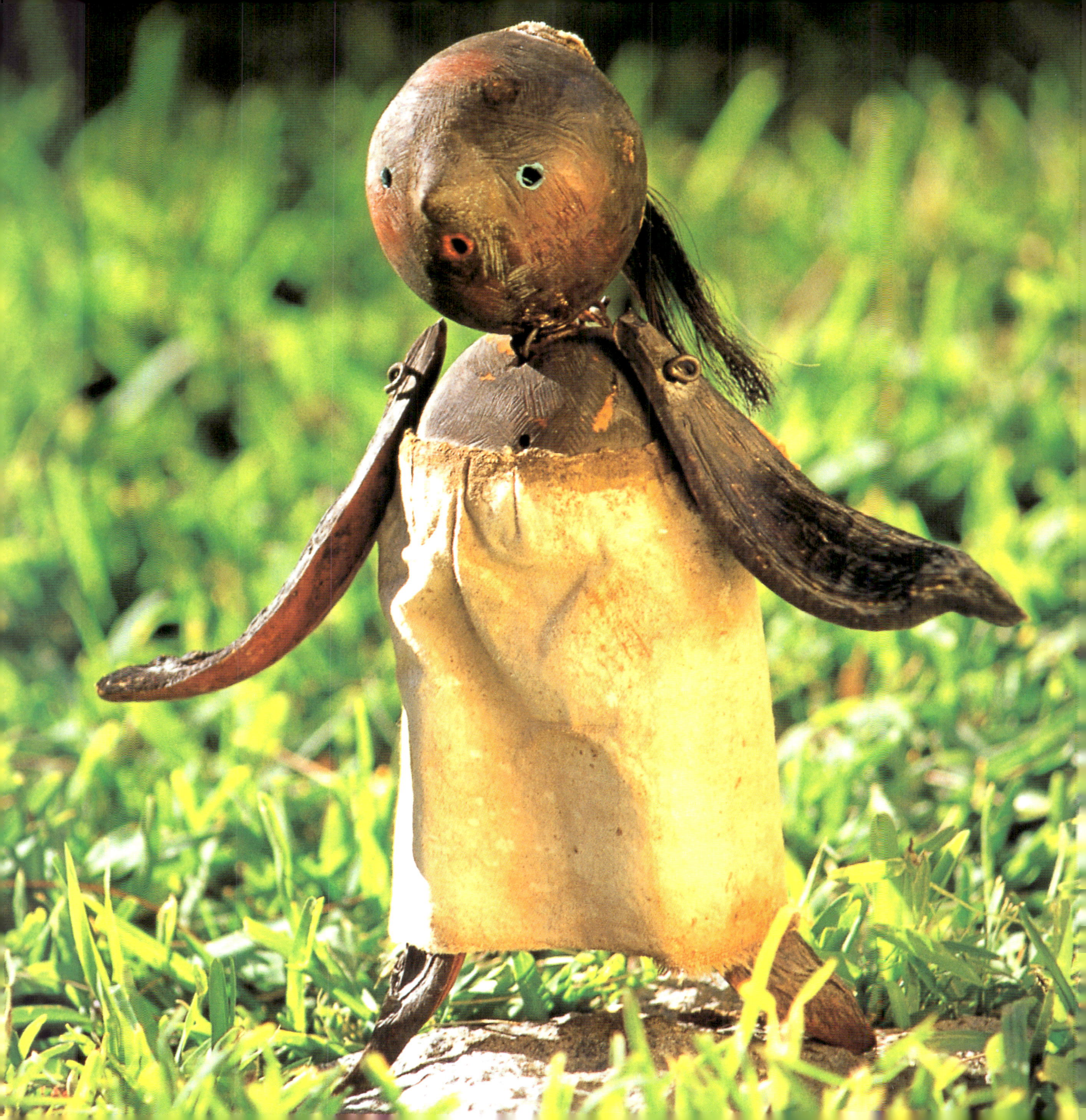

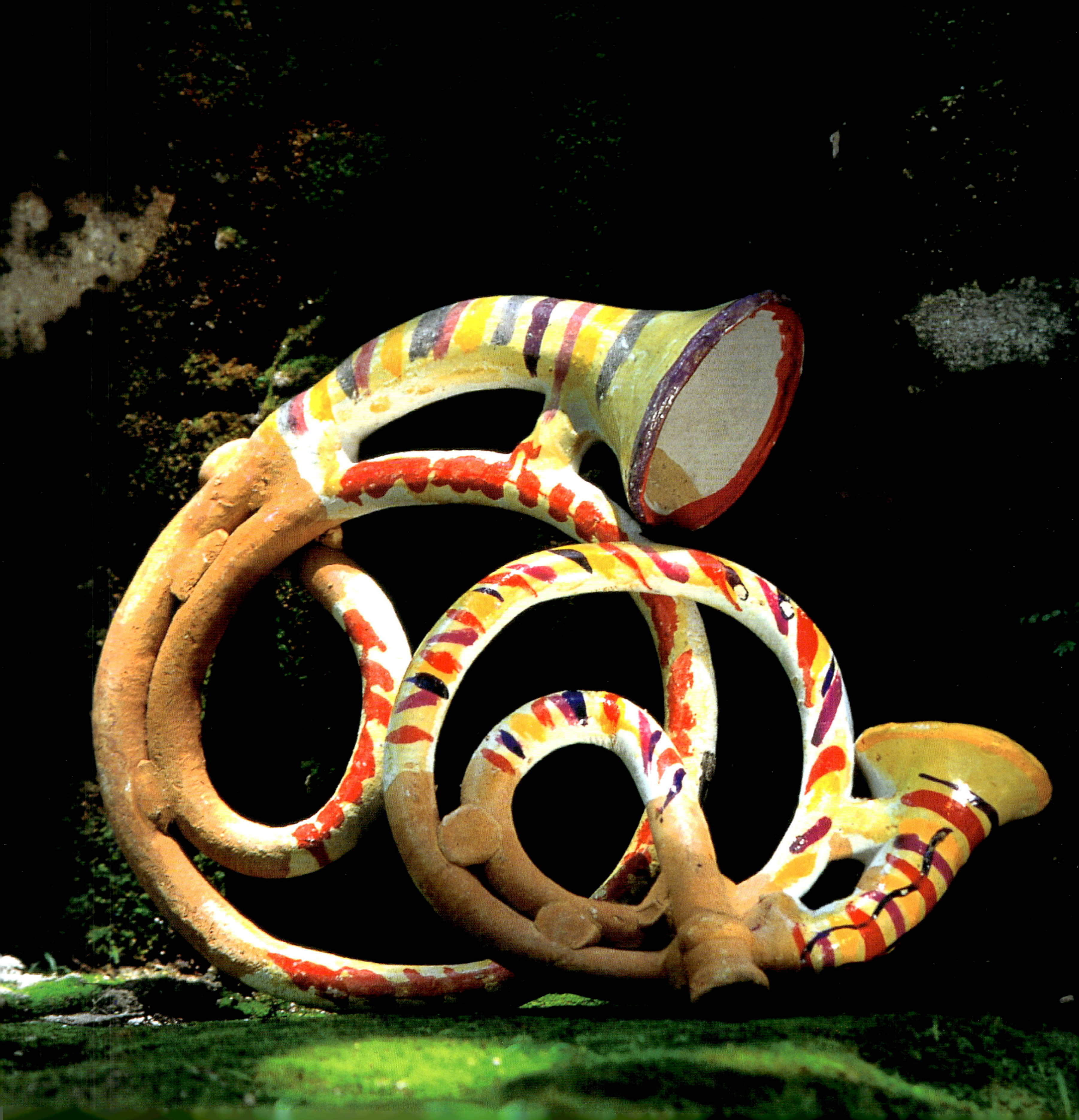

It is well known that in a number of languages the term "play" is used to describe what happens in dance, musical and theatrical performances, and poetry, because each is full of rhythm and harmony, the two most notable qualities that man can encounter, and that he may express. To play, to act, to dance and to make music are means of creating. And, if it were possible, guitars, little drums and tambourines, ocarinas and whistles, tin rattles, cornets and reed flutes, in short, the many instruments that tradition gives to childhood, would testify to the adventures that give them their soul and cadence.

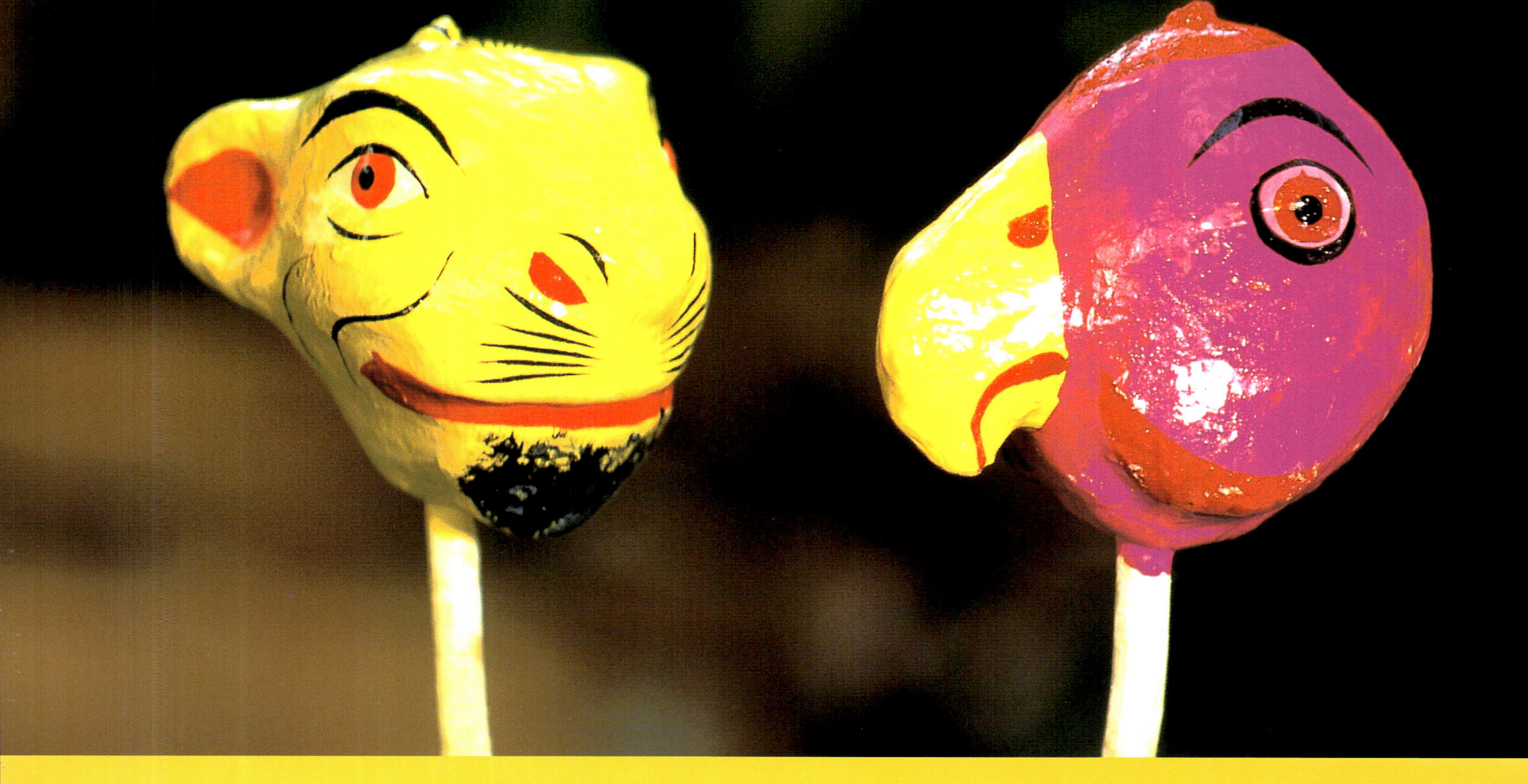

The celebration is now ready,
All that's missing is for the hearts to show up
Disguised as musical instruments

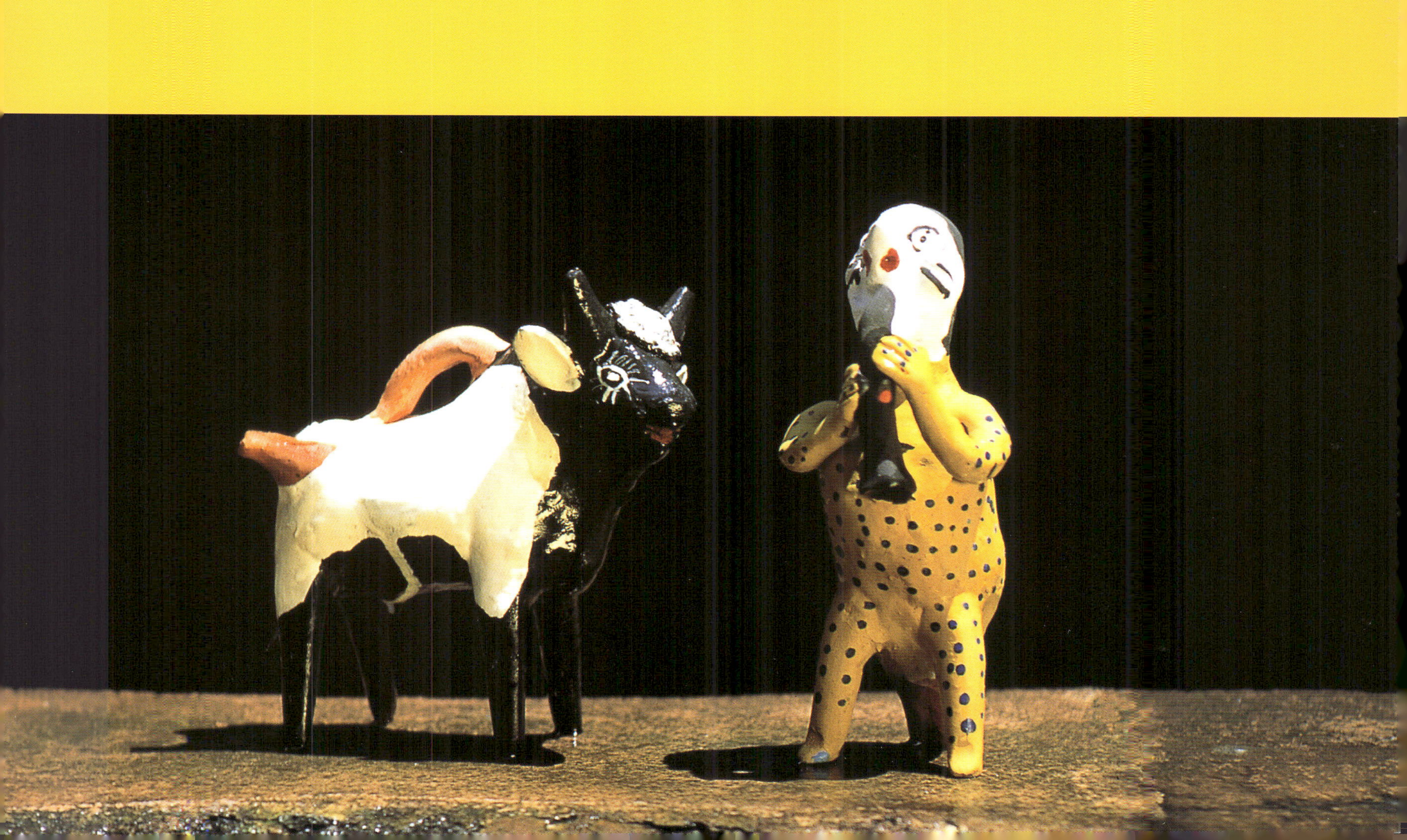

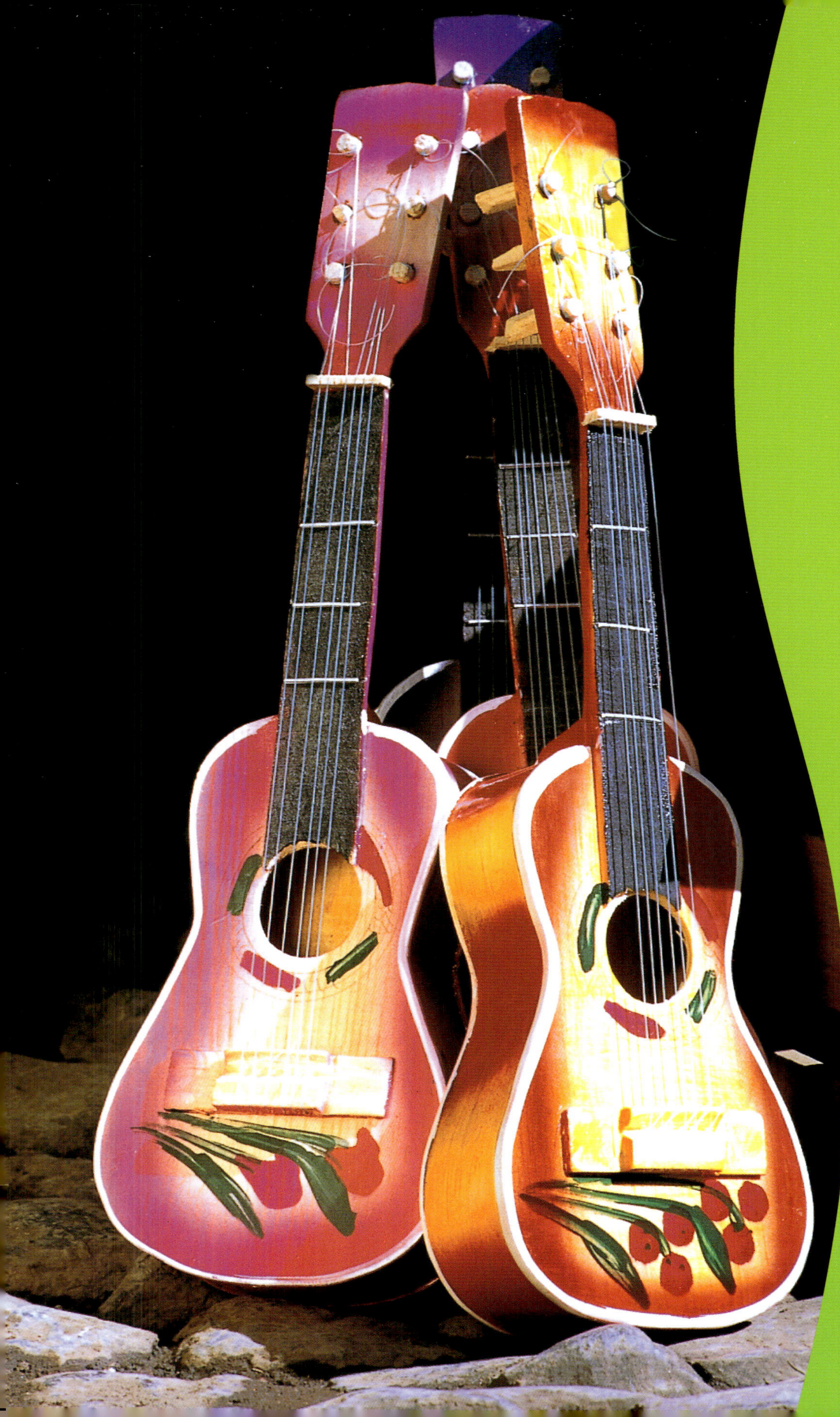

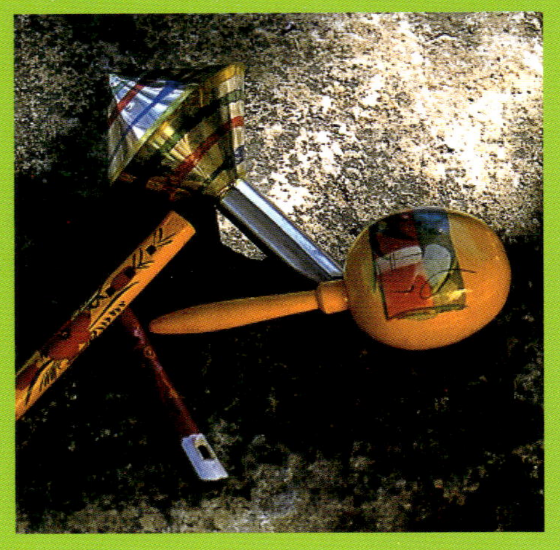

Strange musical flowers
sprouting from the substance
of hollow branches:
soon melodies will toss
their petals into the air.

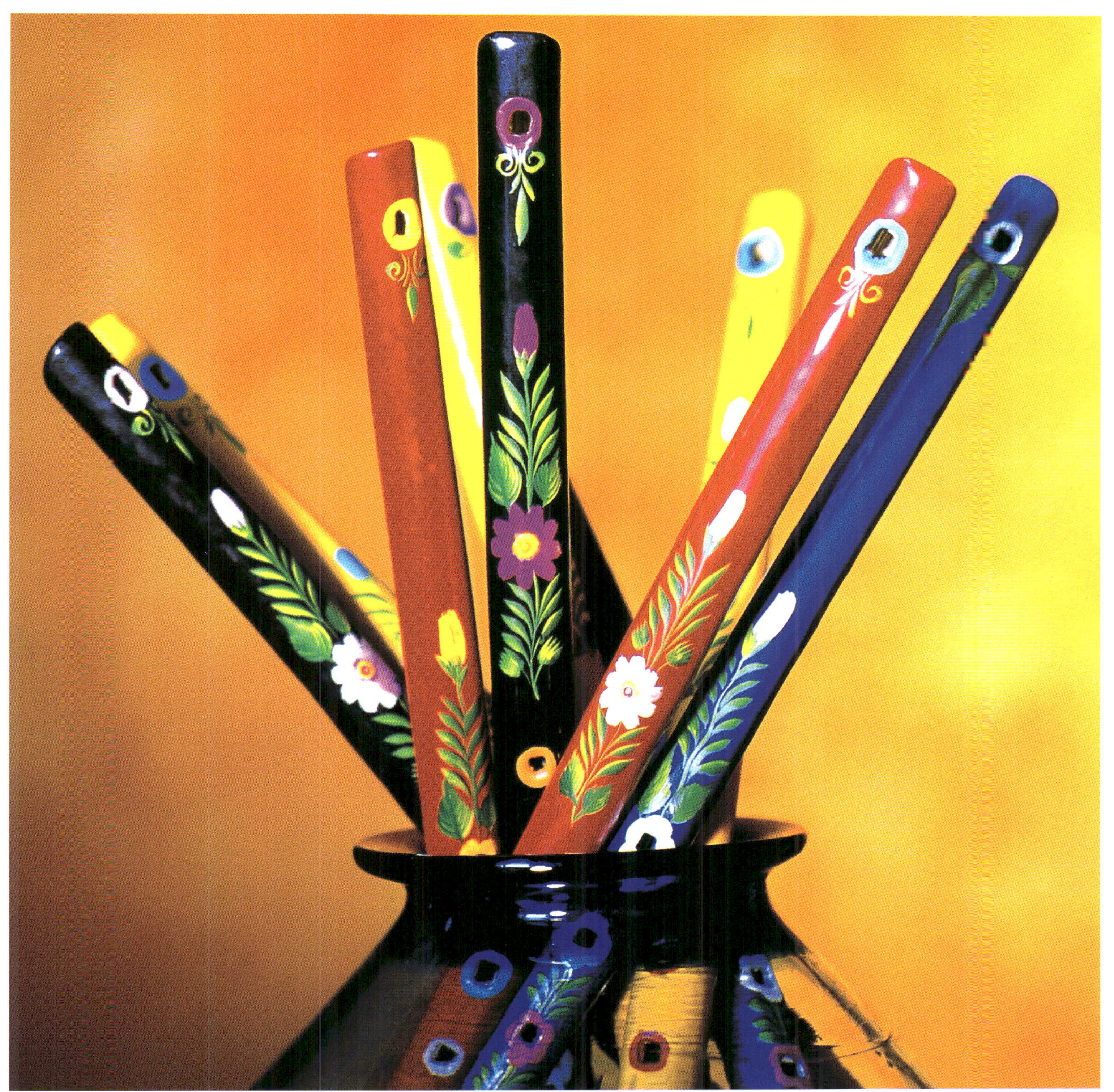

Tin cornets
birds with long beaks
that fill the forest of silence
with metal screeching,
like funnels of joyful sound
becoming infernal clamor.

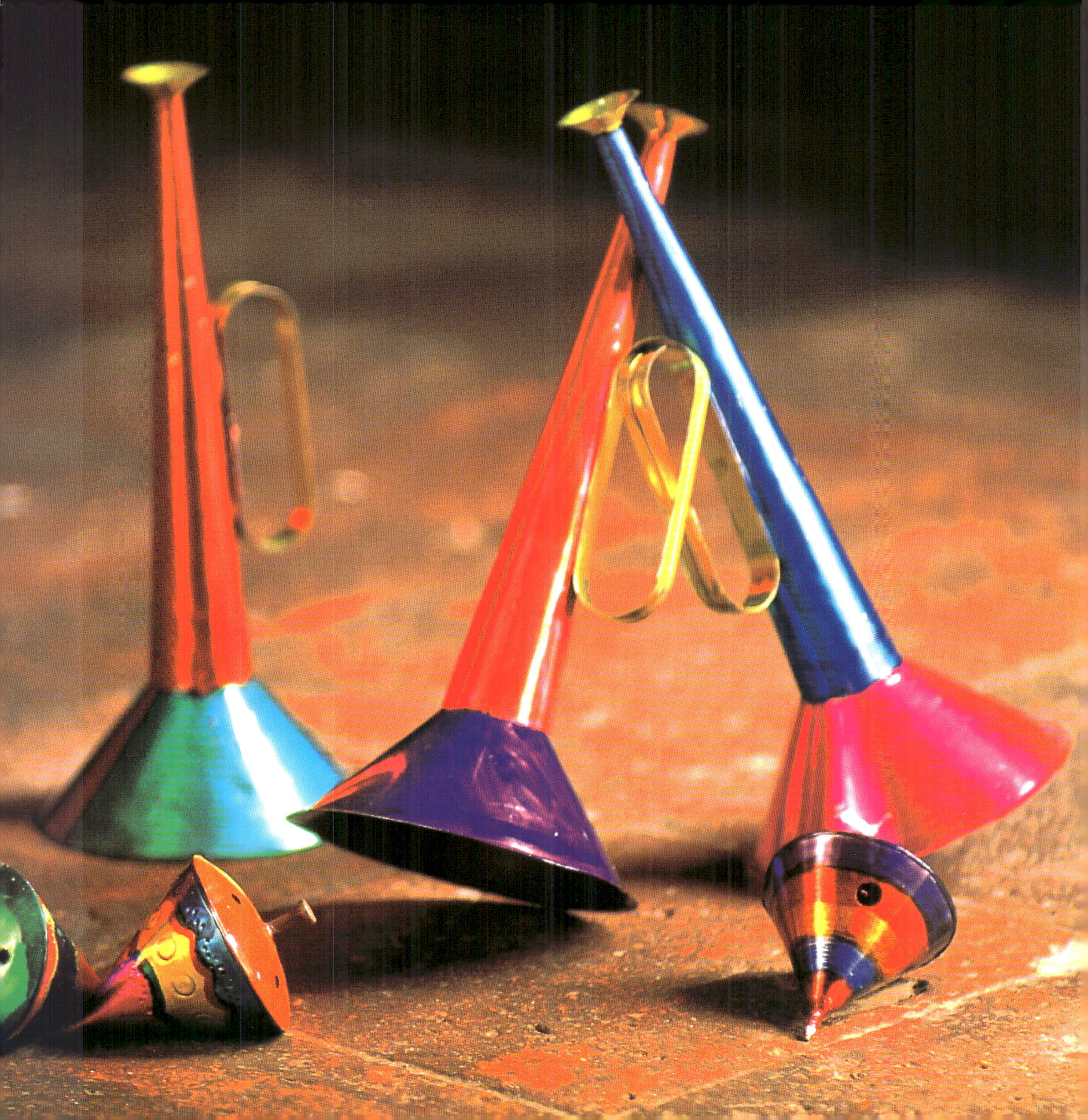

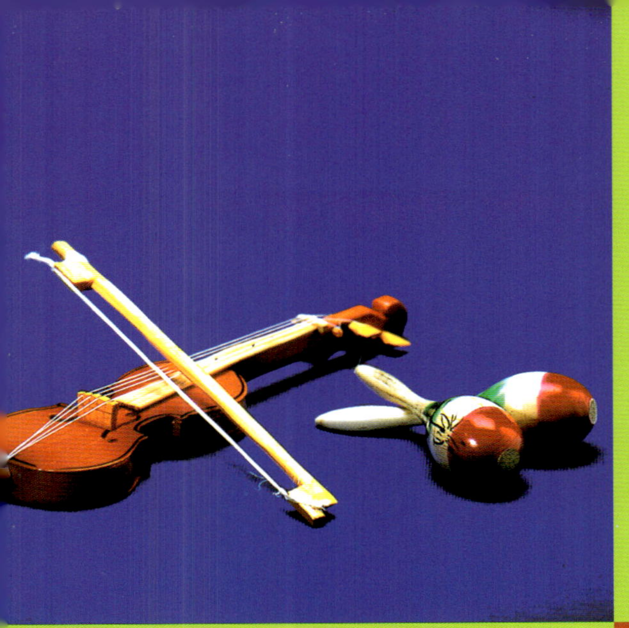

On the musical planet
the inhabitants are shaped
like drums, violins,
flutes or tambourines:

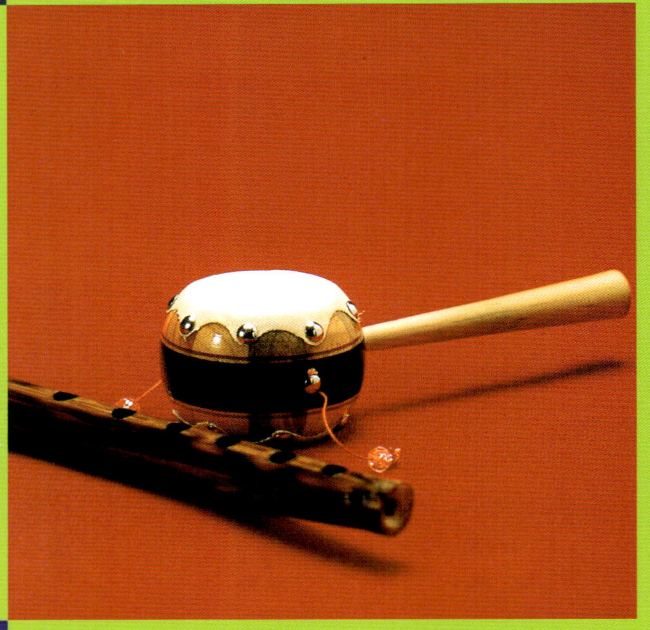

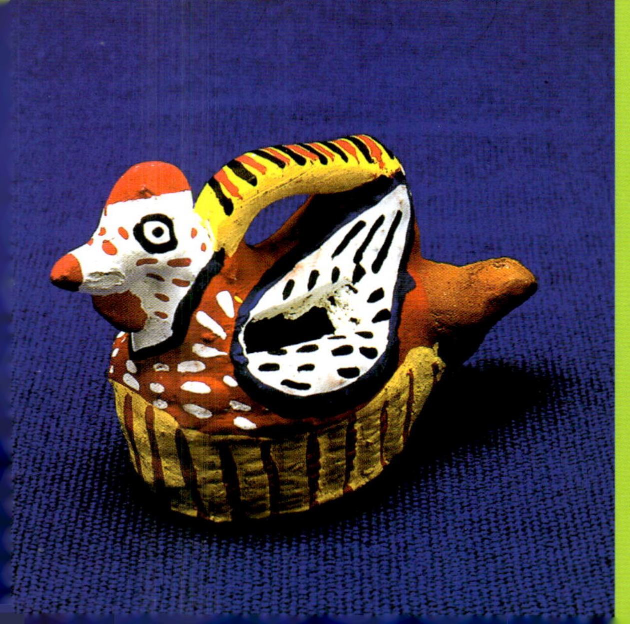

you simply must hear
the noise they make
when they all try to talk
at the same time.

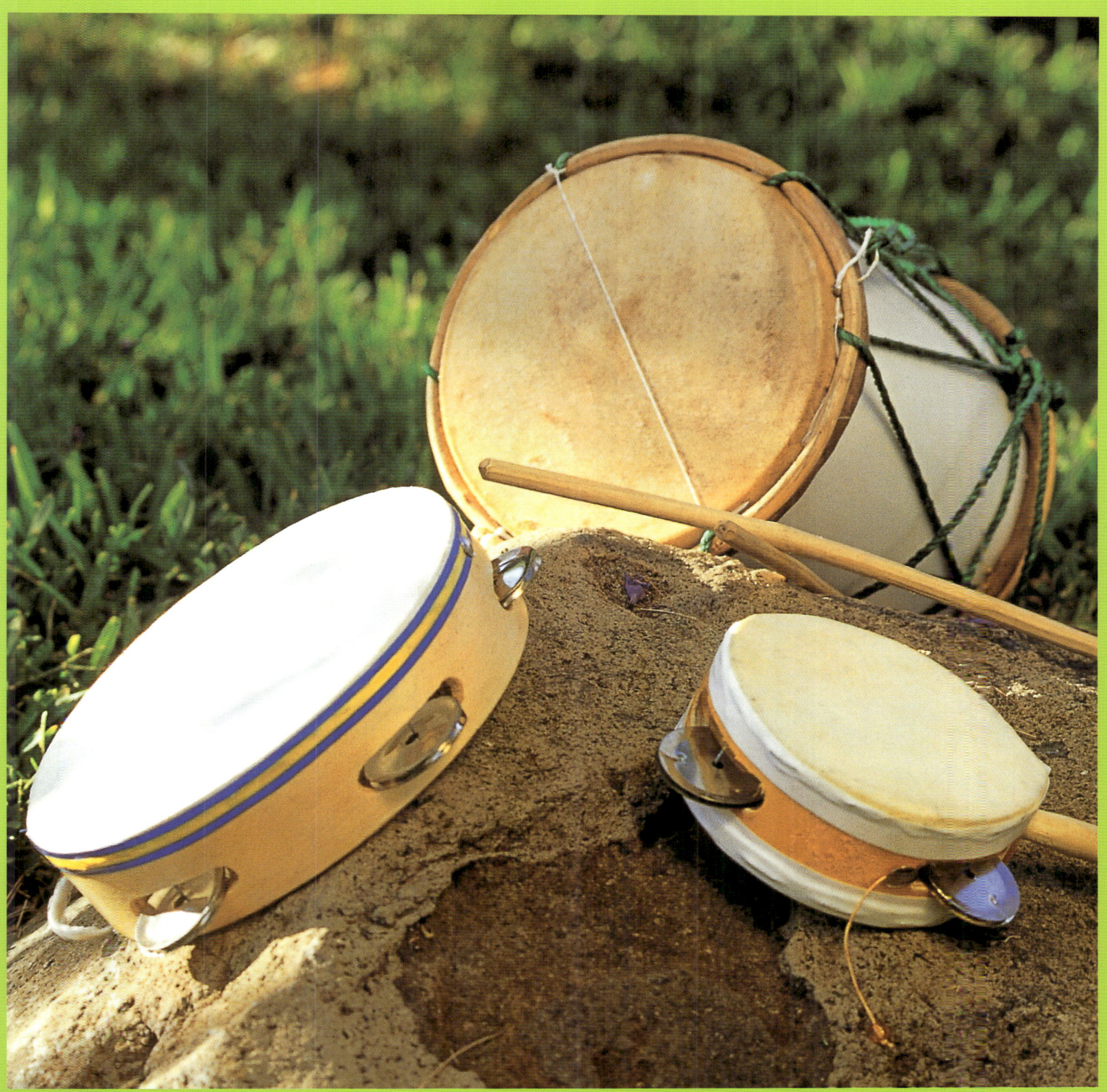

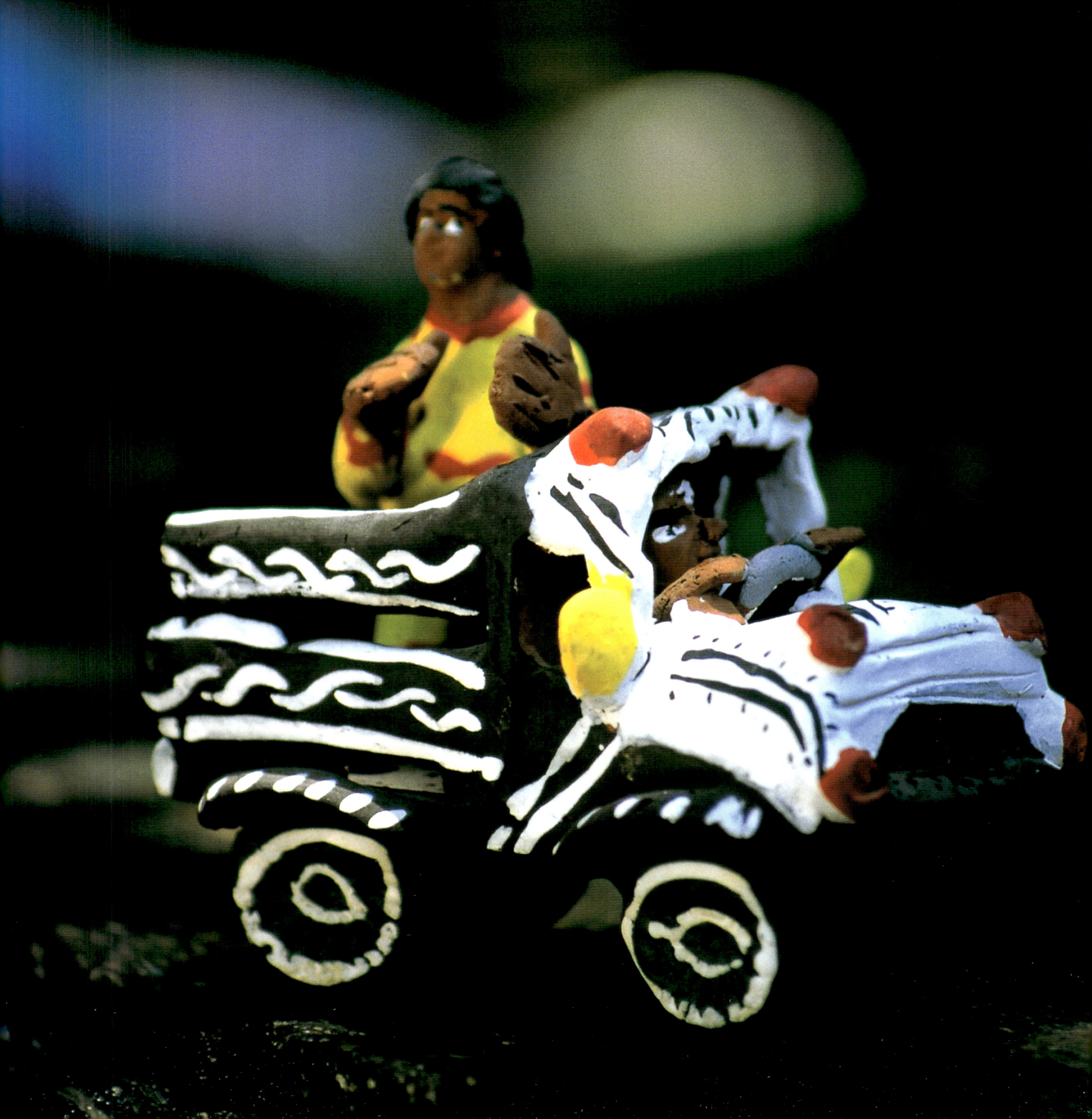

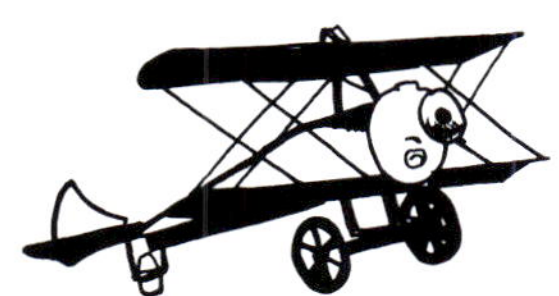

Toys, and play itself, are located somewhere outside the rationality of life's practical details, beyond the zone of utility and necessity. In the world of play, voyages exert a particular fascination, for they unleash the astonishment of coming to know different people and new places.

Because of this, modes of transportation have a special place among childhood toys. Children, embodied in dolls, travel at the velocity and instantaneity of imagination, to the most recondite sites in the universe, in trains, cars, planes, hot-air balloons and rocketships.

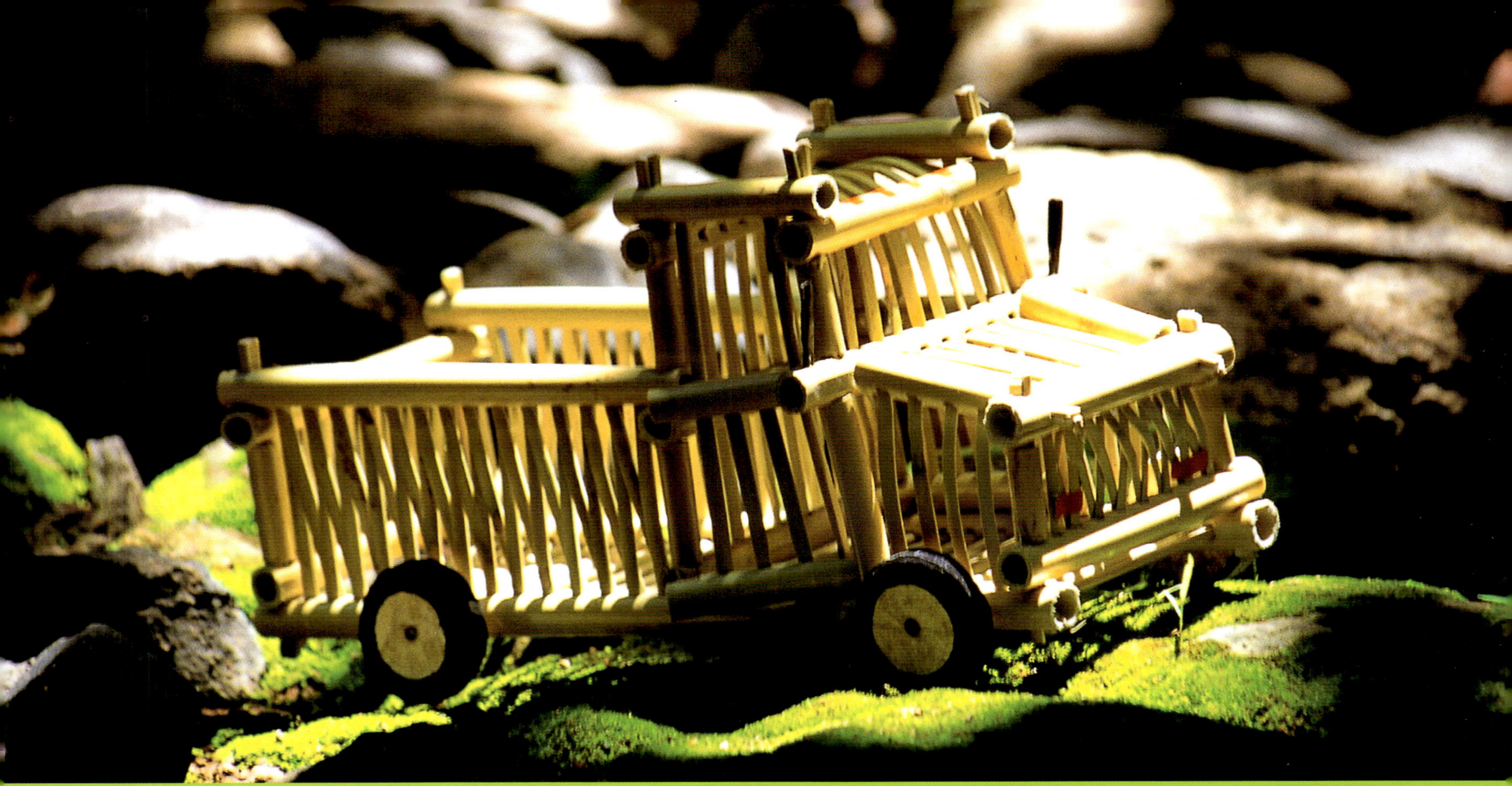

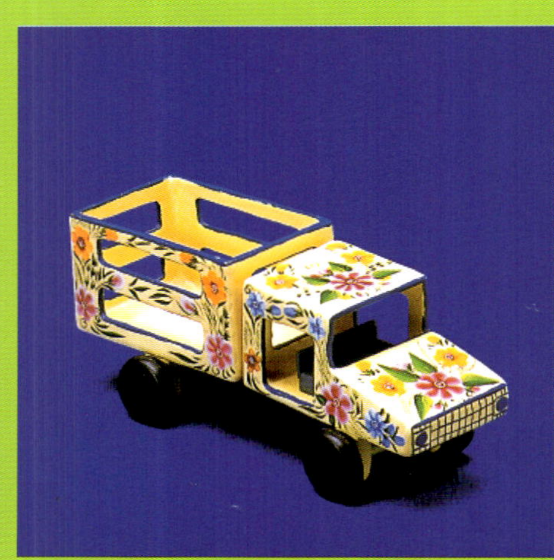

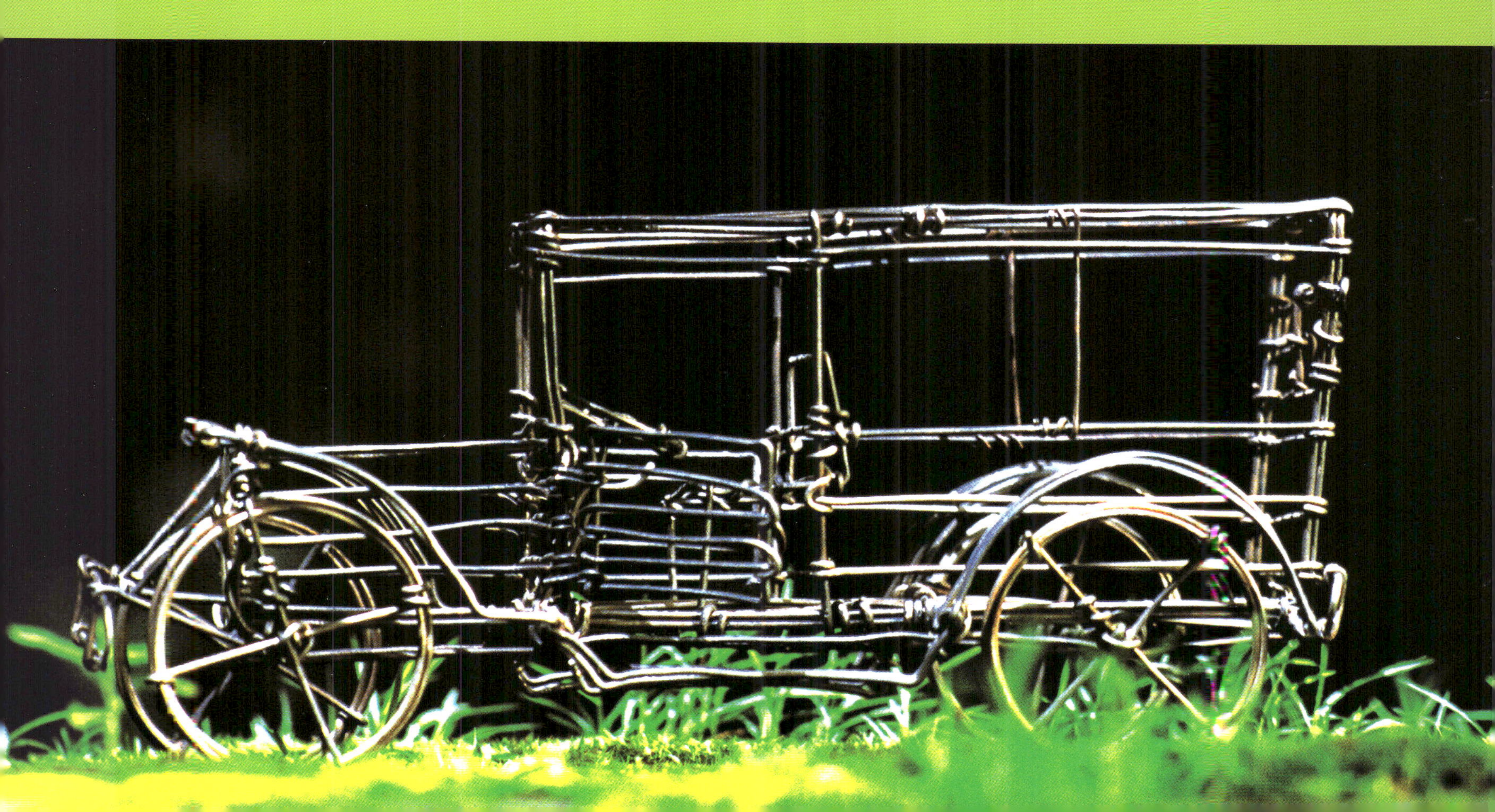

If there were somewhere to go
they would surely take us there,
yearning to share the trip.

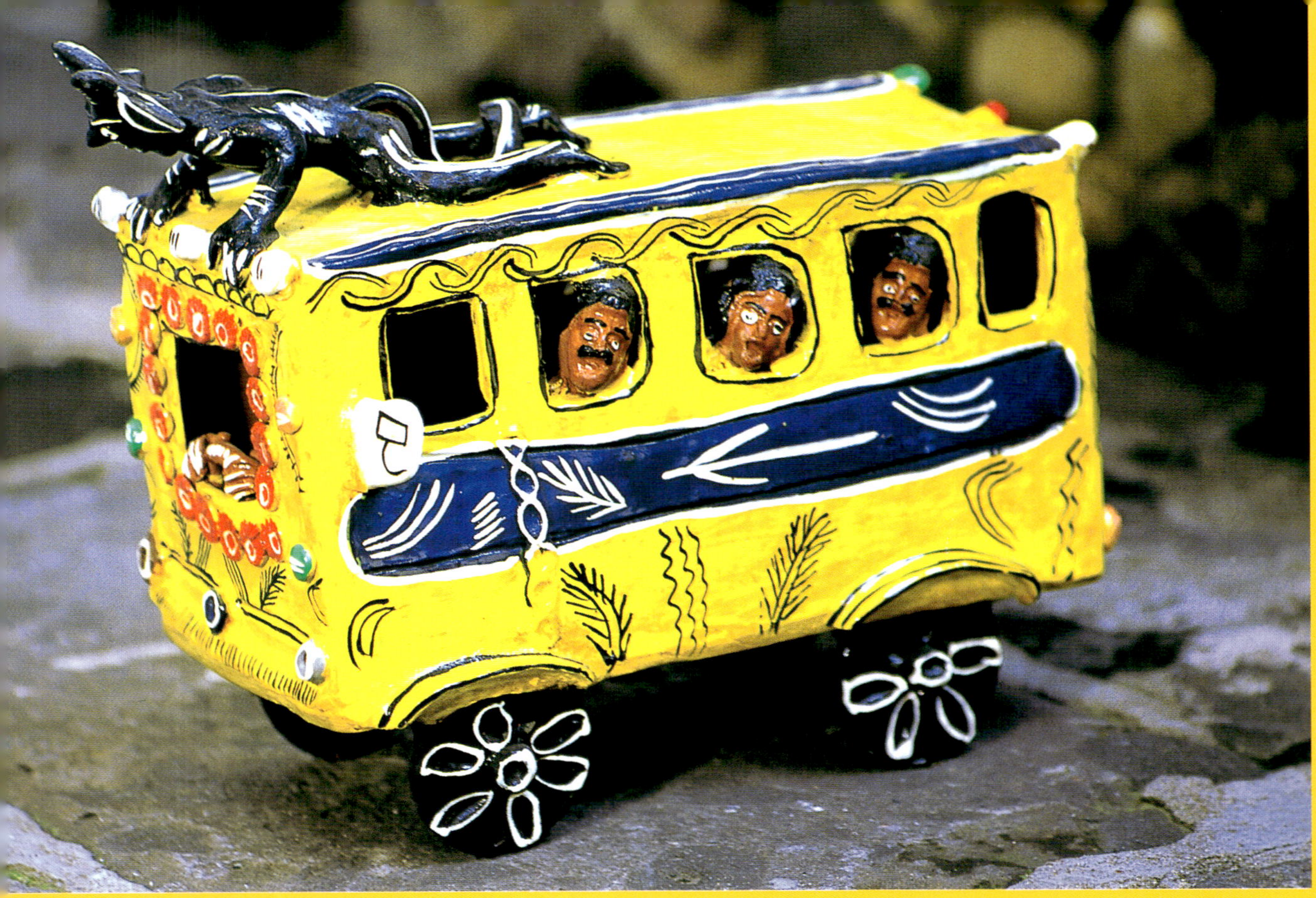

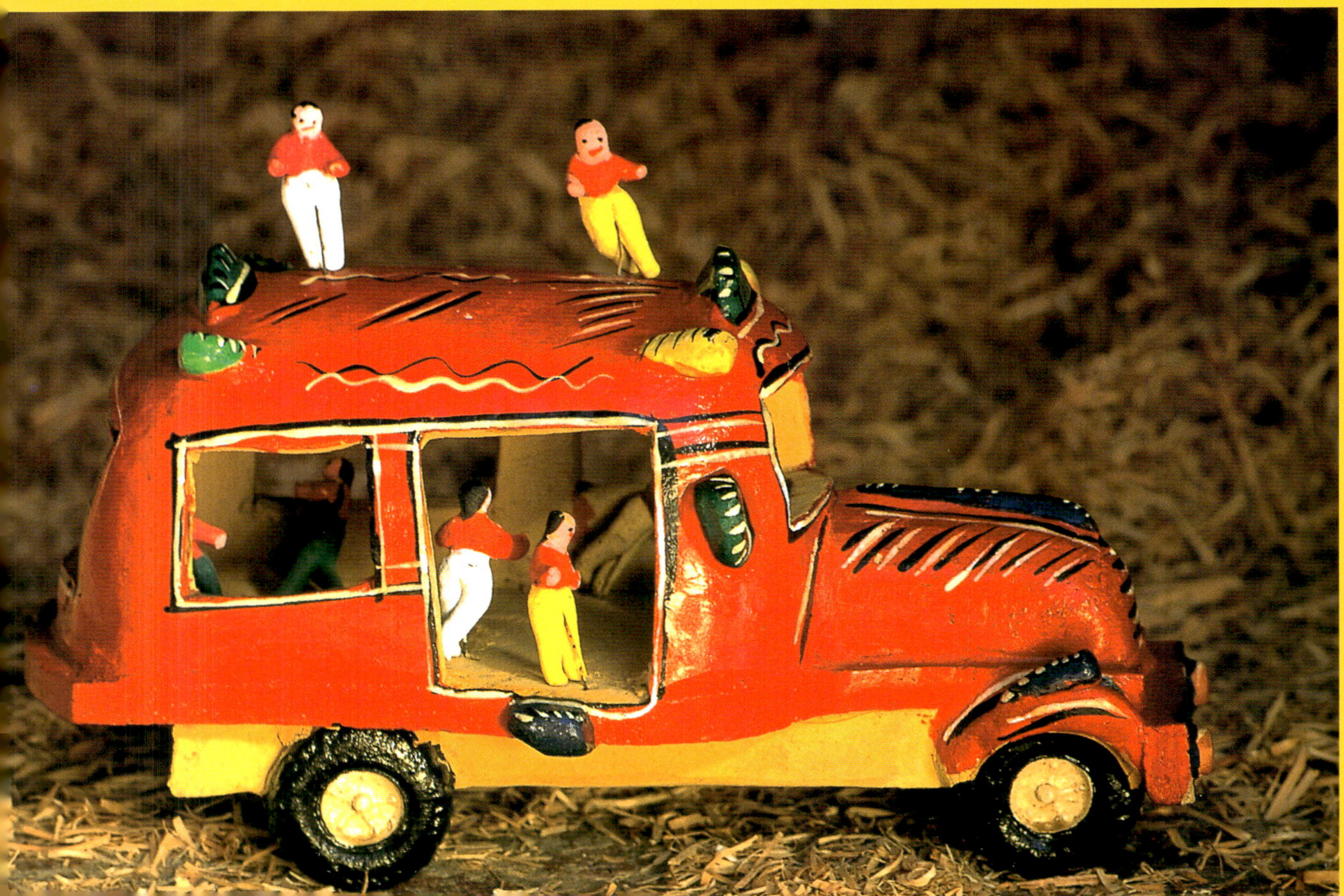

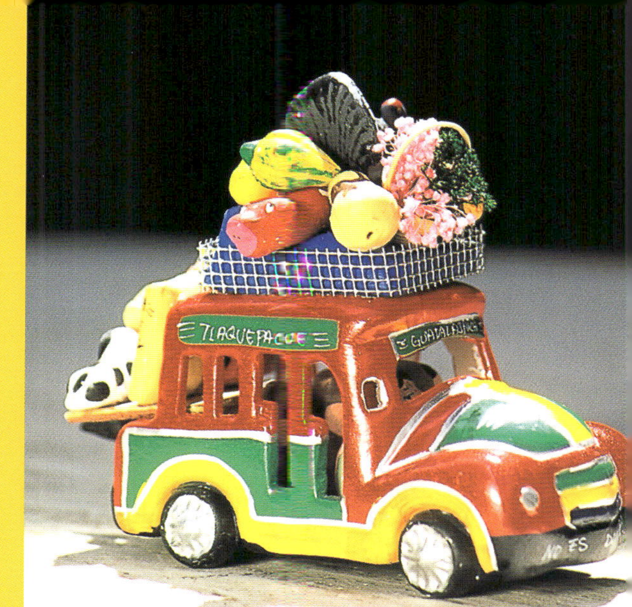

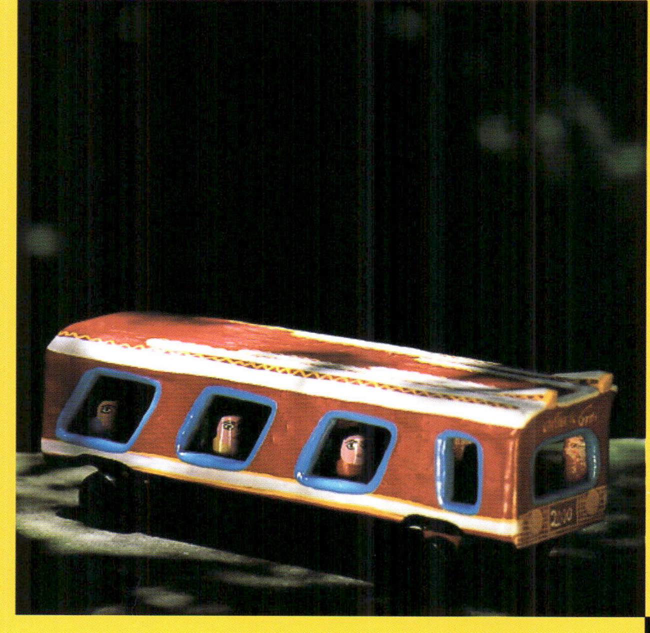

They awake mid-journey
not remembering where they're going
and having forgotten
from whence they came.

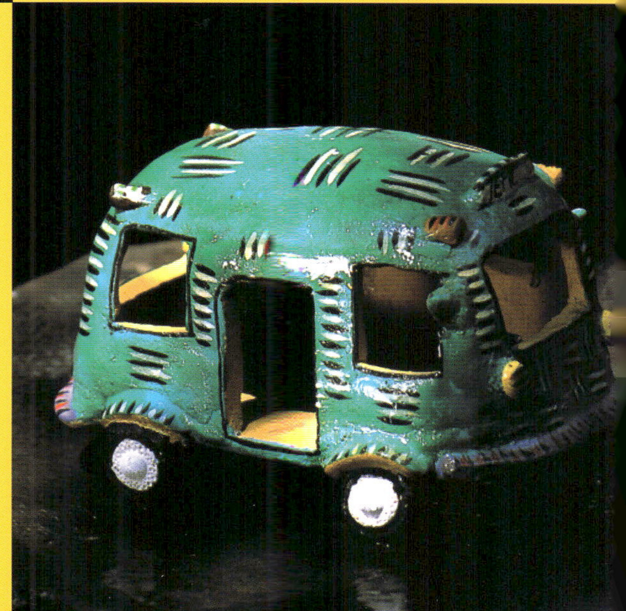

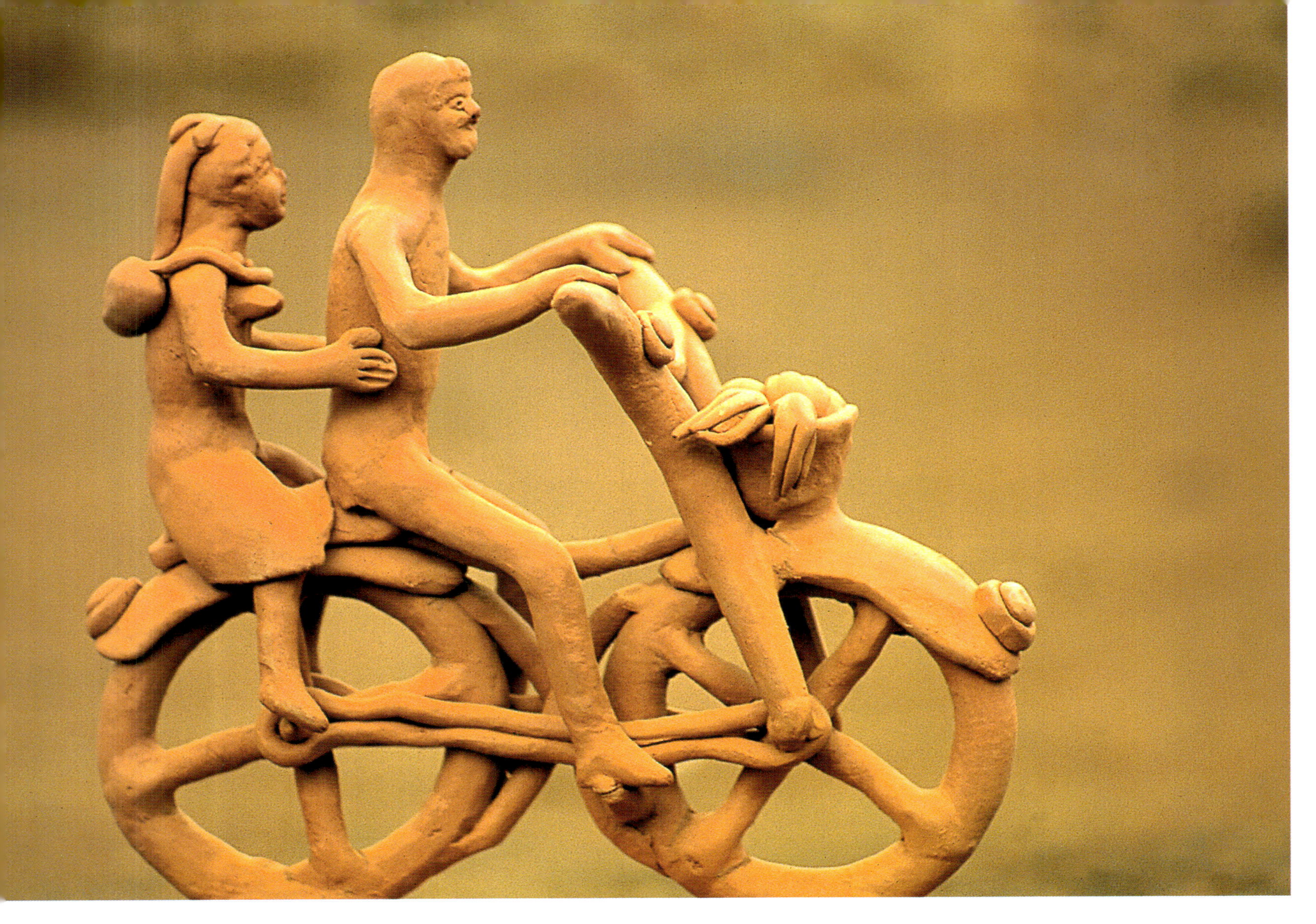

Toys transport dreams if
dreamed some other way
never reach their destination.

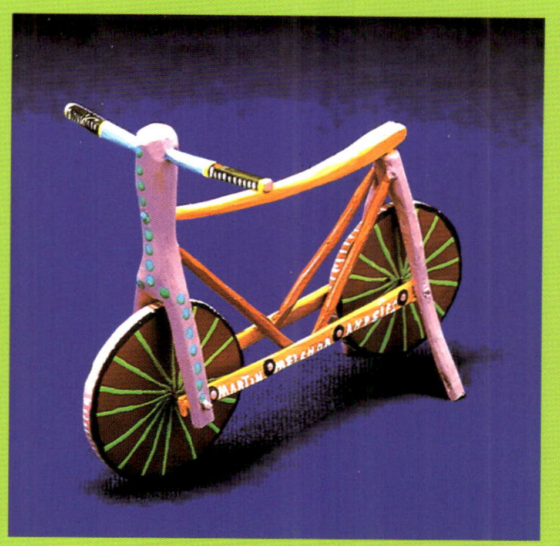 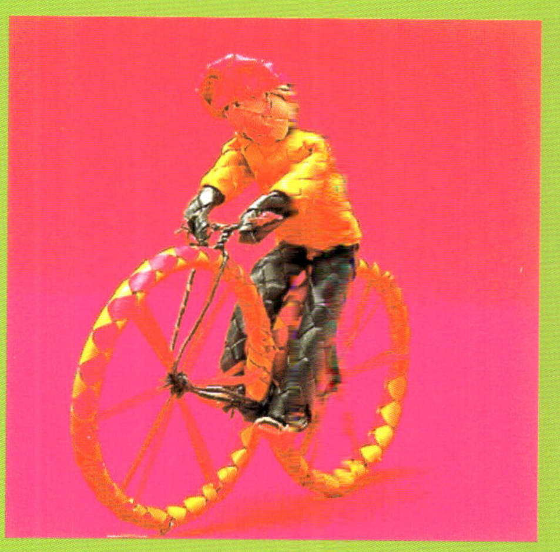

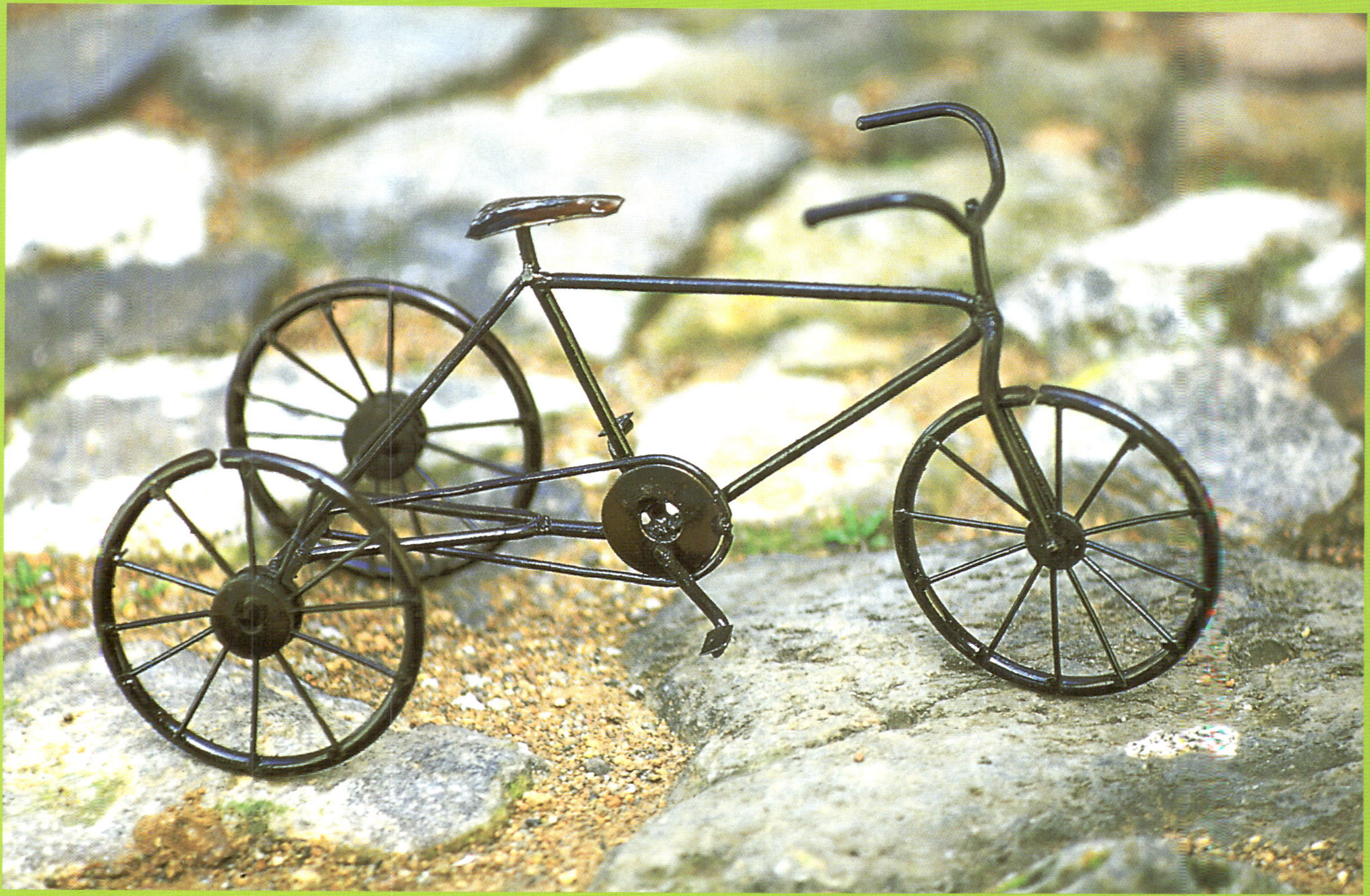

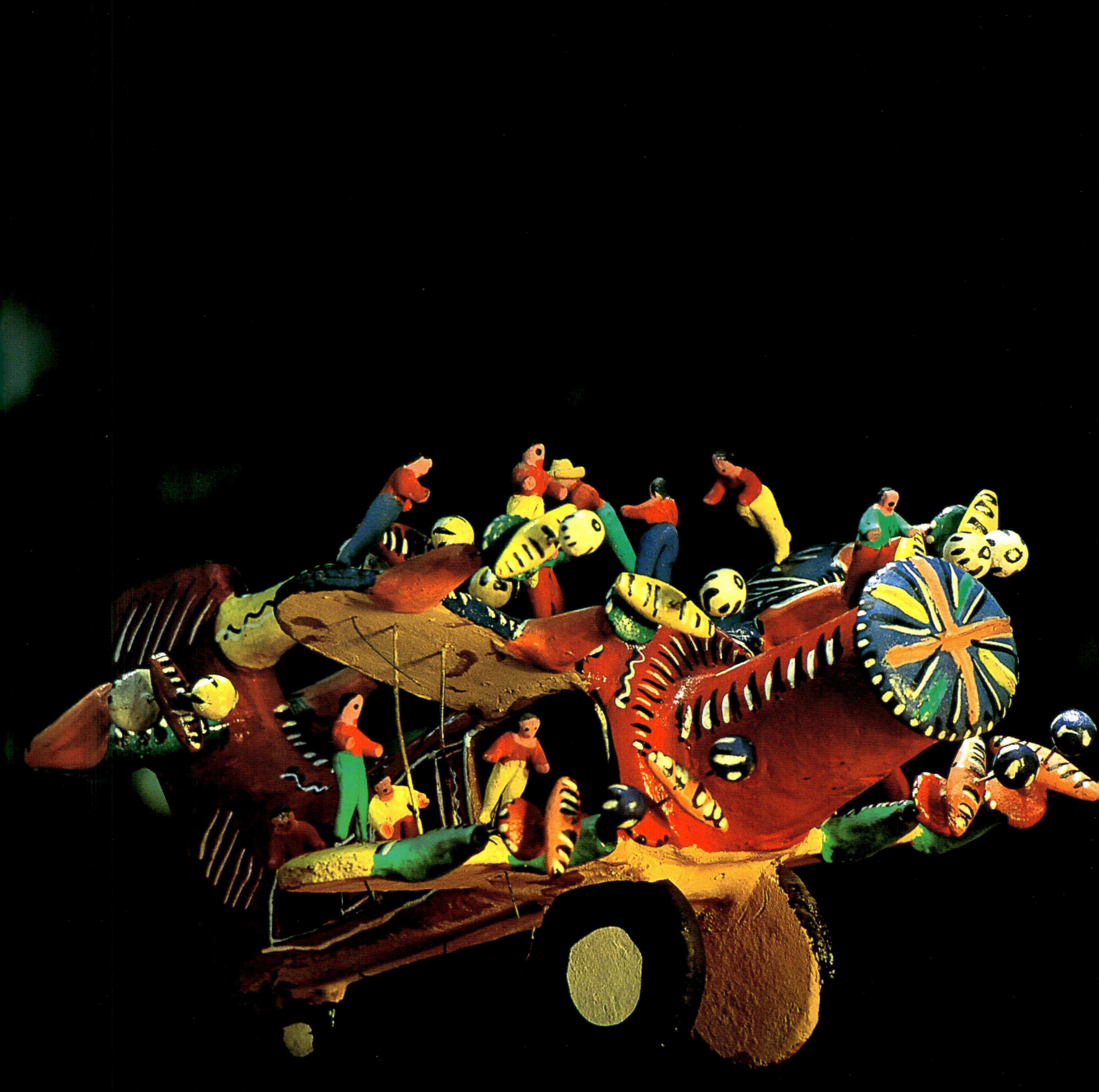

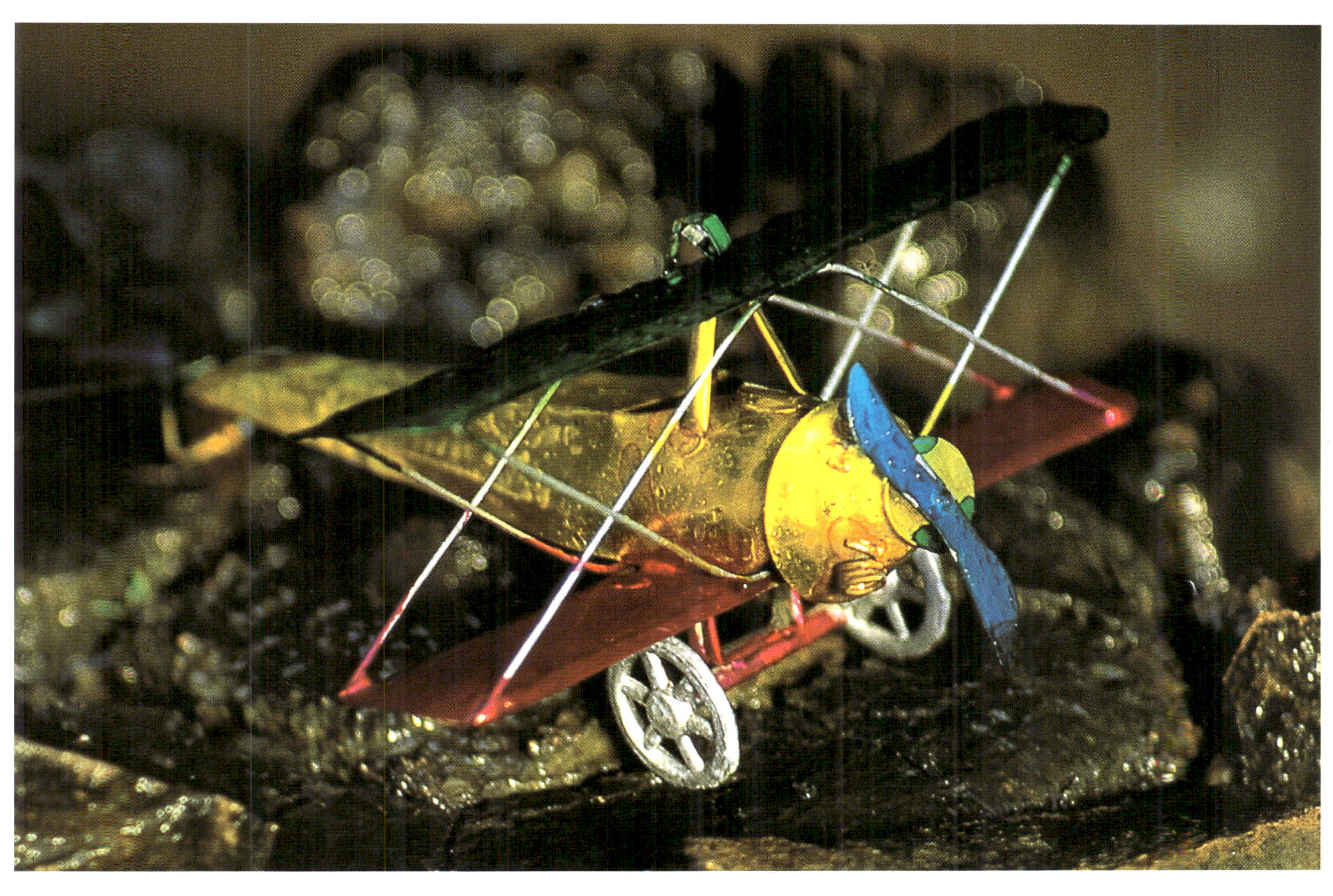

A stripe in the sky
flock of souls
or airplane to neverland.

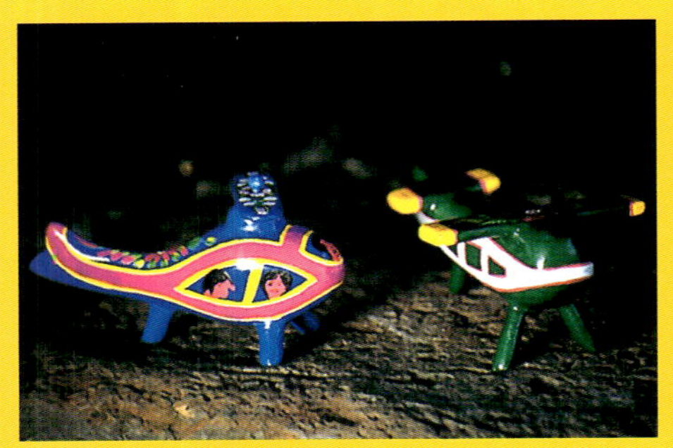

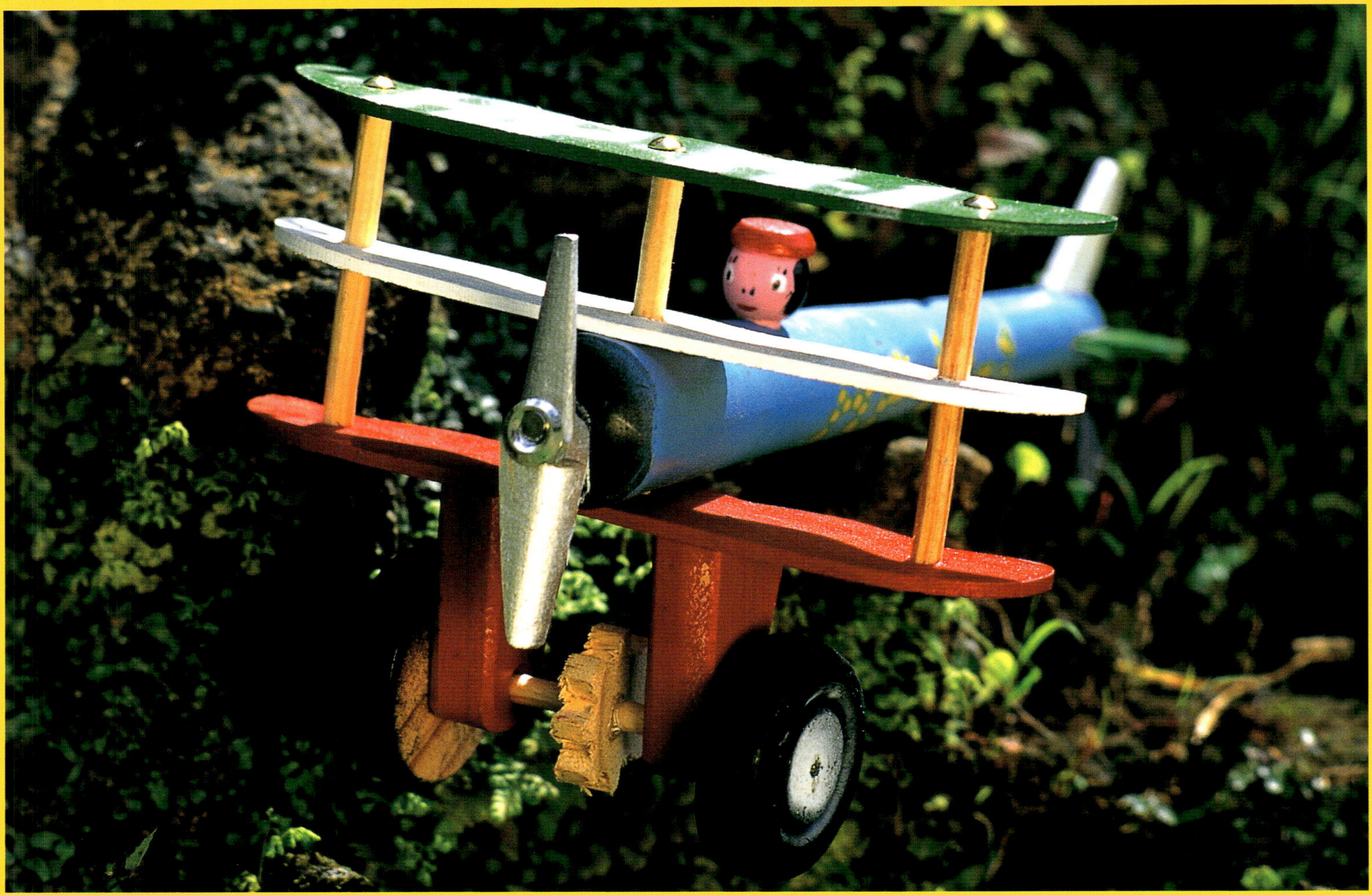

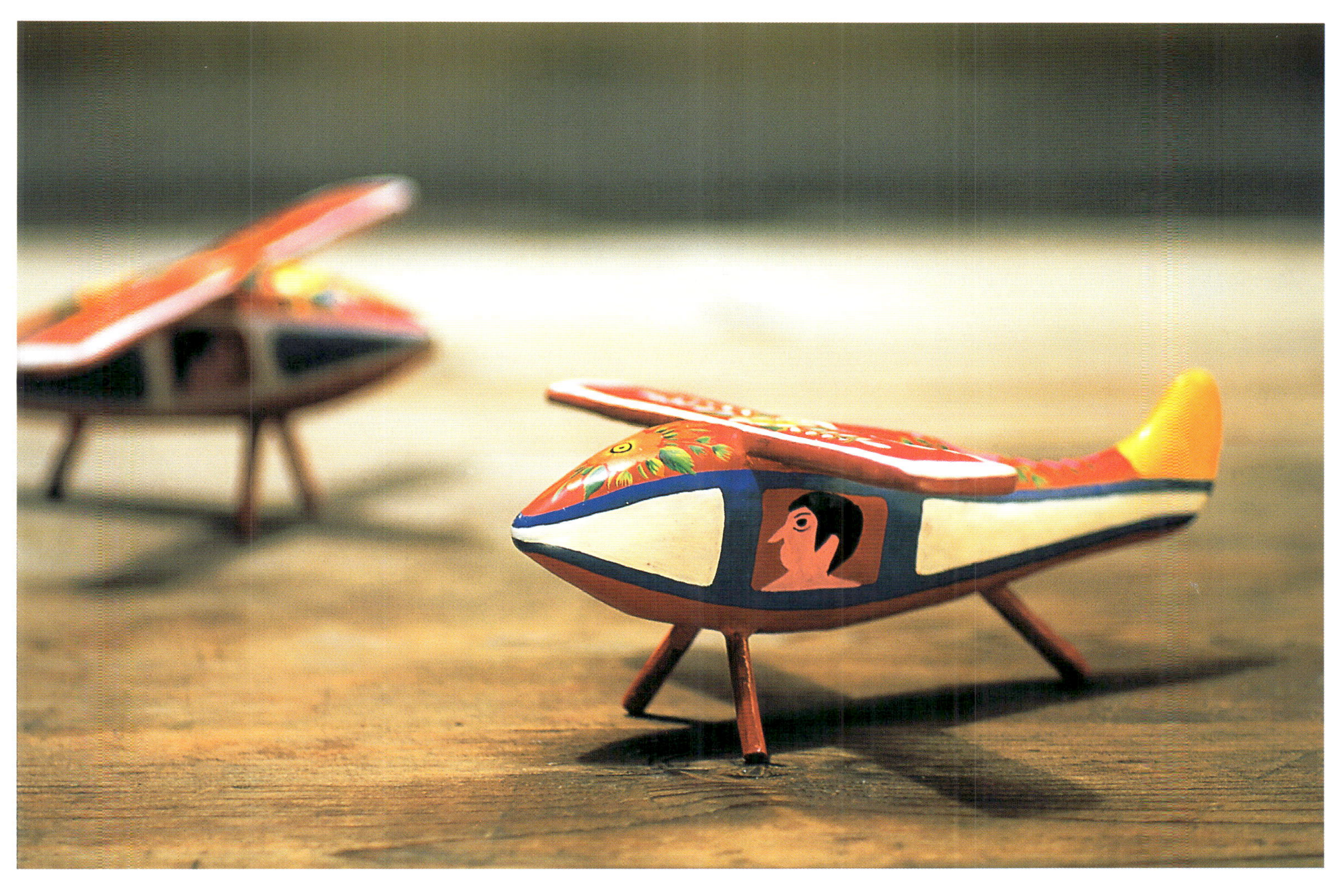

In flight the world looks better,

what's on view is real life in miniature
seen from the majestic eye of the airplane.

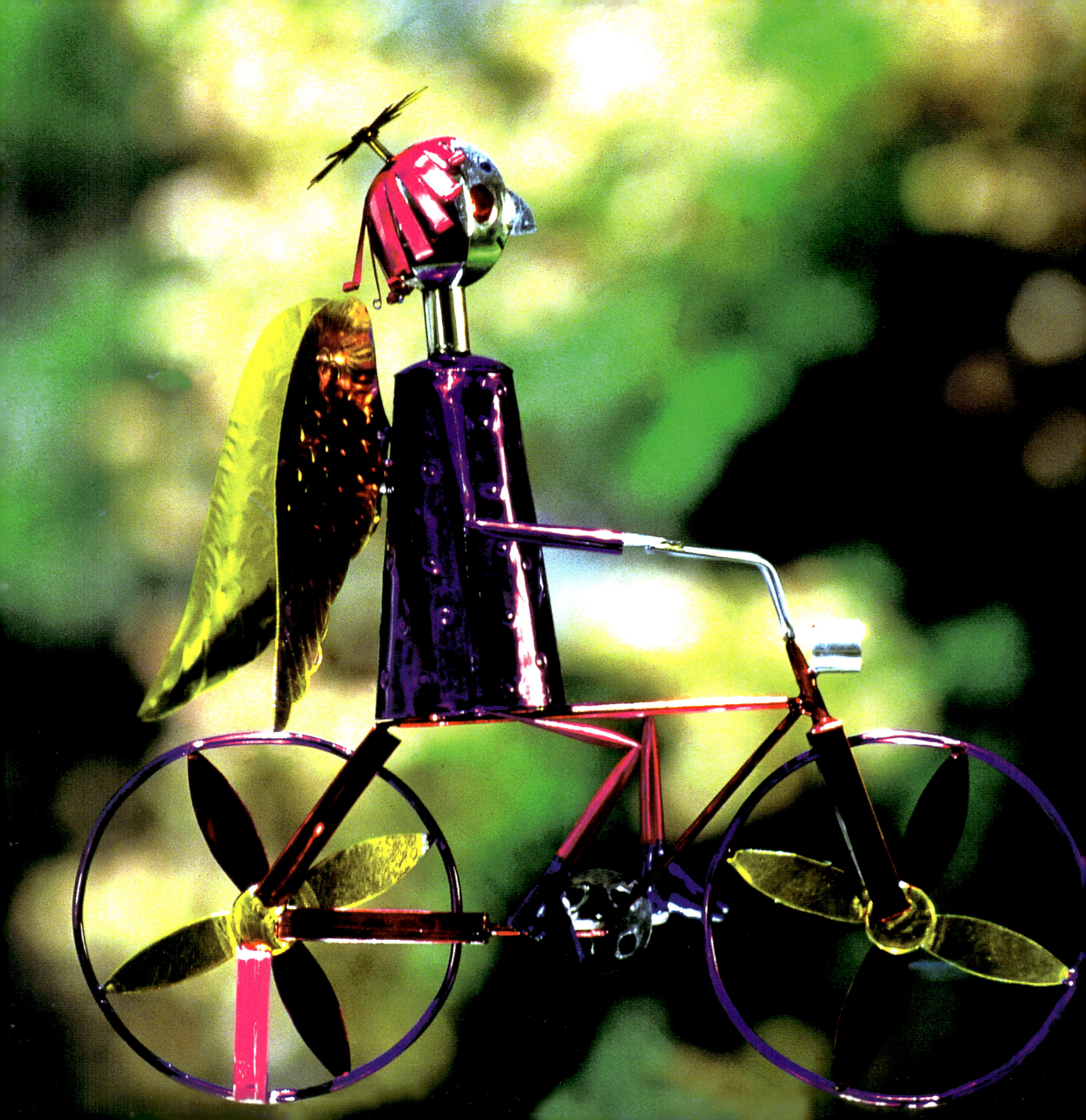

*They have the fortunate desire
of no desire but to be right here,
where all that is, is.*

PHOTOGRAPHIC CATALOGUE

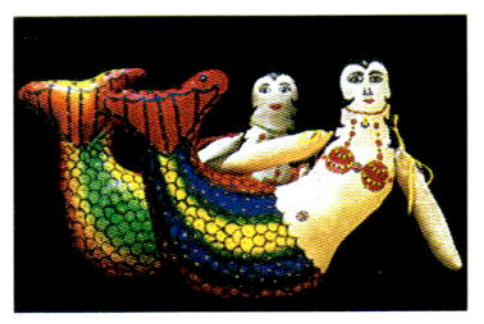

Pages 2 and 3:
Painted Cloth Mermaids
San Miguel de Allende,
Guanajuato.
Photo: *Rigoberto Moreno*

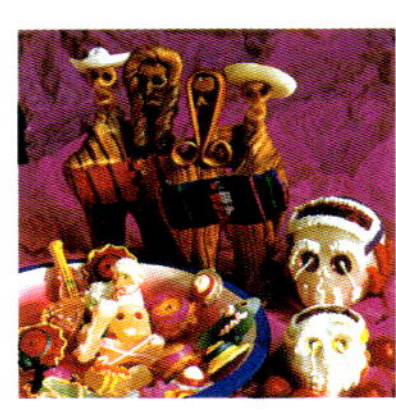

Page 18:
Charamuscas (traditional Day
of the Dead confections),
figures and skulls of sugar.
Photo: *Carlos Díaz Corona*

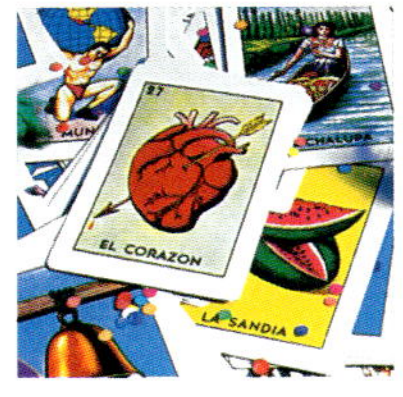

Page 25:
Lottery Game and Confetti.
Photo: *Carlos Díaz Corona*

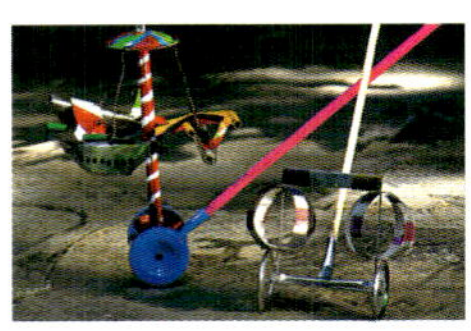

Pages 6 and 7:
Push-Toys on Canes:
Tin roundabout,
State of México.
Tin whirling globes,
Tlaquepaque, Jalisco.
Photo: *Carlos Díaz Corona*

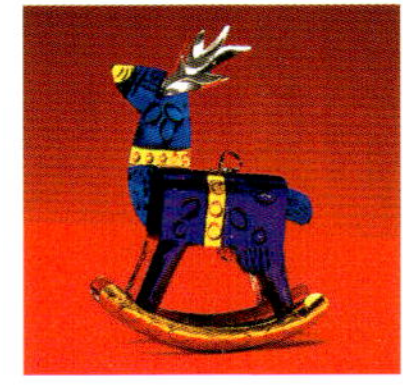

Page 19:
Rocking Horse
of painted tin, Oaxaca.
Photo: *José Martínez Verea*

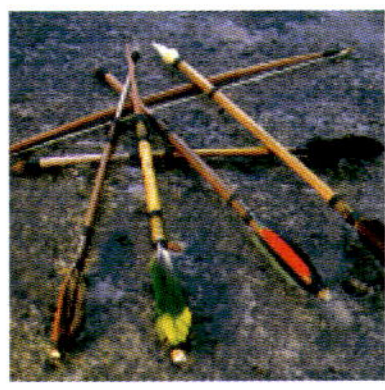

Page 26:
Bow and Arrows, Chiapas.
Photo: *Mauricio Martínez*

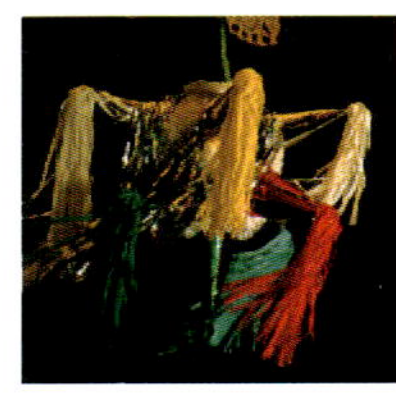

Page 12:
Like a lone shooting star,
the piñata trails its colors.
Tissue paper over clay pot.
Photo: *Rigoberto Moreno*

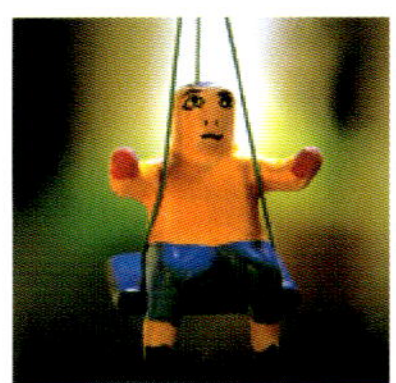

Page 20:
Swing Set (detail),
carved and painted wood,
Guerrero.
Photo: *Rigoberto Moreno*

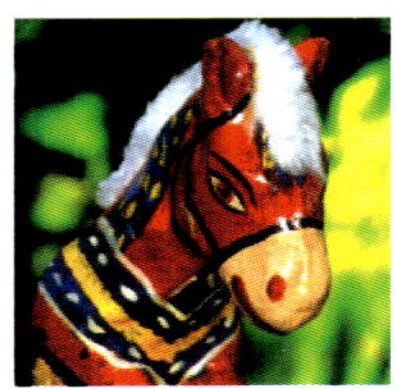

Page 27:
Hobby-Horse
of painted papier-maché,
Guanajuato.
Photo: *Carlos Díaz Corona*

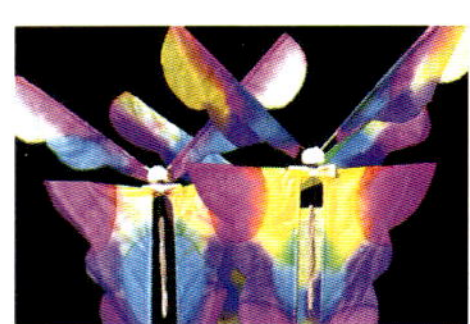

Pages 14 and 15:
Colored tissue
paper butterflies,
State of México.
Photo: *Rigoberto Moreno*

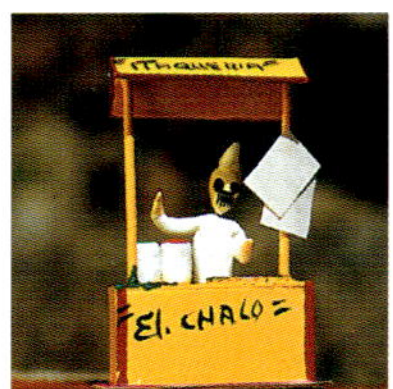

Page 21:
Miniatures of painted clay,
cardboard and wire,
State of México.
Photo: *Rigoberto Moreno*

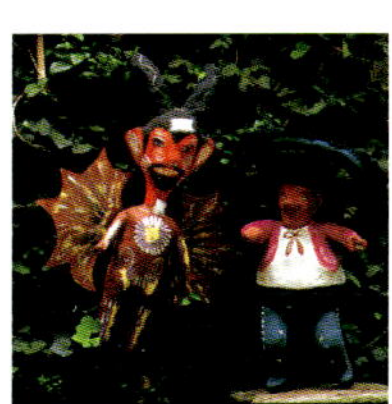

Page 28:
Painted Cardboard Figures
Celaya, Guanajuato.
Photo: *Rigoberto Moreno*

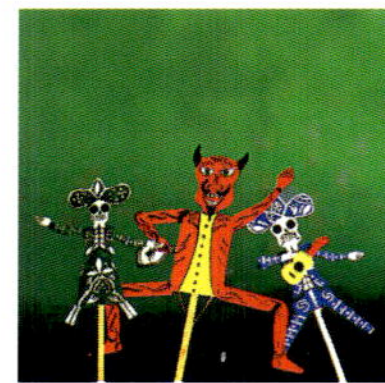

Page 16:
Painted wooden
stick puppets, Oaxaca.
Photo: *Rigoberto Moreno*

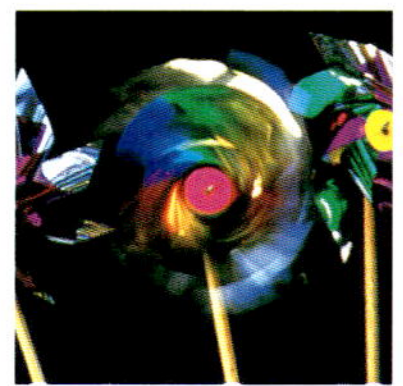

Page 23:
Pinwheels,
metalicized plastic,
Puebla, Puebla
Photo: *Rigoberto Moreno*

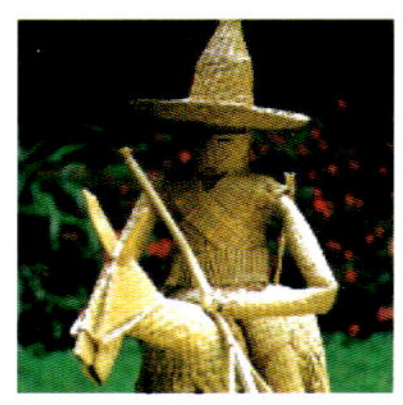

Page 30:
Woven Palm Figure
Pátzcuaro, Michoacán.
Photo: *Rigoberto Moreno*

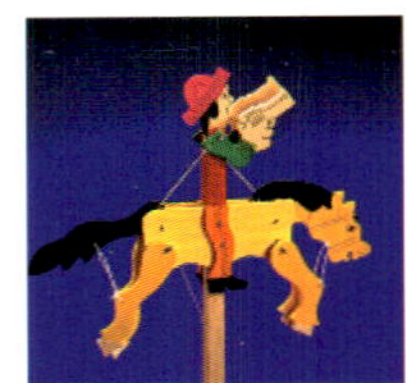

Page 52:
Jointed Stick-Puppet
of painted wood,
Quiroga, Michoacán.
Photo: *José Martínez Verea*

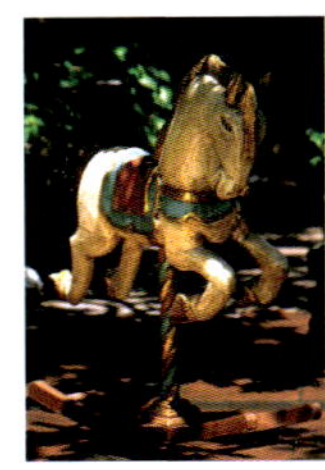

Page 58:
Rocking Horse,
painted wood;
Apaseo, Michoacán.
Photo: *José Martínez Verea*

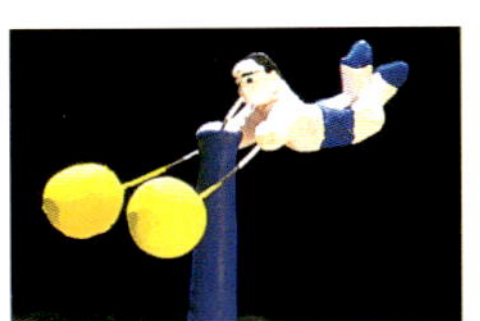

Page 62:
Painted Clay Acrobat
Santa Cruz de las Huertas,
Jalisco.
Photo: *Rigoberto Moreno*

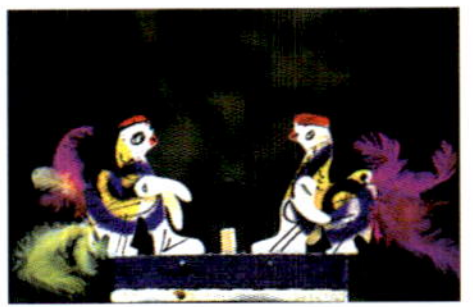

Page 54:
Fighting Cocks,
painted wood;
Pátzcuaro, Michoacán.
Photo: *Rigoberto Moreno*

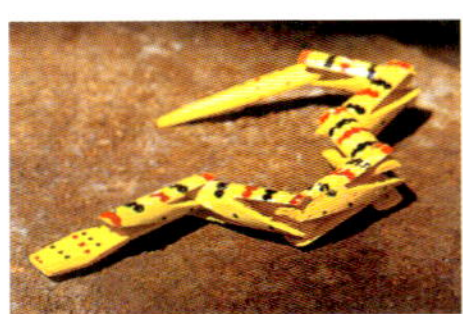

Page 59:
Snake, woven reed;
Quiroga, Michoacán.
Photo: *Rigoberto Moreno*

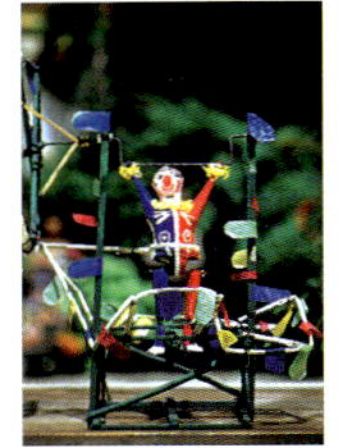

Page 63:
Doll-shaped fireworks-
armature, painted cardboard
and wire; Oaxaca.
Photo: *Rigoberto Moreno*

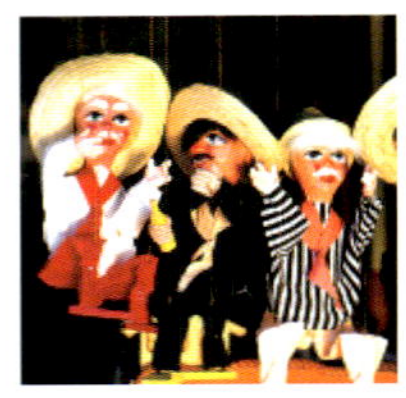

Page 55:
Marionettes of wood
and Cloth;
Morelia, Michoacán.
Photo: *Rigoberto Moreno*

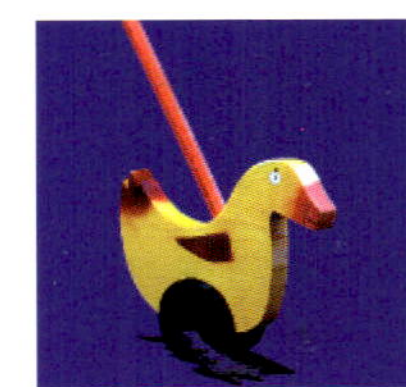

Page 59:
Duck Push-Toy,
wood and rubber;
Quiroga, Michoacán.
Photo: *José Martínez Verea*

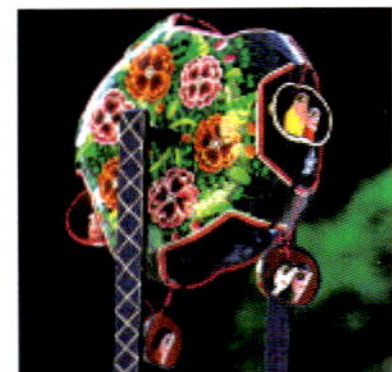

Page 64:
Ferris Wheel of painted and
lacquered gourds, Guerrero.
Photo: *Rigoberto Moreno*

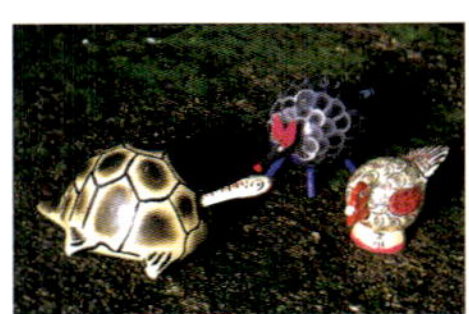

Page 56:
Gourd Animals, lacquered
and painted; Guerrero.
Photo: *Rigoberto Moreno*

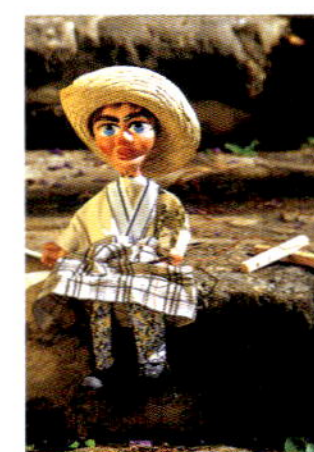

Page 60:
Wood and Cloth Marionette
Morelia, Michoacán.
Photo: *Rigoberto Moreno*

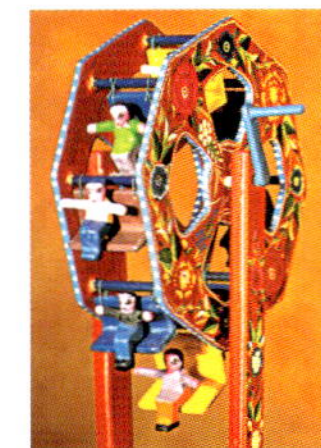

Page 66:
Ferris Wheel of painted and
lacquered wood, Guerrero.
Photo: *Rigoberto Moreno*

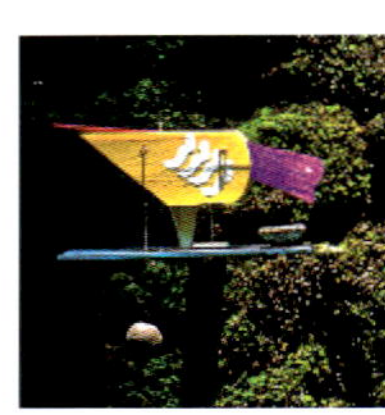

Page 57:
Bird Figure, painted wood;
Pátzcuaro, Michoacán.
Photo: *José Martínez Verea*

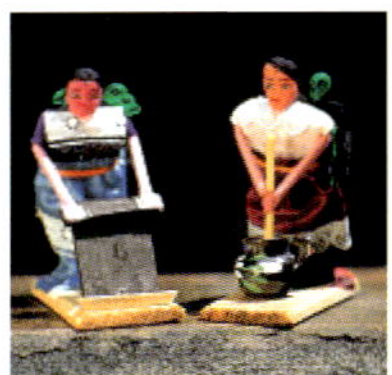

Page 61:
Animated Dolls
of cloth and wood;
Quiroga, Michoacán.
Photo: *Rigoberto Moreno*

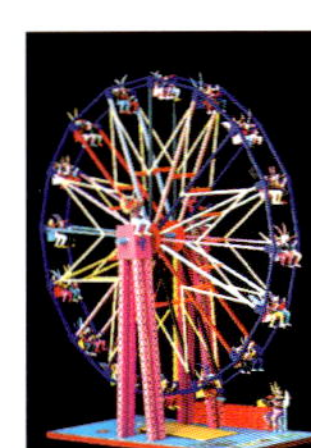

Page 67:
Ferris Wheel
of painted wood, Oaxaca.
Photo: *Rigoberto Moreno*

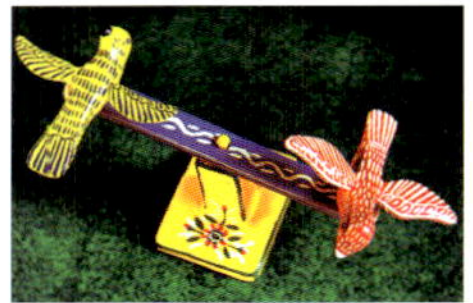

Page 57:
Roundabout with Birds
of painted and lacquered
wood, Guerrero.
Photo: *Rigoberto Moreno*

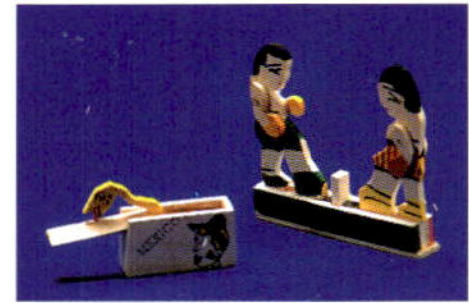

Page 62:
Boxers and Snake-trick of
painted wood, Guanajuato.
Photo: *José Martínez Verea*

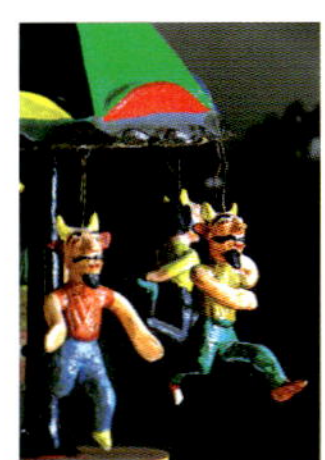

Page 68:
Roundabout with Devils
Ocumicho, Michoacán.
Photo: *Rigoberto Moreno*

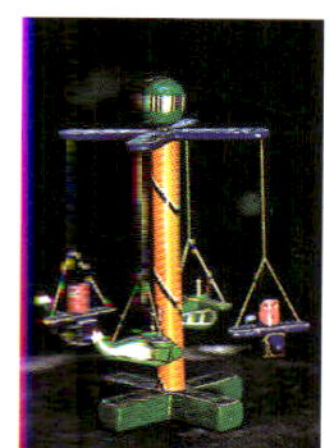

Page 68:
Aerial Roundabout,
painted and lacquered wood;
Guerrero.
Photo: *José Martínez Verea*

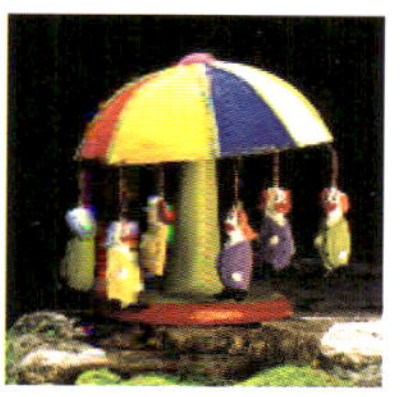

Page 69:
Painted Clay Roundabout
Santa Cruz de las Huertas,
Jalisco.
Photo: *Rigoberto Moreno*

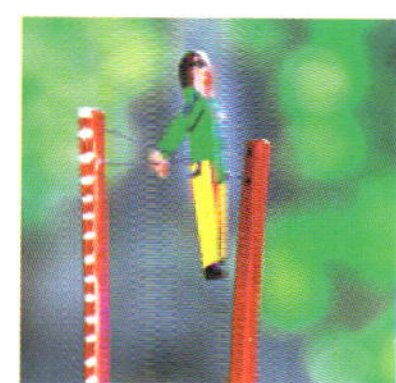

Page 70:
Twirling Acrobat, painted
and lacquered wood;
Guerrero.
Photo: *Carlos Díaz Corona*

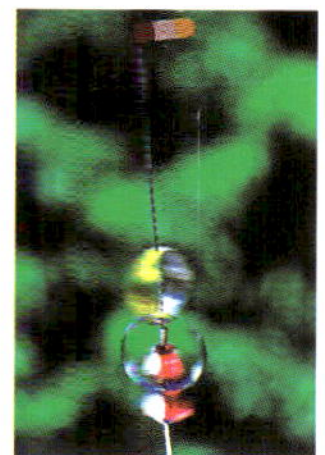

Page 71:
Spinning Rings, tin
hand-toy; State of México.
Photo: *Rigoberto Moreno*

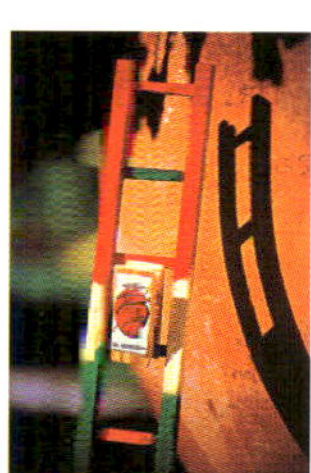

Page 71:
Painted Wood Ladder
Pátzcuaro, Michoacán.
Photo: *Rigoberto Moreno*

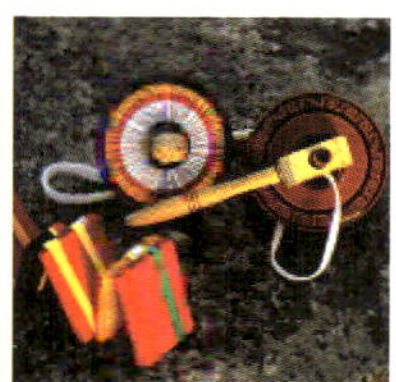

Page 72:
Turned Wooden Tops
and Jacob's Ladder Toy;
Quiroga, Michoacán.
Photo: *Mauricio Martínez*

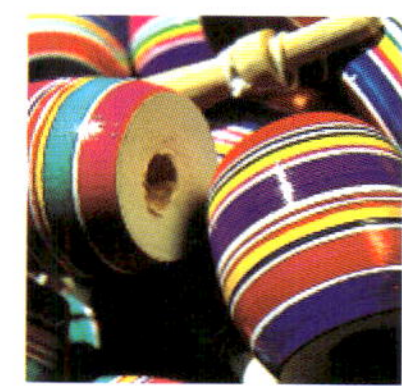

Page 73:
Baleros of turned and painted
wood; Quiroga, Michoacán.
Photo: *Rigoberto Moreno*

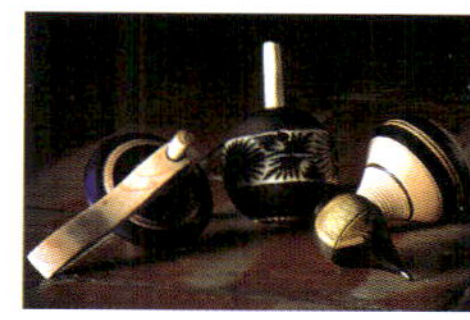

Page 73:
Turned-Wood Tops
Quiroga, Michoacán;
Carved Gourd Top, Chiapas.
Photo: *Carlos Díaz Corona*

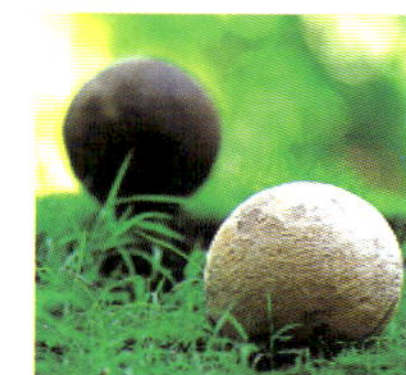

Page 74:
Carved Wooden Balls
made by Tarahumara Indians,
Chihuahua.
Photo: *José Martínez Verea*

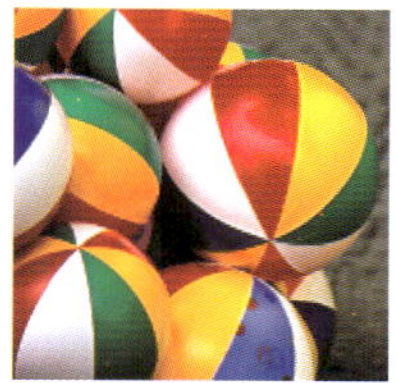

Page 74:
Inflatable Bouncing Balls
Photo: *Rigoberto Moreno*

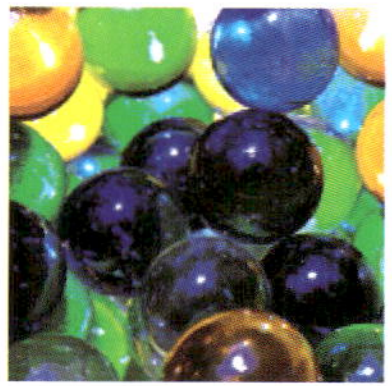

Page 75:
Glass Marbles
Tonalá, Jalisco
Photo: *Rocío Guillén*

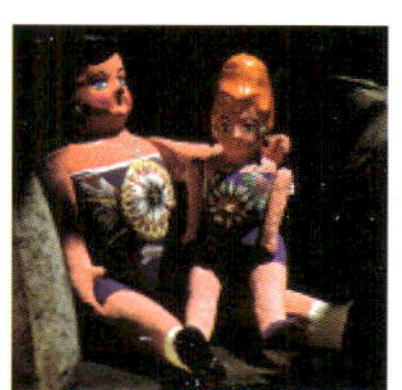

Page 76:
Painted Cardboard Dolls
Celaya, Guanajuato.
Photo: *José Martínez Verea*

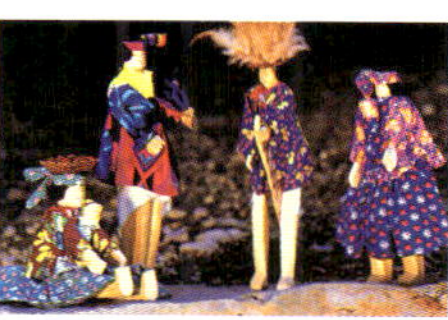

Pages 78 and 79:
Dolls of wood and cloth
made by Tarahumara
Indians, Chihuahua.
Photo: *Rigoberto Moreno*

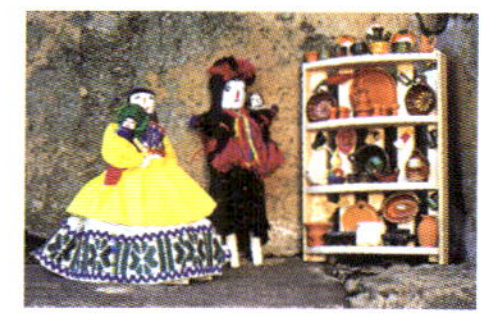

Page 80:
Rag Dolls
Querétaro and Chiapas.
Shelf with clay miniatures,
Tonalá, Jalisco.
Photo: *Carlos Díaz Corona*

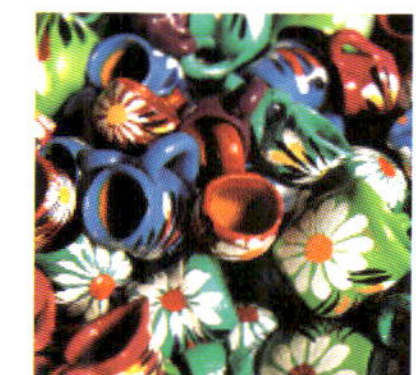

Page 81:
Miniature Pitchers, painted
clay; Tonalá, Jalisco.
Photo: *Rigoberto Moreno*

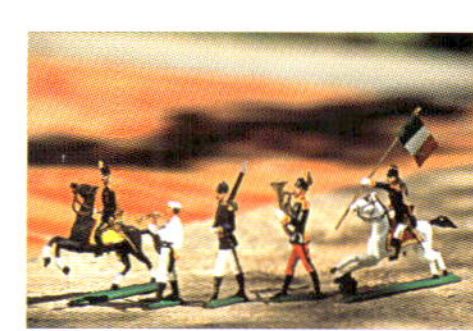

Page 82:
Painted Lead Soldiers
State of México.
Photo: *José Martínez Verea*

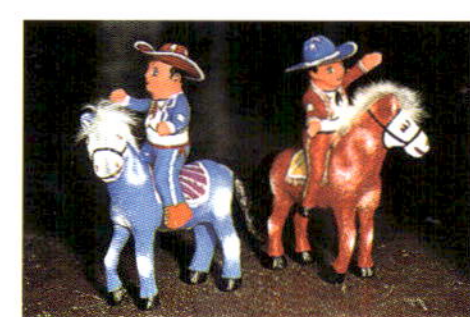

Page 82:
Painted Cardboard Horsemen
State of México.
Photo: *Rigoberto Moreno*

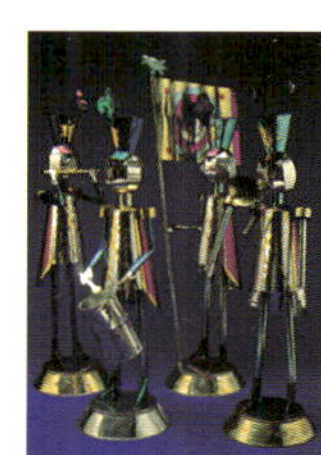

Page 83:
Painted Tin Soldiers, Oaxaca.
Photo: *José Martínez Verea*

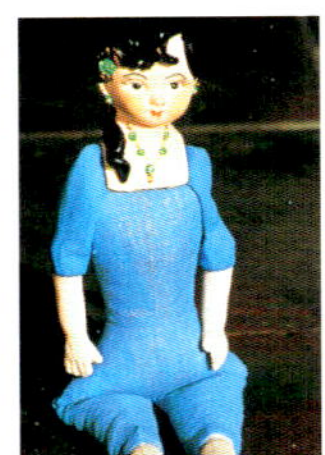

Page 84:
Molded Wax and Cloth Doll,
Tlaxcala.
Photo: *Rigoberto Moreno*

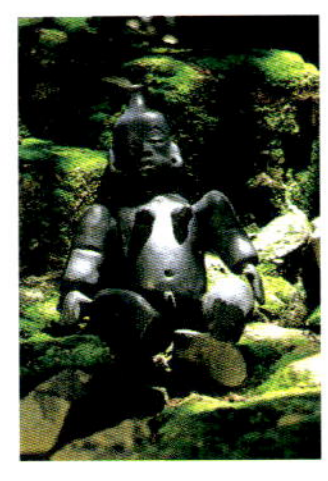

Page 88:
Jointed Doll
of black ceramic, Oaxaca.
Photo: *Carlos Díaz Corona*

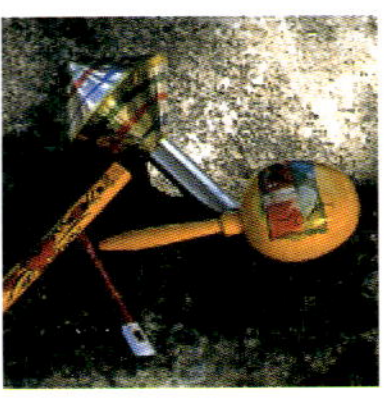

Page 94:
Tin Rattle, State of México;
Wooden Flutes and Maracas,
lacquered and painted wood;
Guerrero.
Photo: *Mauricio Martínez*

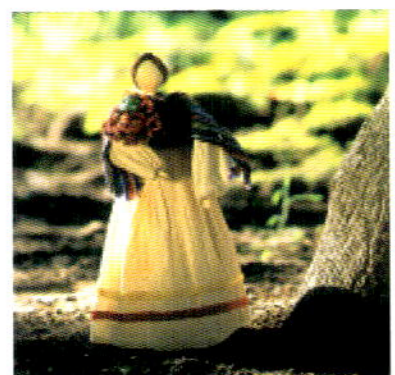

Page 85:
Cornhusk Doll
Tlaquepaque, Jalisco.
Photo: *Rigoberto Moreno*

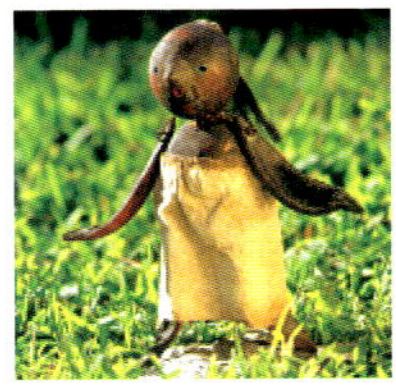

Page 89:
Doll of seed pods, rags
and horsehair, Guerrero.
Photo: *Rigoberto Moreno*

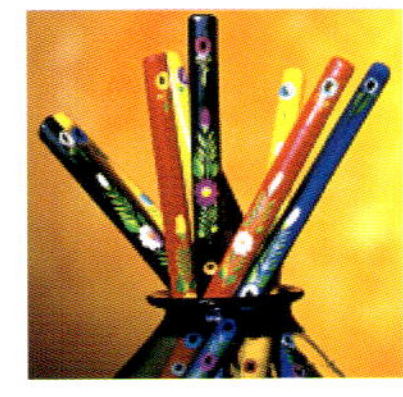

Page 95:
Flutes, lacquered and
painted wood; Guerrero.
Photo: *Rigoberto Moreno*

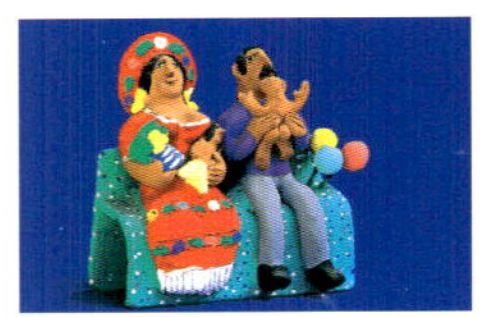

Page 86:
Painted Clay Seated Figures
Ocotlán de Morelos, Oaxaca.
Photo: *Mito Covarrubias*

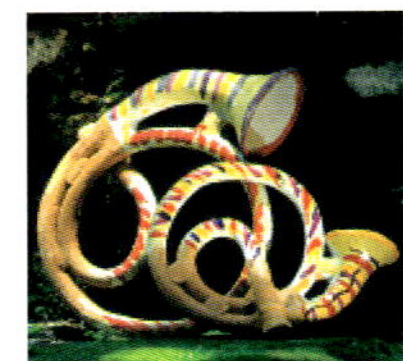

Page 90:
Painted Clay Horns
Santa Cruz de las Huertas,
Jalisco.
Photo: *José Martínez Verea*

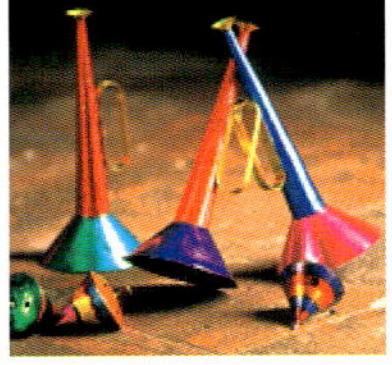

Page 97:
Cornets and Tops,
painted tin; Oaxaca.
Photo: *Rigoberto Moreno*

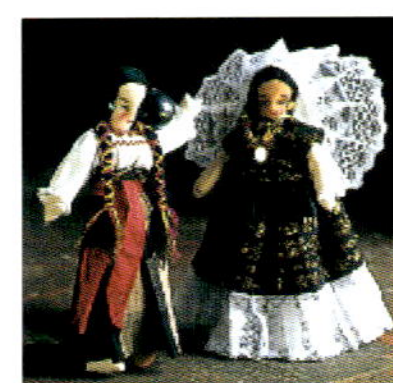

Page 86:
Rag Dolls in Regional Dress
Oaxaca.
Photo: *Rigoberto Moreno*

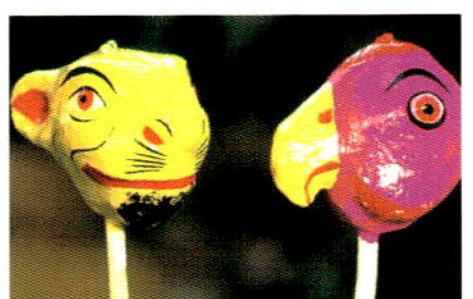

Page 92:
Rattles, painted
papier-maché; Guanajuato.
Photo: *Rigoberto Moreno*

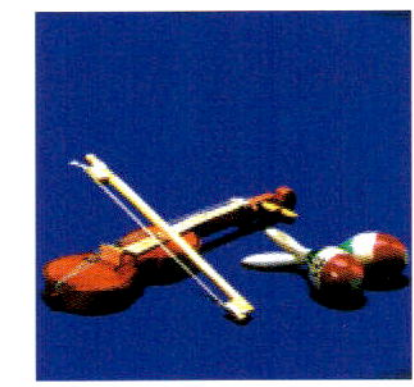

Page 98:
Violin and Maracas,
painted wood;
Quiroga, Michoacán.
Photo: *José Martínez Verea*

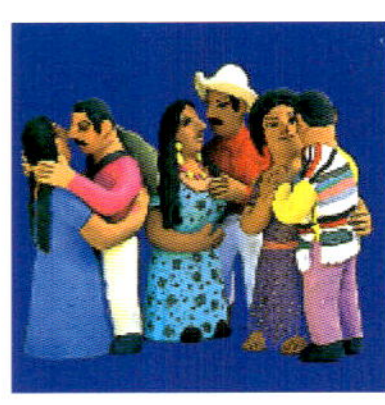

Page 87:
Painted Clay «Dance Hall»
Ocotlán de Morelos, Oaxaca.
Photo: *Mito Covarrubias*

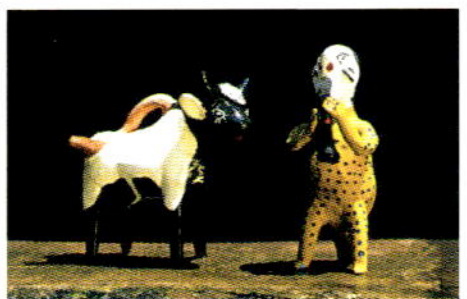

Page 93:
Painted Clay Flutes
in zoomorphic designs,
Ocumicho, Michoacán.
Photo: *Rigoberto Moreno*

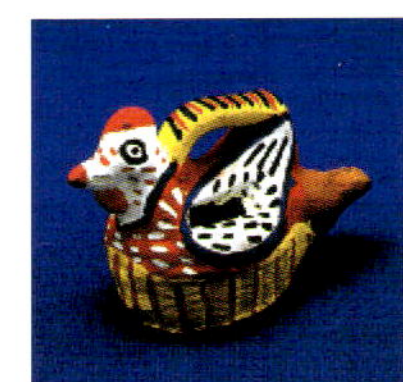

Page 98:
Painted Clay Whistle
Santa Cruz de las Huertas,
Jalisco.
Photo: *José Martínez Verea*

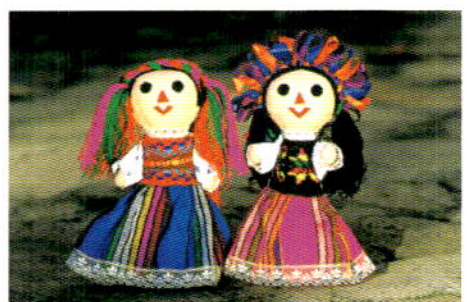

Page 87:
Rag Dolls
Tlaquepaque, Jalisco.
Photo: *Rigoberto Moreno*

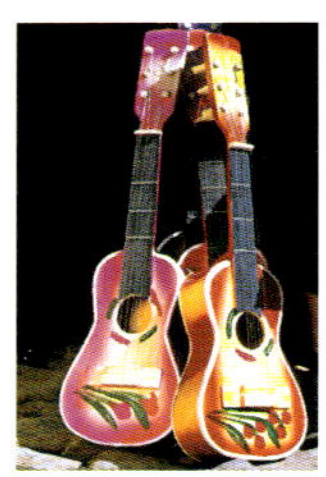

Page 94:
Painted Guitars
Quiroga, Michoacán.
Photo: *Rigoberto Moreno*

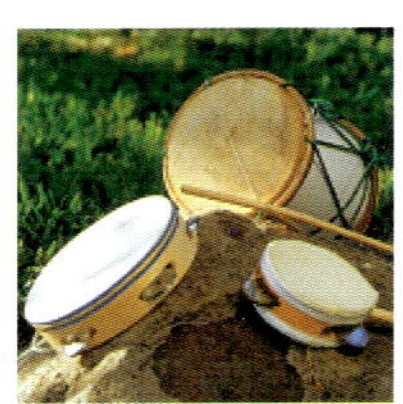

Page 99:
Drums and Tambourine
of wood and leather.
Photo: *Rigoberto Moreno*

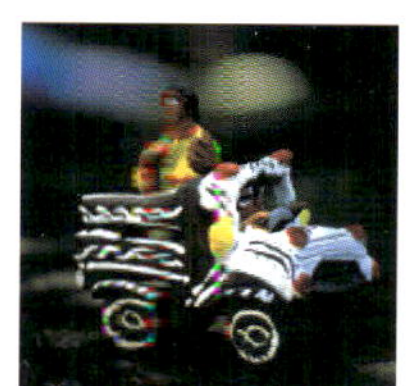

Page 100:
Bus with People,
painted clay;
Ocumicho, Michoacán.
Photo: *José Martínez Verea*

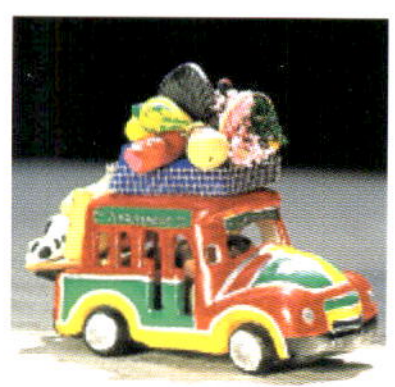

Page 105:
Painted Clay Bus
Tlaquepaque, Jalisco.
Photo: *José Martínez Verea*

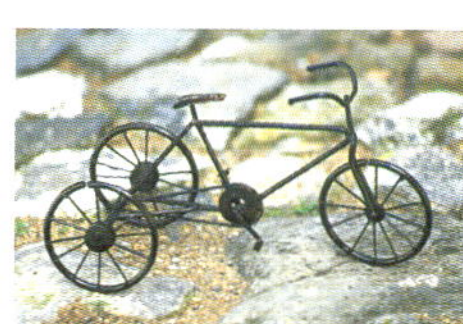

Page 108:
Tricycle of Metal Wire,
Guanajuato.
Photo: *Rigoberto Moreno*

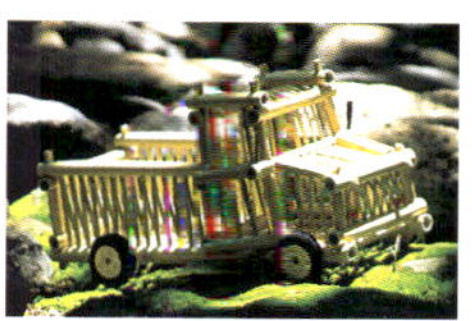

Page 102:
Bus of Reed Slats, Oaxaca.
Photo: *Carlos Díaz Corona*

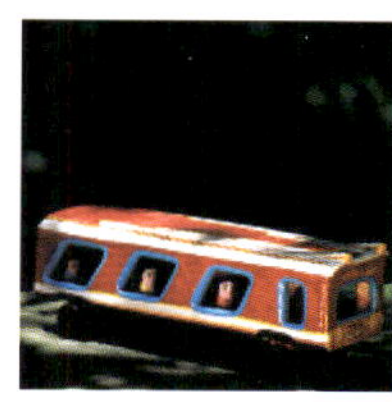

Page 105:
Bus, lacquered
and painted wood; Guerrero.
Photo: *José Martínez Verea*

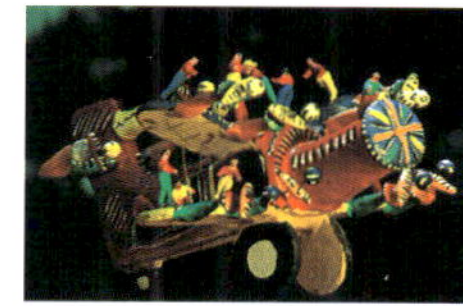

Page 108:
Bi-Plane with People,
painted clay;
Santa Cruz de las Huertas,
Jalisco.
Photo: *Carlos Díaz Corona*

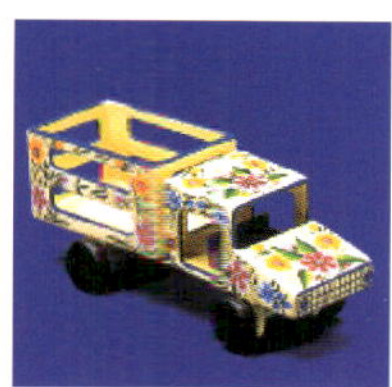

Page 102:
Lacquered and Painted Bus,
Guerrero.
Photo: *José Martínez Verea*

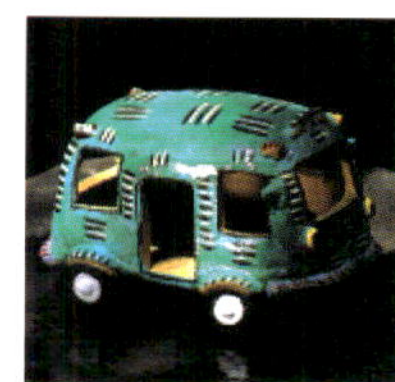

Page 105:
Painted Clay Bus
Tlaquepaque, Jalisco.
Photo: *Rigoberto Moreno*

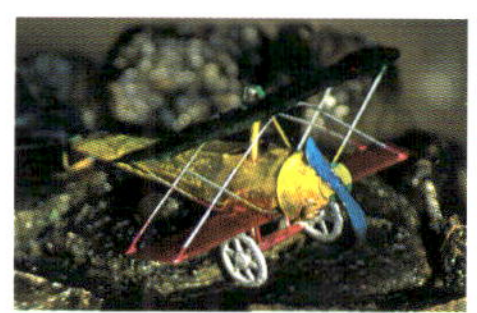

Page 109:
Painted Tin Airplane
State of México.
Photo: *Rigoberto Moreno*

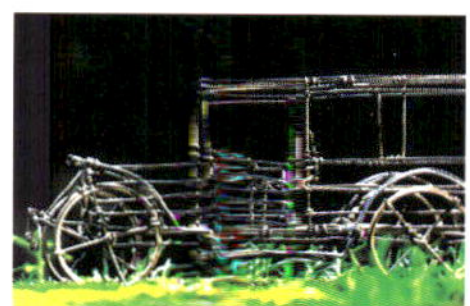

Page 103:
Automobile of Metal Wire
State of México.
Photo: *Rigoberto Moreno*

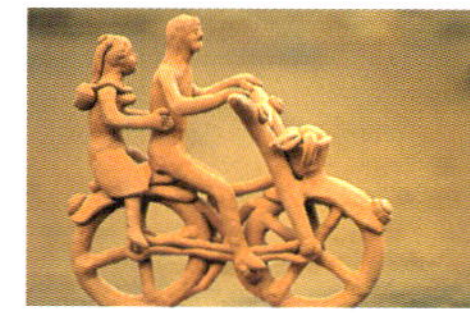

Page 106:
Bicycle of Unglazed Clay
Ocumicho, Michoacán.
Photo: *Rigoberto Moreno*

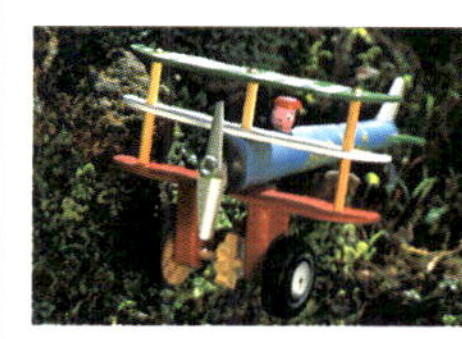

Page 110:
Painted Wooden Airplane
Quiroga, Michoacán.
Photo: *Rigoberto Moreno*

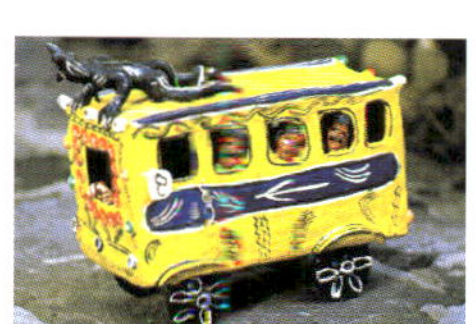

Page 104:
Bus with Passengers,
painted clay;
Ocumicho, Michoacán.
Photo: *Rigoberto Moreno*

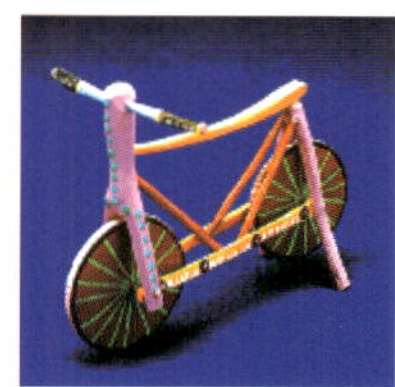

Page 107:
Bicycle of Painted Wood,
Oaxaca.
Photo: *José Martínez Verea*

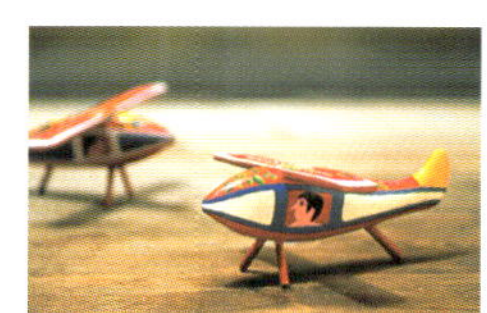

Page 111:
Airplanes lacquered
and painted wood; Guerrero.
Photo: *Rigoberto Moreno*

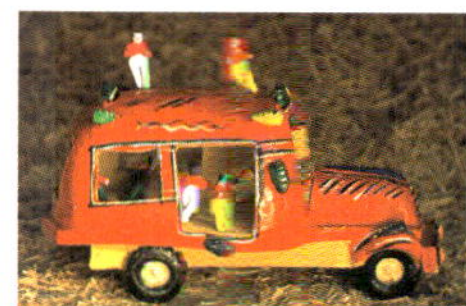

Page 104:
Bus with People,
painted clay; Oaxaca.
Photo: *Rigoberto Moreno*

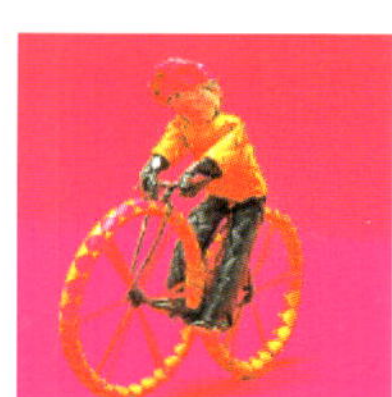

Page 107:
Bicyclist of woven and
braided palm-leaf;
Chicmecatitlán, Puebla.
Photo: *José Martínez Verea*

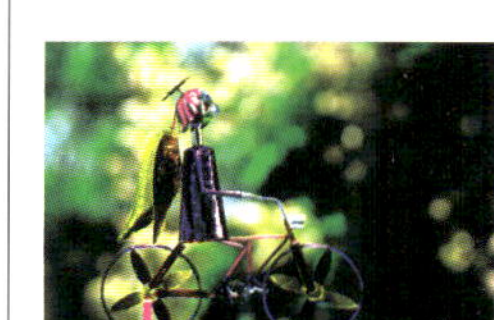

Page 112:
Cyclist Angel,
painted tin, Oaxaca.
Photo: *Rigoberto Moreno*

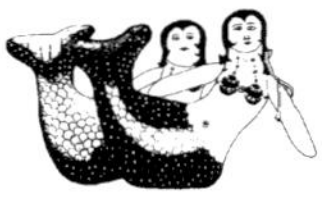